RACEHOSS
BIG EMMA'S BOY

Albert Race Sample

BALLANTINE BOOKS • NEW YORK

The language and descriptions contained in this book do not reflect the personal views or attitudes of the author, and are used solely for the purpose of authenticity.

The names and identity of some of the individuals contained in this narrative have either been omitted or changed and any similarity with the names of persons living or dead is strictly coincidental.

ISBN 0–345–32807–8

Manufactured in the United States of America

First Ballantine Books Edition: January 1986

Dedicated in memory of my mother, Emma.
And to Carol, my wife and best buddy.
For without her love, help, and inspiration this book
would not have happened. But I thank her most of all
for walking back in time with me and holding onto my
hand so Raw Hide and Bloody Bones wouldn't get me.
And to Amber, my daughter and helper.

Contents

Introduction

The mass of men lead lives of quiet desperation.
—Henry David Thoreau

Doing time. Some men do it behind prison walls. Others, imprisoned from within, mark time in a life they are condemned to endure, without promise of fulfillment.

Race Sample seemed destined to do time one way or the other. This mixed-race product of the depression and war years of East Texas was embarked on a course headed away from life's more enriching dreams. Every force pulled him further from the mainstream, so it should have been no surprise when Race became an alien of the free world. It was a pattern more familiar and predictable than destiny itself.

Albert "Racehorse" Sample graduated from seventeen years in prison for three felony convictions at about the same time I graduated from law school. He and some friends were looking for a lawyer to help them start a half-way house for ex-cons. I was looking for some clients. It was the auspicious beginning of one of the more rewarding friendships of my life. In the ten years I've known Race, I have learned from him something about the value of hope.

Most of us face adversity by seeking the strength to overcome it. We admire that strength and often pity those who, lacking it, become more vulnerable to life's retreats. A conventional perspective would even view as desperate, if not failed, a life which invites no hope of that power. Race has been a desperate man.

His escape from that convention, that despair, is the subject of this book. This unique achievement is, I believe, the result of the hope woven into every sinew of his being, creating a unique and powerful insight which makes Race worth loving and his book worth reading.

Race is no longer a desperate man and I am no longer a practicing lawyer. As a judge I now try to learn from Race's example. With each judgment or sentence I pass, on other lives and on my own, there is always that hope.

This book is hardly the culmination of Race Sample's life. It is the prophecy of his soul. I am proud to call Race my friend; my brother.

Michael J. Schless

I

Emma

Prelude

1909 Sunday morning . . . somewhere in Western Louisiana

Standing in front of the mirror, Lillie Barnes hastily fumbled with the pearl-tipped hair pin as she pushed it through the bun in the back. While fitting on the flower-laden straw hat, hurrying not to be late for the eleven o'clock church service, she hollered into the kitchen, "Bama, ya'll hurry up now or we gon' be late!"

"Yes mam, we hurryin Mama."

"Be sho an wipe that baby's face an tie her shoes up."

"Yes mam."

Taking a last quick glance and smoothing down her Sunday gingham dress, she thought about how nice it would be if Son Buddy was here to go to church with them. He was seventeen, the oldest of her four children and already out on his own. Smiling she thought to herself: *but even ef he wuz heah, me an him would be goin roun an roun. That boy got slow as cream risin when it come time to go to church.*

Rushing the children, she called into the kitchen again, "Bama, ya'll bout ready?"

"Yes mam, Mama. We ready."

"Well, cum on now, les go."

Her husband, Charlie, was already seated on the wagon and waiting for them. Cautioning as she turned the skeleton key in the lock, "One uv ya'll betta ketch holt uv that baby's hand so she don' fall goin down them steps." Sally grabbed

3

it—she was eight. Bama was twelve and the baby, Emma, was four.

Charlie, his patience worn thin, said, "Lillie, ya'll hurry up ef'n you want me to drive ya'll down there." He had other plans. As soon as he dropped them off, he was heading straight for the gambling shack. Grumbling still, "Damn, Lillie, it takes ya'll longer to git ready than anybody I ever seen. I been settin out heah nelly a hour."

"Oh bosh," she said, "you ain' been settin out heah no hour. Quit yo fussin. You'll have plenty time to gamble," settling herself on the hard oak seat.

Looking back over his shoulder, "Bama, ya'll hurry up an git in." Sally couldn't lift Emma up onto the wagon bed alone; Bama had to help her. "Ya'll on?" Charlie asked.

"Yessir we on."

"Ya'll set down back there an behave," he ordered.

Lillie added, "Bama, you an Sally bet not let that baby fall out."

Charlie snapped the reins and started the mules in motion, "Cum up heah Jake, Ol Blackie!" whacking them on the rump as they struck up a trot.

Bouncing on the springless seat and holding her hat down on her head, "Charlie, don' git to gamblin an forgit to cum back an git us."

Irritated, he said dryly, "Don' worry Lillie. I won' forgit ya'll."

It was miserably hot and each time the wagon ran over a bump in the dusty road, Lillie complained. "Slow down a little bit Charlie. You ain' gotta be in such a great big hurry to git rid uv us. I'm gon' make a cushion for this hard thang or start brangin me a pillow to set on." She was nine months pregnant and expecting their fifth child any day now.

"Oh shet yo mouth Lillie. I ain' goin all that fas." Aggravated, he coaxed the mules to speed up. They had less than a mile to go after crossing the branch. The mules were trotting at a rapid pace when the front wheel on Charlie's side bounced over a big rut and suddenly rolled off.

Everyone was thrust sideways when the wagon jerked and tilted to the left. Frightened, little Emma started crying. Charlie had his hands full getting the spooked mules to slow down. Lillie grabbed onto the seat tightly with both hands. When she let go of her hat, the wind whisked it away and it was crushed beneath the wheels.

Pulling back on the reins with all his strength, "WHOA! WHOAA! WHOA BLACKIE! WHOA JAKE! WHOAA! WHOA!" The mules slowed down and finally stopped.

"Ya'll awright?" Lillie quickly asked the children. "Is the baby hurt?"

"Yes mam, we awright. No mam, she ain' hurt, she jes scaid," Bama answered.

"You awright Sally B?"

"Yes'm, I'm awright Mama," she snivelled.

It took some slow-doing for Lillie to climb down the jacked up side of the wagon. Nervously rubbing her overswollen belly, she told the girls to unload as she walked around to Charlie's side. While he stood looking down at the wheelless axle she nagged, "I tole you to slow down but you so bull-headed an won' lissen to nobody. At least you could've cum roun an heped me git down."

"Lillie, jes shet up an lemme alone so I kin fix the damn wagon! Sally, go back down there'n git that wheel an roll it up heah."

"Yessir." Sally about-faced and took off down the road.

"Take Emma witcha so she kin git my hat," Lillie yelled. Adding to herself sorrowfully, "I know it's all messed up."

"Yes'm, c'mon Emma."

While they waited for Sally's return, Lillie asked, "Do you thank you kin git it back on?"

"Yeah, I bleeve so," he said while rummaging through the junk he stored underneath the seat. "Gotdammit!" he bellowed. "I thought I had anutha pin but I ain'. Well, ef I kin jes git the wheel back on the axle I'll use a nail, maybe it'll stay on long nuff to git ya'll to church."

Emma had found the hat and ran back eagerly. "Mama, is all broke," she said, handing it over to Lillie.

"Yeah baby, I know."

Sally rolled the wheel up to the wagon and leaned it against the side. Charlie bent down and lifted the bed up.

5

The beads of sweat popped out on his forehead as he strained to keep it hoisted. Realizing he needed help, "Bama git over heah an ketch holt."

Obediently, she rushed to his side and began lifting. Bama grunted and strained shoulder to shoulder with her father. When the heavy oak bed was up a little higher Charlie yelled, "Sally B, roll that wheel roun heah 'n git ready to shove it on." Sally quickly rolled the wheel in front of the axle and stood waiting, but they couldn't raise it high enough before Charlie's arms gave out. "Les ease it down Bama," he said winded.

After wiping away the sweat with his bandanna and catching a breath, Charlie bent back down. "Okay, les try it Bama," prodding, "but this time lift hard is you kin."

"Yessir." Bama drew a deep breath and bent over.

Before they could start lifting, Lillie, with motherly instincts, stepped up and nudged Bama away. She took her place saying, "Charlie, you know this thang's too heavy for that baby to be tryin to pick up."

Shoving Lillie away from the wagon, Charlie snarled, "I didn' tell you to do it! I tole her to do it! Bama git back over heah!"

"Naw Charlie, I dun tole you thas too heavy fo her," Lillie persisted.

Charlie stood up, "Thas whut's th' Gotdam matter now. You pamper these rotten chillun all the time an won' let 'em do nuthin. You the reason they ain' worth a shit."

Angered, Lillie blurted out, "Charlie Barnes, sometimes you make me so mad I could jes wring yo neck off! Lemme . . ."

"You jes git yo ass outta my way!" Charlie screamed. "C'mon Bama."

Unhesitating, Bama tried to heed his order, but Lillie would not relinquish her. She got a lifting hold on the bed. Without looking back, Lillie snapped, "Ef you tired uv foolin roun, les git this thang up. We late enuff as it is."

In deathly silence, Charlie reached into the wagon and grabbed the extra singletree. Gripping one end in both hands like a club, he raised it high above his head, and powerfully crashed it across Lillie's lower back. As she lay writhing and gasping on the roadside Bama took off running for the church to get help. A few minutes later, Lillie was dead. Horror-stricken, Sally and little Emma clung to each other and looked on while their new baby sister was born.

As soon as she got word of her daughter's death, Louduskie came down by train. Her husband had been dead for years, but she brought along the rest of her family for the funeral. Lillie, at thirty-six, was the oldest of her nine children. The other four daughters and four sons, whose ages ranged from fourteen to thirty-two, still lived at home with her. In addition, the clan also had four grandchildren belonging to two of her unmarried daughters, and one daughter-in-law.

After the funeral and the man came and got his wagon and mules Charlie still owed him for, there was no more business to transact. Lillie and Charlie had been renting the house, and the meager insurance policy on Lillie was just enough to cover her funeral and burial. With no reason to remain any longer, the tribe would be leaving in the morning.

Louduskie dug deeper into the large purse, corralling and smoothing out the crumpled dollar bills as she laid them on the ticket counter. Good thing she thought to get some more money from the coffee can before she left; she was buying three extra tickets for the trip back to Big Sandy, Texas. The infant Bama named Elzado, could ride free. "Grandma Duck," as she was known to her grandchildren, held onto the round-trip tickets she bought in Big Sandy for the others, and handed Bama their three tickets for safekeeping.

Apart from the others, sitting on one of the waiting benches to give her feet a much needed rest, Grandma Duck watched her grandchildren playing on the station platform. Noticing they were getting too close to the tracks, she yelled, "Ya'll git back away frum the edge uv that platform!"

Her mind drifted: *we barely makin it off them three acres as it is. Fo mo moufs to feed sho gon' be hard on me an wit that low-down Charlie in jail, he won' be no hep atall. Only reason I'm takin his chillun in's cuz nobody else would. His mama an papa both dead an his fo brothers an sister didn' even show up at the funeral. They ain' nuthin but a low-*

down stankin bunch uv thievin, gamblin heathens whut ain'
hit a lick a' work since they be grown. An Son Buddy can't
keep 'em. He jes a porter livin in the backroom uv a hotel
where he works at in Gilmer. He never did git 'long wit that
ol' devil an got away quick as he could. First time Lillie Mae
cum draggin him up to my house, I tole her then. She wuzn'
nuthin but a baby, not even eighteen. Ever'body in town
knowed bout his drankin, fightin an gamblin an carryin on:
Bless my po child's heart, she wouldn' lissen. Hard as I tried
Lord, she jes wouldn' lissen. She's in yo hands now Lord,
rest her soul.

Louduskie's shoulders sagged and her tears flowed freely. While dabbing them away, she heard the train whistle in the distance. She stood and yelled, ''Git back frum that edge! Rat now!'' They scampered over to their mothers and started shouting and pointing at the huge rumbling mass of steel.

Bama quickly covered the baby's face with the blanket to protect her from the swirling duststorm the engine kicked up as it went by. Emma's dress blew over her face as she gleefully jumped up and down, excited about her first ride on a ''choo-choo.'' When Grandma Duck heard the porter's ''All aboard!'' she gathered ''her'' flock together at the coach's boarding steps and stood to one side, making sure everybody got on. Then she boarded.

Afterwards Bama stepped on carrying Elzado in one arm and lugging a cardboard suitcase. Sally helped Emma up the steps and they trailed behind Bama as she looked for seats. She found two with the backs already flipped the right way so they could sit facing each other. Taking a window seat, Bama told Sally to sit next to her so the active Emma could have the whole seat to herself.

The train slowly pulled out and then picked up speed. The telephone poles went zooming up through the window. Emma was taking it all in and merrily swinging her feet back and forth when she asked, ''Sally B, how cum Mama didn' go on th'choo-choo wit us?''

''Cuz she can't Emma. Mama dead.''

''How cum she dead, Sally B?''

"Cuz th' preacher say it wuz time for God to cum 'n take her away to heaven."

"Is God gon' let her cum back?"

"Naw, she ain' never comin back."

"Well, God ain' nice an I don' lak Him no mo if He ain' gon' let Mama cum back frum heb'n."

Rocking Elzado motherly, Bama gently scolded, "Sally, ya'll hush up. Emma, you look out the window at th' moo-cows," quickly turning her face toward the window to keep them from knowing.

When Emma saw some she pointed out the window exclaiming, "Look Bama! Look! There go sum moo-cows!"

"I saw 'em Emma."

"How cum you cryin then?"

"Watchin moo-cows thru a train window always make me cry."

"Oh," Emma answered and looked back out the window.

1 |||||||||||||||||||||||||||||

When the Barnes girls walked into the house, Grandma Duck told them to wait in the hall. She went into another room, put away her hat and purse, and returned. At fifty-six, she was a robust giant of a woman, standing nearly six feet tall and weighing over 200 pounds. Ill-tempered and worn out from the funeral and trip, she didn't mince words.

"Ya'll kin cum to the table to eat afta we git thru. Bama, fur as I'm concerned, them chillun b'long to you an you gon' hafta keep that baby quiet. I heah enuff cryin in this house. You gon' hafta see afta 'em. I dun raised all the younguns I'm gon'. Sally B kin hep you wit ya'll's washin an ironin. She kin tend to them other two while you hep in th' kitchen wit the cookin."

With hands on her hips, Grandma Duck towered ominously over the girls as she continued, "I'm tellin ya'll rat now, I ain' gon' put up wit one bit uv ya'll's foolishness. An ya'll bet not be sassin out nonea these grown folks roun heah neither. Ef you do, I'll burn ya'll's hind-ends up. Do ya'll heah me? Did you heah me, Bama?"

"Yes'm, Grandma Duck."

Beckoning for them to follow, "Ya'll cum on in heah an put ya'll's thangs up under onea these beds."

Bama's arm was cramping from holding Elzado for so long, and she asked, "Grandma Duck, where kin I lay the baby down?"

Pointing to the open entry door, "Take her in yonder an lay her on onea them beds. Make sho you put sump'n else under her so she won' pee all over ever'thang."

"Yes mam."

Grandma Duck's final order came as she fixed her eyes on Emma, "An Bama, you keep this lil' ol' Charlie-lookin devil outta my sight!"

The paintless, wood-framed house, weathered gray with age, had an arched tin roof and no porches. The ground around it was feet-packed hard and bald. All the grass had been trampled away. The water well was in the back yard. The old house had four medium-sized bedrooms. Two were on either side of the hall which led through the kitchen to the back steps. For the married son and his wife, the brothers rounded up enough scrap lumber to build a shack with a separate entrance onto one of the back bedrooms.

All the bedrooms, except Grandma Duck's, were overcrowded with beds and single metal cots, with only narrow trails for passageways. Elzado slept in the bed with Bama and two aunties. Sally and Emma slept in the kitchen on two single canvas fold-up cots shared by four other children.

Little by little the Barnes girls were subjugated to being the family Cinderellas. When the inside work was caught up, it was on to the washing board and tubs. Then the garden had to be hoed and the hogs slopped.

With free time on her hands, Grandma Duck taught Emma to tie her shoelaces and button the back of her dress. For a teacher's aid, she used a thin board that she had driven a nail through at one end. Every morning when the children were getting dressed Grandma Duck called Emma up to her and pecked her hands with the nail-board while she desperately tried to button her four back buttons. The pecking ended when they were all buttoned. She got the same lesson while tying her shoelaces.

When Grandma Duck let her go, Emma ran crying to her surrogate mother with her bloody hands. Bama took her to the well to wash the blood away and dried them gently with the tail of her dress. Standing behind the well, Bama held her closely, stroking her hair and consoling, "Shhhh, hush now. Don' cry Emma. Hit's gon' be awright," while crying herself. "You know whut Emma?"

Her lips still quivering, "Naw, whut Bama."

"Onea these days when I git growed up I'm gon' have a great big o' house to live in wit room enuff fur everbody. When I do, I'm comin back afta ya'll."

"I wanna go wit you Bama."

"Ef you hush cryin, I'll cum back an gitcha real quick."

"Awright," wiping her nose with her arm.

"You go play now."

"They won' play wit me Bama."

"How cum?"

"They call me Charlie-lookin devil an won' play wit me."

"Well play by yosef." Looking toward the back door, "I gotta go fo Grandma miss me."

There was hardly elbow room on the cot with the three of them sleeping in it. Emma scooted as close to the edge as she could, trying to get out of the puddle of piss that hadn't seeped through yet. Reaching back, she tugged some of the raggedy, wet quilt they shared over her cold back. In an effort to squirm further away from the wetness, Emma slung her arm and leg over the side and lay sleeping, exposed to the chilling night air.

When it felt like somebody was turning her over, she opened her eyes to see who was tucking in the flimsy quilt. It was her mother! In the second it took to wipe the sleep from her eyes to get a better look, Lillie had disappeared.

Emma untucked the quilt, jumped off the cot, and tiptoed over to Sally's cot. Shaking her vigorously, "Sally! Sally! Sally B, wake up!! Wake up Sally B!! Mama cum back! Wake up Sally B!! You said she . . ."

One of Sally's cotmates interrupted, "Emma, ef you don' go back to bed Grandma gonna whup you!"

The many trips Sally made to and from the well drawing up and toting wash water had taken their toll. She was dead asleep. Emma crawled back onto her cot. She got a whipping the next morning from Grandma Duck anyway when her bunk rats ran and told, "Emma peed the bed."

A few days after Bama, now eighteen, took some jars of

Grandma Duck's watermelon rind preserves to the County Fair, she ran off with a soldier and got married. Her leaving didn't even put a dent in the overpopulated household. Grandma Duck's two oldest daughters stayed neck and neck producing another baby apiece and the two youngest had come up with three between them. Seems like every time they had a revival, her daughters got full of the "spirit" and had another one on the way.

After Bama absconded, Grandma Duck tightened the screws of vengeance down on Emma six more notches. She got a "whuppin" almost daily from Grandma Duck and the "grown folks" were unleashed to fill in the gaps.

Grandma Duck walked in the kitchen; Emma knocked over her glass and buttermilk spilled all over the oil cloth covering on the table.

"Git up frum that table an clean up that mess you made. You triflin heifer!" Hovering over Emma, watching her wipe the tablecloth with a dishrag, Grandma Duck yelled, "You ol' Charlie-lookin devil you! Don' cha lemme ketch you settin at my table no mo til I tell you. Frum now on, you eat out on them back steps." Shaking her finger, "You heah me?!!"

"Yes'm Grandma, I heah you," she bristled and flashed a quick, defiant look.

Enraged, Grandma Duck grabbed the iron skillet from the stove and drew it back, "Don' cha be astandin there rollin them eyes at me. You betta gitcha ol' Charlie-lookin sef outta heah fo I bus yo brains out," she shouted.

On an errand to the store Emma was hailed down by one of Grandma Duck's church member neighbors, "Emma."

"Yes mam?"

"Stop by heah baby," beckoning her to the porch. "Heah, take this quarter an brang me a small box uv KC Baking Powder when you cum back. An you stand there an wait cuz you got some change comin."

"Yes'm."

"Now git!"

When she delivered the baking powder, the woman handed her a dime and thanked her for doing the errand. On the way to the house, mad and frustrated, Emma kicked the

13

road, "I sho wisht she hadda give it to me on my way *to* th' store."

She quickly crawled under the house and hid her dime on one of the rafters, then went in. With an overabundance of anxious errand runners on stand-by, it took a while for her turn to rotate around again. Until it did, she checked on her dime two or three times a day.

Inside the store, "What else you need today, Emma?"

"An Grandma wonts a dime's worth uv Rough On Rats."

"Gotta rat problem, have ya?" walking around to the other counter.

"Yessir, Mr. Riley. They be gittin pretty bad."

After scooping the yellow, mealy-looking rat poison from the barrel and putting it in the small paper sack, he weighed it. Looking at the scales, "Well, that looks lak a whole dime's worth. This'll surre git 'em. You tell Duck I said be careful wit that stuff." Folding down the sack, "An don't git any on your hands, you heah?"

"Yessir, Mr. Riley. I ain't."

When Emma hit the straightaway for home, she started running to keep from being too late. Closer to the house she started walking again. Before she left for the store, supper was on the stove and everybody was sitting out in the yard waiting for it to cool. She was glad to see they were still there.

As soon as she walked in the yard, Grandma Duck asked, "Didja git ever'thang I tole you?"

Not slowing down, "Yes'm, I got it."

"Take it on in there an set it down an cum on back outta th' house."

"Yes'm."

The oblong pan of cream corn Grandma Duck had cooling on the stove-top was still plenty hot as she dumped the whole sack in. Hearing somebody coming, there was no time to get a spoon and she burned her fingers while stirring it frantically.

Out on the yard, Emma casually played her way up to Sally and Elzado. Without raising suspicion, she had to tell them before Grandma Duck called suppertime. "Sally B, les you an me an Elzado go over by the well 'n play."

14

When they got to the well, she motioned for them to squat down behind it so Grandma Duck couldn't see them.

"Whut is it Emma?" Sally asked.

"I got sump'n to tell ya'll."

Glad to be in on the secret, Elzado wanted to know, "Whut is it?"

"Ya'll bet not eat nonea that corn we scraped."

"Why Emma?"

"Never mind why, I'm tellin ya'll, don' eat none."

"But why Emma?"

"Cuz it'll kill ya'll, thas why."

"Whut'd you do to it?"

"Never mind Sally. Jes don' eat none uv it. An ya'll bet not tell nobody neitha."

The threesome sat down on the back steps waiting for the others to finish eating. All the while, Emma glanced nervously through the screen door and couldn't sit still. Puzzling it over in her mind: *from the way that man wuz tellin me bout how much poison Rough On Rats is, they outta be keelin over dead in their plates any minute now.*

Everytime she quit watching, Sally or Elzado asked anxiously, "Whut they doin Emma?"

"Nuthin yet."

When Grandma Duck's army finished she called, "Sally, Elzado, ya'll cum on to th' table 'n eat."

They were too scared to eat anything and sang back, "We ain' hongry Grandma."

"Suit ya'll's sef. But don' be ramblin roun in this kitchen afta while lookin fur nuthin to eat."

"No mam Grandma, we won't."

Emma fixed her pan, minus the corn, and sat between them on the back steps and ate. Disappointed, she wished she had her dime back. In a few minutes Grandma Duck called them, "Sally B, ya'll git in heah 'n clean up this kitchen."

"Yes mam Grandma, we comin."

After supper, as usual, the rag buckets were lit to smoke the mosquitos away. Grandma Duck and her swarm sat outside in the cool of the evening. With the kitchen cleaned, Sally, Emma and Elzado joined them.

Over the noisy playing of the smaller children, Emma heard Grandma Duck cry out, "God, I'm so sick," as she held her stomach.

Then another, "Me too."

And another, "Mama, my belly's crampin me to death."

One by one, they began sweating, moaning like sick cows, and vomiting all over the yard.

Nudging Sally, "C'mon," Emma said, "les play lak we sick too."

They lay down and started rolling around on the ground holding their bellies, groaning, and giggling. Elzado wasn't putting on a very good act mimicking the others, and drew Grandma Duck's attention. With sternful eyes, she looked at Elzado for a minute and knew she was "jes puttin on." Then she looked at Emma, then at Sally. Then back at Emma again.

Pointing her finger at Emma, "Ain' nobody dun this but that ol' nasty, stankin Charlie-lookin devil! That heifer dun sump'n to our supper."

"No mam, I didn' Grandma," Emma defended quickly.

After Grandma Duck puked again, she hollered, "Sally B, run down yonder an tell Doc Hines I say cum rat away. An don' you tarry!"

As Sally turned to go, "Take Elzado witcha."

"Kin I go wit 'em Grandma?" Emma asked eagerly.

"Naw. You set yo tail down over yonder where I kin see you. You low-down heifer."

By the time Sally and Elzado got back, that Rough On Rats had Grandma Duck and her gang's bellies swole up like balloons. When Doc Hines got through pumping them out, he had enough shit to fill up a wagon.

In a few days when Grandma Duck recuperated, Emma took her "whuppin" with a smile. Even though things didn't go as planned, it was a whole dime's worth.

"Sally B wuz always so quiet an shy; it sho surprise everbody when she got saved at the revival. She kept it a secret long as she could, but the spirit wuz in her an kept gittin bigger an bigger til she got shame-faced an run off wit that jackleg preacher who filled her wit it."

Sitting together on the back steps, "Emma, les run off," Elzado urged. "Bama an Sally B been gone so long. They ain' never comin back afta us," she said forlornly.

"I know they ain't."

"Well, les run off then! I'm tired uv doin all th' work an me an you gittin all th' whuppins, specially you. Grandma hates you! Look at my back, Emma," pulling down the neck of her tattered dress to bare the rows of freshly inflicted coat-hanger welts.

"I know Elzado," she said, looking at her shoulders, "mine looks th' same way, but you too little to run off."

"Naw, I ain' too little! I'm big is you is, an I do much work as you do."

"I know that, but you still jes 'leven, Elzado."

Emma, at fifteen, had blossomed. Though her 5'5" frame was slim, it bore the signs of womanhood, and her long dancer legs were striking. She kept her wavy, reddish, dark-brown hair in a braid that hung midway down her back, exposing an interestingly beautiful face. The tiny moles dotting her cheeks were unignorable and accentuated the dark, intense eyes and pouted lips.

Unlike her sisters, Emma took her caramel-colored complexion and hair from Charlie's light-brown Cajun-Negro side of the family. Bama, Sally, and Elzado, with their kinky black hair and dark-mahogany skin, resembled Lillie and the rest of Grandma Duck's offspring.

Grandma Duck was crowding seventy. She wasn't as agile as she used to be, but just as hateful. Because she'd gotten too short-winded she delegated "Big Auntie," her oldest daughter, full authority to do all of her "personal whuppin" while she oversaw to make sure it met her satisfaction.

Big Auntie was still sitting at the kitchen table while Emma and Elzado cleaned off the dirty supper dishes. She was just as ornery as Grandma Duck and Emma decided now was as good a time as any. She had been wanting a chance to talk to Big Auntie away from all the others.

As she raked the leftovers into a bucket for the hogs, "Big Auntie?"

"Whut!"

"I wisht you'd make them ol' boys a' your'n stop meddlin me."

"They be meddlin me too," Elzado chimed in.

"You shet up Elzado!" Big Auntie barked.

Looking up at Emma, who stood across the table, Big Auntie asked with indignation, "Meddlin you how?"

"They puttin they hands up under my dress, pinchin my titties an stuff."

Big Auntie pushed her chair back abruptly and stood up. "You jes shet yo lyin mouth!" she shouted angrily. "They ain' dun no such a thang! You low-down cow, nonea my boys wouldn' even look at you!"

"They did Big Auntie!"

"I tole you to shet yo mouth! I been seein you sassy-wigglin yo behind up an down in that hall."

"Naw I ain't, Big Auntie!"

"Why you ol' Charlie-lookin devil you!" coming around the table to get at her, "You bet not spute my word!"

They clashed together and the noise of their battling soon brought Grandma Duck. Emma was fighting Big Auntie like a tiger-cat and had her down on the floor. Grandma Duck rushed in, hitting at her until Emma grabbed the butcher knife off the table.

Holding them at bay, with the long-bladed knife poised in a striking position, she threatened, "Ef ya'll cum up on me, I'm gon' stick ya'll's hearts out. I ain' gon' take no mo whuppins!" easing her way out the back door.

2 ||||||||||||||||||||||||| [   ]

"Mutherless chillun sees a hard time, when they
    muther is gone.
Mutherless chillun sees a hard time, when they muther
    is gone.
They don't have noooo place to go; they jus keep
    runnin frum door to door.
Mutherless chillun sees a hard time, when they
    muther is gone."   *Old Song*

Emma didn't stop running until she got to the railroad trestle. She stayed under it all night long, and as soon as the
dark lifted at dawn, she got on the railroad tracks and hoofed
it the twenty miles to Gilmer. Son Buddy was not hard to
find. He was still living in the back room of the same hotel.
He'd been working and living there for so long, he was practically a landmark.

He could offer Emma no refuge. His quarters were too
small for two people; besides, the manager of the hotel
wouldn't allow it. However, he did know that the owners of
the dry goods store were looking for some live-in help and
offered to take her there.

"Thas awright, Son Buddy. You needn' do that. Jes tell
me how to git there, I'll find it."

Emma walked up to the lady behind the counter,
"Mam?"

"Yes, can I help you?"

"Yes mam, I wuz by the hotel awhile ago an the porter
over yonder say the folks who own this store wuz lookin for
somebody to work. Is you th' one?"

"Yes, I am. Well, that is, me an my husband," smiling.

19

"We need somebody who can live-in. It's just me an Jim an our three year old boy. We been dropping him off at a woman's house, but we'd rather somebody be at home with him while we're gone. We spend most of our time here in the store," adding, "usually when we get home, I'm dead on my feet and need some help with him at night."

"I kin do it Miz . . ."

"Swift. My name's Mrs. Swift and that's my husband Jim over there," pointing to the man behind another counter.

"Miz Swif, I kin do it."

"What's your name?"

"Emma."

"Emma, do you know anything about taking care of smaller children?"

"Oh yes mam, I growed up in a house full uv 'em."

"Where you from Emma?"

"Big Sandy," dropping her head.

"Why you in Gilmer?"

After taking a long breath, "I run away frum home Miz Swif."

"Why on earth you do that?"

"Cuz they whupped me all the time for nuthin." With tears streaming down her face, Emma showed Mrs. Swift her scarred back.

"Why would they do a mean thing like that?" she exclaimed.

"Well, Miz Swif, afta my daddy kilt my mama, me an my utha three sisters had to live wit Grandma. She already had utha chillun uv her own an didn' want us to begin wit. An afta the two biggest got grown an lef, Grandma got meaner an meaner to me an my baby sister. We didn' have nobody to go to or take up for us or nuthin an got whuppins all th' time."

Sympathetically, "Emma child, you just stand right here and I'll be right back," and fetched her husband.

"Jim, this is Emma. She's gonna be living with us and taking care of Bobby Joe."

After hearing his wife's version of Emma's plight, he looked her over and smiled. "That's fine Irene, but first we got to find her some clothes. I'll take her home and let her git herself cleaned up." Looking back at her, "I bet you'd like that, wouldn' you Emma?"

"Yessir."

"Come with me then."

With Emma cooking, the Swifts started taking turns coming home every day to look in on Bobby Joe and eat a hot lunch. It was Jim's turn and he was seated at the table. Emma had her back to him putting some things away in the cabinet.

"Emma."

"Yessir?"

"You honestly bout the prettiest colored gal I ever saw."

"Thank you, Mr. Jim."

Soon after, Jim started giving her money and getting more than just a hot meal when he came home, while his wife tended the store. And, in addition, Emma could go to the dry goods store and Jim let her pick out anything she wanted. She quickly learned that a white man was willing to pay for "it."

In her off time, when she went to town, Emma expanded her profitable "trade" beyond Mr. Swift. Stopping by to visit Son Buddy, the conversation drifted to her pretty clothes. "Emma, I thought you wuz workin for them people for jes room an board. Ever time I see you, you got on sump'n new. Where you comin up wit all them pretty new hats an shoes an dresses?!"

"It ain' nonea yo bizness where I got 'em frum. I sho as hell didn' git 'em frum you!"

"You didn' answer me. Where you git the money for that stuff?"

"Mr. Jim give it to me."

"Whutcha do to git it?"

"Nonea yo damn bizness!"

"Emma, you bet not be no whorish gal, messin roun wit that white man an takin money frum 'em!"

"Who you to talk?! You been livin a few measly miles away frum us all this time an NEVER cum see bout us, not one time! An you ain' NEVER raised a finger to hep us! So don'cha be tellin me shit!!"

SMACK! The hard slap across the face sent her reeling. Soon as she cleared her head, Emma lit into him forcing him over backwards. Realizing he had a ferocious wildcat on his hands, he used his fists a couple of times to get her off.

Emma's dress was torn and by the time she got to the Swift's house, her bloody lip had swollen to twice its size and the bruised skin under one of her eyes was bluish-black. Still angry, she hurried straight through the house to her back room. Jim looked up from his newspaper in time to see her going past, and got a glimpse of the torn dress. He went to her door and knocked.

"Emma, can I come in?"

"Yessir," she sniffled.

When he entered and saw her bloodied face, "What on earth happened to you? Who did this?" he asked angrily.

"Nobody Mr. Jim."

He called out into the kitchen, "Irene, come in here and look at what somebody did to Emma."

Irene got a wet towel and was wiping her face when Jim said, "I tried to git her to tell me who did it, but she won't."

"Well Jim, maybe she don't feel like talking about it right now. Why don't you go on out and let her lay down for awhile."

Her shiner had turned good and black by the time Jim came home for lunch the next day. Refusing to let it drop, "Emma."

"Yessir?"

"Tell me who did it."

"It wuz my brother." And she told him why.

The next week Son Buddy was found dead, with a bullet hole through his chest, in his little room at the hotel. After a "thorough" investigation, the authorities were unable to come up with a suspect for the murder. Emma was questioned, and she said she knew nothing.

Emma took a seat in the back of the little church and wouldn't sit close to them at Son Buddy's funeral. Grandma Duck and her bunch had the three front benches on both sides of the aisle filled with family. As she dressed for the funeral, Emma had only one thing on her mind, raised the corner of her mattress and got her savings to which Jim

Swift and a few others had so generously contributed. On her way out, she stopped by the kitchen doorway, "Mr. Jim, Miz Swif, I'm gone."

Grandma Duck was watching her masses like a chicken does a hawk. It was clear she didn't want them to even look around at her. Finally, Elzado got the chance to glance back long enough for Emma to catch her eye and gesture to go outside. She quickly passed the word down the bench to Grandma Duck, "Elzado gotta pee."

Looking down the bench at Elzado, Grandma Duck whispered loudly, "G'on! But you hurry up an git yo behind back in heah, an don' be talkin to that ol' Charlie-lookin devil!"

Soon after Elzado left the church, and Emma caught Grandma Duck not looking, she left. She met Elzado on the outside and they stole away. Emma had their getaway prearranged. She handed the driver the thirty dollars for their fifty-mile trip and they settled in the backseat of the car. Elzado asked excitedly, "Where we goin Emma?"

"We goin to Longview. They havin a oil boom up there, an men is comin' frum ever where bringin lotsa money wit 'em. Don' worry. I got some saved up to rent us a house til we kin git started."

"Emma, I don' care ef we ain' got nuthin. I'm jes so glad to git away!"

"I know Elzado. I wuzn' gon' leave you behind again."

They were dropped off in downtown Longview. Neither had ever seen so many people in their entire lives. Car horns honking, wagon-mules rearing, and all the folks scuddling about had their hearts racing with excitement. The town was flourishing. After finding a place to stay, it was time to sit down and go over the game plan. Elzado was ready and willing as she listened to Emma's teachings.

"The first time you may have to grit yo teeth. Lak I did wit Mr. Jim. But afta that, you git useta it an it don' hurt or nuthin. White men want to git thru quick is they kin an go cuz they don' want nobody knowin it. You kin put on a little baby whine an they'll give you jes about anythang you ask fo. They always in a hurry, so the only thang you gon' git frum 'em is money. An thas all we want! Soon as he gits

23

thru, suck yo belly in an git up an pee that stuff out. We gon' git us two uv them long pocketknives an we don' never wanta be on our backs at the same time. Understand?''

Elzado answered with a laconic ''yeah.''

''While I'm doin it, you stand guard an be ready to use that knife. When you do it, don' be scaid, I'll be guardin fo you. We gotta stick together an not git separated frum each utha. You understand?''

''I unnerstand Emma an don' worry, I ain' scaid. Not half as scaid is I wuz to eat that corn you put poison in that time.'' They hugged and laughed in remembrance of the occasion. Even though Elzado was big for her age, she wasn't quite fourteen when they hooked up as a team and took to the oil fields.

The roughnecks welcomed them with open arms and billfolds. Very seldom did anybody give them a hard time. When they did, it usually was the foreman rushing somebody back to work so he could take his turn in the tool shed. Their notoriety spread quickly. The other whores in town even noted how much ''guts an gall'' it took to be out in the fields tricking, ''jes the two uv 'em.'' Danger or no danger, the team kept hiring the taxi driver to take them from one site to another, and wait.

Taking it directly to the frontlines, they were shortstopping the traffic before it got to town. They bought plenty of baubles and beads and pretty clothes, and eventually filtered into the ''streets'' mainstream. Soon thereafter, Baby Norris joined their team. She was five or six years older than Emma, didn't have a steady man, was tired of waiting on the tricks to come to town, and had the guts.

By now, Emma was well known in the fields and heralded as everybody's favorite. She always made a lot more money than Elzado. Emma and Baby Norris were about the same build and complexion, and she was passed off as the third sister. To enhance her chances at a greater share of the tricks, she and Emma dressed alike to confuse the ''bulls'' who picked her thinking she was Emma. But Emma had enough tricks to keep them both busy.

Even though the tool shed business was very lucrative, it was getting old and the trio started having the workers come to the little shotgun house instead. With a few tips from Baby Norris, Emma got in touch with the right people and expanded her enterprise to include bootlegging. As soon as the other whores found out about the crowds that came to her house for a "good time," they started coming too.

Emma got a piece of cloth and hung it over the open doorway separating the one small room from the kitchen. She bought a cot and placed it just inside the kitchen beyond the curtain. Then she laid down the law to the visiting whores. "Don't ketch no tricks in my house an take 'em off somewhere else. You found 'em here, leave 'em here. When you wanna trick an I ain't usin it, you kin pay me to use the cot in the kitchen. An don't be rollin no drunks, it give my house a bad name." Even though Elzado had moved out and was on her own living with a white man in the North Cut Heights, she was still tricking and spent much of her time at Emma's.

Emma's good-time house was fast becoming the most popular place in town. The bootlegging business was going well and, with the other whores hanging around, the shotgun house was always crowded with oil field workers, black and white. This soon brought the gamblers. "Where there's hoes an boozin, there's sho to be gamblin," Baby Norris explained. That's how Emma met Allen.

He was a tall, good-looking black devil, so black his friends called him "Blue." He was street-wise and smooth as butter, a touch of arrogance mixed with caution. His worldly manner ofttimes betrayed his mere twenty-three years. His expensive, tailored clothes fit snugly, accentuating his slim, muscular frame. He was a gambler by profession and always won big at Emma's.

She had smoked him over on several occasions when he was down on his knees shooting dice. Aside from his outright handsomeness, she was magnetized by his gambling skills. When he propositioned her about paying her to let him "manage all the gamblin," she jumped at the chance to enter into the contract.

He started coming early and staying late. For the first time Emma was infatuated and didn't view him as just another trick. She dropped her guard and fell head over heels for Allen. He soon took up permanent residence and they worked as a team. She tricked on the cot and took care of the bootlegging while he cleaned up with the dice. All the money that came in the house, stayed there, one way or another.

Emma realized that Allen was making more than she was and much quicker. However, many times after he'd won all the money in the game at her house, he left and went somewhere else to gamble, only to lose. When he got broke at the other places, he sent his hat by a runner for identification, and she sent money back to him. He wouldn't quit until he used up all of her money too.

Being in the hole was tampering with the bootlegging business. With both of them broke, she had to accelerate her tricking to come up with the money to pay for the loads of whiskey. It was becoming increasingly apparent to Emma that he was blowing it faster than she could make it. They began to argue about it more and more. "Hell," she told him, "I don' need nobody to help me fuck it off! I kin do that by mysef."

It was late morning when he finally made it home. Clothes rumpled and his eyes blood-shot, he'd been up all night gambling. She noticed it right off, it had looked so good on him, "Where's yo hat?" she asked, as he headed into the kitchen.

Stalling for time, he hated to face her, "Whut'd you say Emma?" in between swallows from the dipper.

"I said, where's yo hat?" She had paid sixty-five dollars for that Borsalina.

"I hocked it last nite."

"To who?"

"Aw, I let Pinch hold it for twenny dollars; I'll git it back this evenin'."

She'd been up and down all night herself, waiting on customers who dropped by for bootleg whiskey and getting up to send him money. Propped up in bed on her elbows, as she talked to him, "Say, you don' look real tired to me," wheeling out of the bed, "I'm gon' git the crap blanket an spread it down on the flo. You gon' teach me how to gamble an shoot dice, right now. I'm sick uv this shit!" She spread the army blanket out and got down on her knees. "C'mon, you got some dice in yo pocket, gitcha no-gamblin ass down here,'' she taunted.

He whined and hem-hawed around awhile, but in hopes of soothing ruffled feelings, agreed reluctantly, "Oh, awright. First off,'' picking up the blanket, "you don' want it spread all the way out lak this, it's too thin,'' folding it into a four by four square. "The softer the surface, the easier it is to control the dice when you roll 'em, lak this,'' demonstrating. "You don' want 'em bouncin roun lak this,'' as he precariously threw them out on the blanket. "You want to hold 'em wit yo fingers lak this, an jes rollll 'em easy lak this. Jes sorta push 'em 'cross the blanket so they stay together an tumble side by side. You hafta learn how to control the way they roll wit yo fingers. You wanna keep 'em rollin side by side an not let whutever you got locked in th' middle cum up.''

Taking the dice, one in each hand, he showed her what he meant. "Look, I got a three an a two in th' middle,'' joining the two together. "I'm gon' roll 'em so they stays where I put 'em.'' He "rolllled'' them time and time again and the three and two never showed up. "Anutha thang, they's forty-two dots on a pair uv dice, three sevens on each one.'' Rotating them in his hand, "See, all the dots equal seven. You got five-deuce seven, four-trey seven, an six-ace seven. So . . .''

She interrupted, "If you know alla that an kin do it so good, how cum you git broke all th' time?''

"Cuz Emma, you know well as I do, most uv th' white-folks an nigguhs that hang aroun over heah don' know shit bout gamblin. They be jes havin fun an don' hardly know one dice frum anutha. You kin git away wit cold-blood mur-der in a game wit them.''

"How cum you can't do it when you be gamblin in them utha games?''

"Cuz they won' letcha set 'em an roll 'em lak that. All uv them nigguhs know how to gamble, an all uv us know how to roll. So they serve 'em to you. Every time you shoot 'em out there, the houseman or whoever's runnin the game, picks 'em up, shakes 'em an puts 'em back in yo hand. You ain' got a chance to set 'em an you be goin on luck. Spe-

27

cially when we be shootin on a hard pooltable cuz them dice be tumblin ever which way.''

"Well, if they won' letcha do whut you showin me, whut the hell do you keep goin over there for an luckin off all our money?''

He looked at her for a moment, "I guess for the same reason you keep on trickin. C'mon, les git back to whut I wuz tellin you. The best way to learn bout the bets is to watch the game. You bet the straight-make on six an eight, an you bet the bar on four, five, nine, an ten. When you throw seven . . .''

Emma went to Shiver's Drugs and bought several pairs of dice. All during the day when she wasn't busy, she devoted her time to playing with the pair she carried in her hand, squeezing them, matching them, fitting them and learning to hold them the "right way." When the crap games at the house started, she got down on her knees and watched. When the game ended, she practiced on the blanket by herself. She had emulated the roll down pat, and could "rollll" them across the blanket so close together they looked like they had been stuck with glue.

Emma added the third dimension to her repertoire. No longer was she a mere observer, she had served her apprenticeship. Now when she got down on her knees at the blanket's edge, she got down there to gamble and "run" the game. Allen's managing steadily diminished and she took over. She loved it and gambling became her life's blood. Dedicating herself to the perfection of her talents, she became a whiz with the craps and was "lucky as a shithouse rat" in the eyes of the other gamblers.

Along the way, she developed into a pretty fair card shark. She dealt Maude, Georgia Skin, Poker, Blackjack, Kotch, and was a damned good Koon-Kan player. Allen had been a good tutor and as soon as she learned the ABC's of gambling, he taught her how to cheat. Explaining, "The first 'law' in gamblin is 'know how to cheat an know when you bein' cheated.' " She knew how to "pike" under each card off the bottom or from the middle of the deck without anyone ever noticing. It was hard for them to imagine such a good looking woman cheating. She also developed a gift of gab for distraction purposes when she was performing her quicker-than-the-eye-could-see card antics.

Even though she became very adept at cards, her passion was shooting craps. She learned to use every trick in the book to throw her opponent off balance and make him break his rhythm. Anything to distract. She'd put on her sexiest dress and a pair of her best black gun-metal hose. She flashed a little dab of thigh and leaned forward enough to let them have a quickie at the breast. When she got the attention she was after, she made her move with the dice, "the hull-gully," setting them as she quickly scooped them up to make her "Hudson" shot. She released them with a side motion killing the die she had cupped in her little finger and careening the other one out with top-spin English. Coming out, that die she cupped in her little finger always stopped on five, eliminating the possibility of throwing "craps," a two, three and twelve.

Most of the time she was the only woman in the game, but she cursed just as loud, squabbled just as much, hit, got hit, and hit back. She was just as cold, hard, callous, cunning, and tough as need be, with a natural sense of humor to get by with it. They'd fight one minute and be back gambling and drinking the next. Involving herself in the whole game environment, when the players were bally-hooing and passing the bottle, she took her turn and got just as mean and ornery as the rest of them. When that fire-water hit the pit of her stomach, and her shot came, she started "talking" to the dice.

First roll, coming out, "Oh! Don't forgit ta take the dough! ELEVEN! Bless joy, there it tis!!" Snapping her fingers as loudly as she could with each roll, Emma begged for each point incessantly.

Coming out again, with her Hudson shot, first roll, "Oh! Don't leave me here! Take me witcha when you go!" Got nine for a point, "I bet I bar it."

"You got a bet Emma—you don' bar it. Shoot 'em."

Emma rubbed the dice on the blanket, back and forth, talking to them.

"C'mon Emma, quit fuckin roun' an shoot th' damn dice!" the fader said, admonishing her.

"How cum you in such a great big hurry for me to make nine on yo ass?" she quipped, still rubbing the dice slowly and deliberately to antagonize.

"C'mon Emma! Shoot th' fuckin dice!" he said gruffly, irritated by her delaying tactics.

Going for nine, "Oh Lady! Please be good. Quinine! is a bitter dose! Oh Alek! Iron, you cold black shine! Oh Baby! We ain' but NINE MILES frum home! NINE! times outta ten!"

Still no nine. She stops and rubs the dice again. In the meanwhile, she looks around at the players, "Bet somebody some mo I bar nine."

"Thas a bet, Emma. Brang 'em on."

"I'm fixin to make nine on ya'll's asses. Watch me make it wit six-trey. EVER! now an then you meet a stranger. STOP! an invite him in." Nine.

Got eight for a point. "Oh Ada! Black gal. Let! yo hair hang down! Oh Ada! Ross wuz a pacin good hoss!" Sweat rolling down her face, "Oh Baby! don't leave me here. Cum back an git me. Oh! if you please! Ada!! frum Decatur, the county seat a' Wise. EIGHT! babies too soon!"

Taking another big swig from the bottle, gets ten for a point, "Oh! Tennessee Toddy! All asshole an no body! Oh BIG BEN! Bend double. OH BEN! Bend down an lift it up. OH! Tom Pane, thas Black Annie's ol man!"

Five. "Oh, Fantail Fanny! Fanny Fites! Ugliest woman in the North Cut Heights! Oh Phoenix! Arizona. OH! lemme off! AT! your next stop . . ."

Emma and Allen were making "damn good money." When the crap games ended, they had most, if not all the money. A band of regulars, black and white alike, made coming to their place to drink and gamble a daily ritual. The workers, gamblers, and whores kept money in circulation at the house all the time. With it rolling in, Allen got Pinch to come over and run the house for two or three days so he and Emma could get away.

Allen loved to show her off at other gambling places and they'd take special train excursions to Shreveport regularly. At some of the games gamblers bet $500 on a shot, shooting on a pooltable! Allen took her there to let her see all the excitement of a big bettor's game. But Emma couldn't content herself to stand at the table and watch.

During one of their trips she could take it no longer and threw up fifty bucks. All the players shied away from such a small amount. "Say," she said righteously, "don't stand there an look crazy. Somebody fade me. They's plenny mo where that cum frum. I kin make mo money in fifteen minutes then ya'll seen all day!" Looking at Allen, "Ain't that right Baby?"

"Thas right, Baby."

"I got somethin that'll sell when cotton an corn won't." She had them laughing with her. All she wanted was just ONE shot!

Finally one of the players decided, "Hell, I'll fade a pretty woman lak you ANYTIME. I got you faded fifty. Shoot 'em."

She had never shot craps on a pooltable before, but she knew the dice would be bouncing. Just like Allen had said, it was pure D luck. Rubbing the dice gently on the green felt until she was ready, her first roll was a natural.

"Shoot the hundred," Emma snapped.

"Shoot 'em."

Eleven, a winner. "Shoot the two."

"Damn!" the fader said, and tossed up $200 more. "Shoot 'em agin. I gotcha one mo time."

Eight, and she made it. "Somebody else kin fade her. She's too heavy for me."

She pulled down and shot $200 again and caught FOUR! Gamblers generally hate four and hope to never catch it! It was her favorite point! She bet her other $200 that she'd bar it. She took two or three more shots and got all the money Allen had in his pockets, and bet that. Still not satisfied after a few more rolls, Emma wanted to bet some more. She KNEW she was going to make that four. They had no more money to bet. She paused a moment to rub the dice on the felt, then looked around at Allen, "Lemme have yo coat."

"Whut fo?"

"Never mind, jes pull it off an give it here."

He began to take it off, but very slowly. She had paid Louie Rickey, the tailor, $500 to make Allen's imported

31

camel hair overcoat. When he handed it to her, she threw it up on the table and gave a brief on the overcoat. One of the players opened it up and saw the Louie Rickey label and asked, "How much you wanna bet ginst it?"

"Three hundred."

"Hell naw. I'll go two an no mo."

"Put it up."

More than a thousand dollars was riding on four. She threw them out on the table and the ace stopped immediately. The other spun off down the table and was still spinning as she hollered, "Oh! Little Britches! C'mon!" It settled on three. She won BIG that night and became famous for making "Little Britches." The nightly game at the good time house ended and everybody was gone. Allen had something on his mind, "Emma?"

"Yeah, Blue?"

"I wantcha ta stop trickin wit them white men."

"Why?" she asked coyly.

"Cuz I thank me an you oughta git married. How long we been livin together? Three . . . fo years?"

"Yeah, been bout that long an thas the way we need to keep it. That way, you don' own me and I don' own you. Anyhow, I thought you wanted me to do it. Thas whut I wuz doin when you met me."

"I know Emma, but . . ."

"Say, we don' have to git married for me to stop trickin wit them white men," she interrupted. "But jes cuz you want me to, I'll quit."

"I ain' for no bullshit Emma. I mean bizness. I wantcha to stop doin it."

"Awright, awright, I'll stop; I won' do it no mo." With a quizzical smile, Allen searched her eyes for the truth. "I won' Blue, I swear I won'."

The depression was on the horizon and things were "gittin tighter'n the little E string on a cheap guitar." Both of them hustling barely maintained their style of living and paid for the whiskey. Bootlegging had fallen off considerably after the oil fields trade slacked off. In order to keep on buying Allen a new Borsalina whenever she felt like it, Emma started back to "seein" one of her old standbys, Mr.

Albert the cotton broker. Unbeknownst to Allen, she met him somewhere two or three times a week.

Lying beside Allen early one morning, the spirit moved within her; she had to do something quick. She rolled off her side of the bed and started vomiting.

"Whut's th' matter Emma?!" Allen asked, half-awake.

"Damn! I'm sick at my stomach!"

"Whutcha want me to do?"

"Jes git me a wet rag so I kin wipe my face. I'll be awright in a few minutes."

"Whut the hell you eat? I been tellin you bout eatin all that damn garlic an pepper an onions an shit."

She threw up again. Regaining her composure after flopping back down on the bed, "I ain' been that sick since I wuz a kid an et all them half-green huckleberries. G'on back to sleep, I'm awright now. Musta been somethin I et."

Later that day, she sneaked off to see Doc Falvey. After telling him about the vomiting, he examined her and broke the news, "Emma, you're pregnant." Speechless, she just stared blankly. She'd missed the count! She ought to tell Allen; no she ought'n. She decided to just sit on it awhile.

The time had come, "Say Blue, I been thinkin bout whut you asked me, you still wanna do it?"

"Do whut?"

"Git married."

"Do you?"

"Yeah."

"Les do it tomorrow! I know where we kin git our blood tested."

"Okay. I love you Blue."

"I love you too, Baby," and he held her tightly.

After a couple of months, Emma began to show, and Allen commented, "Hey Baby, you suuure gittin full roun th' middle!"

"I got ever reason to be," she toyed. "I'm pregnant."

"Since when?"

"Since you know when! Wuzn' you there?"

"Well, I'll be damned! I'll jes be damned!" he shouted with joy.

They moved into another shotgun house with wider

rooms. It was located right behind the old, condemned cala-boose. The regulars still showed up, as usual, but today they were asked to go outside and be quiet. Doc Falvey was in-side. Waiting nervously, Allen mingled in the yard drinking with the others to keep warm.

After Doc Falvey cleaned the baby, he laid it in Emma's arms and left to make the announcement. Then she got her first look at what the stork just "brung." "Aw shit!" she ut-tered in dismay, "white as the drifts uv snow."

Doc Falvey walked out on the small porch, "It's a boy."

Allen rushed inside, took one look, and knew it "wudn' his'n." He wheeled around and walked out on her that snowy Friday afternoon at 3:20 in 1930.

> "I wuz born in a lion's den,
> and suckled by a bear . . .
> I growed two sets uv jaw teefs
> and a double coat uv hair."

II

Big Emma
and Me

3 ||||||||||||||||||||||||||| [   ]

1934

Emma was busy tricking seven days a week. Our house was only a couple hundred feet from the railroad tracks and a hundred yards from the T & P Station. It was a real convenience for the engineers, firemen and brakemen who left their trains for a quickie. When she had "company," I sat on the steps and waited.

There wasn't much for me to do during the weekdays, except get up late at night and sell an occasional half-pint. The weekends were totally different and sleep was out of the question. Emma rose early on Saturday mornings and got me out of my cot in the kitchen to help her with the preparations for the long weekend stand.

She fixed our Saturday morning special: two cans of sardines piled high with hot peppers, a big white onion, cheese and crackers. "Gitcha a fork an cum on." I loved eating out of her plate; the food tasted better.

As soon as we finished, I helped get the scrub waters ready for the wooden floors that already looked bleached from too many scrubbings. My job was to watch the water from the outside hydrant so it wouldn't overflow the buckets while Emma carried the full ones into the house. When we had enough water she began her ritual of "preparin" it by pissing in the buckets after adding a half can of Eagle lye. This was for good luck she said. I watched out the front door and we'd pretend we weren't home if a woman came to the house before a man. The first person in the house after the piss and lye scrubbing had to be a man because "if a woman cums in first, it puts a jinx on the house."

The next step was getting the gambling area set up. An old, green army blanket was spread in the middle of the floor. When unfurled, the thinly worn "crap" blanket was clearly marked U.S. in the center. No matter how it was folded, the cigarette holes always showed causing a special house rule to be made, "Cocked dice in the hole don't go." Emma tried her best to protect it, but serving combat duty on the front-lines was hazardous.

Emma thoroughly briefed me on my jobs before the crowd arrived. I sat on the case of bootlegged whiskey bottled in half-pints until somebody wanted one. I collected the money and gave each customer a dipper full of water to wash it down with, if they bought it by the shot. Between sales, I kept a sharp lookout for the police and kept an eye on the dice when they rolled off the blanket so nobody could switch in some crooked ones. When Emma was shooting, I watched the cigar box she kept her loose change in so nobody would steal from her.

After a short wait, the gamblers came and Saturday got kicked off with a bang. The twenty-five or thirty black and white gamblers down on their knees were crammed elbow to elbow around the crap blanket. At least a dozen more hovered over the shooters, placing bets over their shoulders. The small shotgun house, with one room and kitchen, was bursting at the seams. Sometimes, the gambling, tricking, drinking, squabbling and occasional fighting went right on into the next day without ever stopping. Many times, Allen came over to gamble. I knew by the way she treated him that he was somebody special.

When there was a lull in the whiskey selling, I watched the dice as they were propelled across the blanket. When Emma's shot came, I tried not to act like I was paying any attention. I knew she didn't want me pulling for her because it made her have "bad luck." Without fail, when she missed a point she had bet pretty heavily on, she glowered straight at me and ordered, "Boy, carry yo jinky, peckerwood-lookin ass in that kitchen an git outta my sight!"

I stayed awhile, but eased my way back into the crap room to take a peep out the curtains for the police. I lingered in the room too long. After missing another point, her eyes found me. "Don't ya'll shoot til I git back," she said as she got up. "I need to take care uv some bizness in the kitchen for a minute." Goosebumps popped out all over me in dreaded expectation.

When she reached a certain quota in her drinking her bitterness surged and I was the target. None of the gamblers dared to interfere, especially after that time Lakey spoke up, "Emma, you ought not to whup 'em lak that." She flew into a rage and stabbed him in the shoulder with an ice pick and threw him out of the house for "meddlin."

Beyond the curtain I stood waiting. She walked into the kitchen with the coat hanger and slowly began stretching it out. "Take off yo clothes."

"Mama, I won' do it no mo. Pleeze Mama, don't . . ."

"I tole you not to call me that! Call me Emma! Now git that shit off. Right now!" When she finished dealing with me, she returned to the crap game and started shooting again.

Soon realizing she needed me, she called me back to the crap room, "Git me my bottle."

The gambling went on into the night. The house was dark except for the kerosene lamp on the kitchen floor and the one placed near the crap blanket. Terrell Latham had been "swinging" the craps all evening and Emma cursed him with every breath. He hung around every crap game in town and never had more than two dollars to lose. After he was broke, or claimed to be, every time his turn came he sold it to a gambler on the other side of the blanket who already shot. If somebody wanted to give him two or four bits for his turn, well and good, but the players to his right were kept waiting, including Emma.

When he'd swing the craps it caused confusion, and she lit in on him. "Terrell, you ain' lost but two chicken-shit dollars an I'll be a muthafucka if you gon' swing the fuckin dice ever'time they git to you. They's some mo nigguhs who want to shoot an can't for you holdin up the Gotdam game!"

Unfortunately for Terrell, he got a little too drunk. After a long evening of swinging the dice and getting cursed out, he flopped down in one of the cane bottom chairs and passed out. Everybody and his brother went through his pockets and this time he really was broke.

The game was finally about to end, with Emma winning most of the money. There were only a couple of players left trying to wrap up the scrappings. Emma had quit shooting and I noticed her staring at Terrell with a mischievous look on her face.

She got up and walked into the kitchen, discovering that our two kittens had shit all over the floor. She rolled several turds onto a piece of paper with the stove poker and brought them back into the crap room. Using a small stick, she smeared it all over Terrell's face, especially heavy around his nose and mustache.

I started laughing but she cautioned me not to be too loud and wake him up before she finished. The few gamblers left in the game had stopped shooting and were watching her too, snickering and trying to keep from laughing out loud. She had figured out an acceptable way to get back at Terrell for being such a nuisance.

When she finished, she opened a bottle on the house and passed it around while everybody waited. After a few minutes, Terrell's nose began to twitch. With closed eyes, he started wiping his nose and mustache, rubbing his chin and scratching his head. Each time he went through those motions, he spread the shit more and more. Now it was even in his hair. The stink in the room was almost unbearable.

At last Terrell opened his eyes and after a few moments of collecting himself, he finally said in a half-drunken stupor, "Gotdam Emma! You needs ta git rid o' dem fuckin cats! Looka heah, dem liddle cocksuckers dun shit all over me!"

I laughed so hard I cried, and forgot all about the zinging of the coat hanger.

If some player in the game happened to catch her fancy, she wasn't slow about giving him the glad-eye. I knew the moment it happened. She mellowed her intense gambling expression into a sexy, sleepy-eyed bedroom look, and flashed it to him like a lightning bug, "stick aroun." When

40

she mixed business and pleasure, she'd have two games going at the same time, never missing a shot in either.

It didn't matter who she kept for her late night lover or how eager she was to go to bed with him, he had to wait his turn. After the others were gone, she told him, "I gotta take care uv my o' man first." She was never too tired and it was never too late. After they'd pulled a long tour of duty, she picked up the old crap blanket, shook it out, and painstakingly folded it up and laid it to rest underneath her pillow. With her "o' man" bedded down, it was on to the next item on the agenda.

To get me to go to sleep in a hurry, I got the Raw Hide and Bloody Bones bedtime story. Rushing me beyond the curtain to my cot, "You betta git you some salt and take it to bed witcha so Raw Hide an Bloody Bones won' gitcha! He loves to git little boys who don' go to sleep lak they mama's tell 'em to.

"Bloody Bones is BIGGG! BIG as a bear. An got big o' bloody chunks uv meat hangin all off uv him! An some loooong sharp claws an big red eyes, wit blood drippin all down 'em! An slobberin blood all out his mouth. He creeeeps up on you at nite, an if he ketchcha not sleepin, he'll smear you wit his big o' bloody hands, an you'll turn into a big scab an die!!

"Only way you kin keep him off you is to throw some salt on 'em an he'll turn yellow an melt away lak a snail do. But if you don' wanna meet him face to face, you betta go to sleep quick! An that way, he won' cum afta you. But jes in case, you best take that salt box to bed witcha."

"Yes mam, I got the box an I'm gon' eat sum too! Emma, kin I keep the lamp on turnt down low?"

"Naw, blow that lamp out an go to sleep befo' Bloody Bones cum."

I covered my head hiding from Bloody Bones. The squeeking bedsprings quickly lullabied me to sleep . . . until somebody knocked on the door and wanted a half-pint. I handled all the late, late traffic from my cot office. Usually, I woke up on the first knock and moved quickly through Emma's room to answer the door before the knocking disturbed them. Digging into the flour barrel in the kitchen for the half-pints, I waited on the customers, collected the money and dropped it in the fruit jar, lay back down and re-hid from Bloody Bones under the covers.

Tuesday, things were slow; we closed up shop and went to bed early for a change. I was asleep on my cot when she came in and woke me up, "Shhh, be quiet an lissen. The police is outside. You start cryin the minute they cum thru the door. If you cry, they won' take Emma to jail."

When I heard the heavy knocking on the door, I got my cry ready. The voice was gruff, "Open up this Gotdam door, it's th' law!"

Very quickly she opened the door and stepped back to the center of the room, gathering me close to her. Feigning fear, I started whimpering. I knew all three of them by name. They had been here before. All three were notoriously well-known for their "head cuttin."

"Yessir, whut ya'll want?" Emma asked politely.

"You know damn well whut we want gal!" Mr. Thrasher shot back angrily. "You got sum bootleg whiskey in heah an we gonna find it or beat hell outta you!"

"Naw sir, they ain' nonea that stuff in here," she denied fervently.

They began tearing the place apart. After looking under the bed, in boxes, in her trunk, and everywhere they could think of, one of the deputies was really getting irritated and took a swing at Emma. I let out my biggest, best cry. For the moment it worked. They wanted her to stop my loud screaming.

During the pause in the action, Emma got a chance to collect herself and go into her command performance, "I'm jes a po ol' workin gal tryin to make a livin an raise this half-white baby. I don' steal or do nonea them bad thangs them utha nigguhs roun here do an I NEVER give the laws no trouble."

Mr. Killingsworth bent down to me, "Is there any whiskey in this house, boy?"

"No Sir!"

Not missing a trick, "An jes look at him ya'll. He's onea yo own. Tell 'em how old you is baby."

"I wuz born rite behind th' ol' jailhouse in nineteen thurty on a Friday at three tweeny th' seventh day uv Febewary. It wuz sleetin an snowin. Gregg County Presink Number One. Hoot Garner is th' Shariff, I'm fo years old.''

It took many a lick with the coat hanger to get it in me, but after I had it down pat she could shake me at four in the morning and I'd rattle it off in my sleep.

She had them until Mr. Thrasher noticed the loose planks in the center of the floor where we were standing. He told us to move over. They lifted the planks and there it was, two cases of half-pints! I looked at her and she looked at me.

This was one of the few times whiskey was in our house and I didn't know it. When I said "no sir," I thought we were sold out. The delivery man had brought it without my knowing.

With a look of "ah ha, we gotcha now" on his face, Mr. Bell yelled, "We're takin yore ass to jail!"

"Whut am I gon' do bout my boy?"

"Leave him wit a neighbor. I don't give a damn whutcha do wit him, yore ass is goin to jail," Mr. Bell reaffirmed.

"Please Sirs, Whitefolks, whutever ya'll do, don' make me leave my baby wit nonea these niggers roun here," she begged. "Look at him, ya'll. If you wuz a nigger, would you want to keep him?"

There I stood like Mary's little lamb, with my light-colored skin and hazel eyes staring up at the three of them so innocently.

"Alright, git him dressed. He's goin too," Mr. Bell conceded.

Emma took me behind the curtain. As she helped me get into my cowboy outfit and boots, she whispered, "They ain' gon' keep *us* in jail long."

While the other two loaded the whiskey into their car trunk, Mr. Thrasher told me he would let me blow the siren on the way. I was tickled pink to be going to jail with Emma. She sat in the back and I sat on Mr. Thrasher's lap up front, blowing the siren all the way to the jailhouse.

After booking her in, they were ready to take us upstairs to the cells. I felt the sweat in the palm of her hand as she clutched mine tightly. She was constantly telling me to be a big boy and not to be afraid. I told her I wasn't scared, but

43

that didn't seem to help much. She was getting more nervous by the minute.

On the walk to the elevator leading up to the cells, she told me not to be afraid and not to cry. I kept saying I wasn't and I wouldn't. Inside the elevator, she said it again nervously. When we got off, she said, "Don' cry baby, an don' be scaid, Emma's right here."

When we got to the cells, they had to decide where to put me. It took awhile, but they finally chose a cell across the hall from her. One of them went to the kitchen part of the jail and returned with a wooden apple crate. He told me if I stood on it, Emma and I could see each other. After locking our two cell doors, they left.

I heard the elevator going down. Standing on the box, I could see Emma looking through her bars at me. "You scaid baby?" she asked.

"No mam, Emma."

I heard the panic when she yelled, "Well, I'm Gotdam sho scaid, an I'm gon' cry!" She screamed and hollered so loud the jailer and two deputies came back up quickly. Emma was in hysterics.

They descended again to call the sheriff at his home to find out what to do. By this time, I was yelling and sobbing uncontrollably, at Emma's instructions. "Don' let me do all the fuckin cryin an hollerin by myself!" After a few minutes, they were unlocking our cells.

"Git the hell outta there," one of the deputies said as he unlocked our doors.

On the elevator ride down, Emma asked for her whiskey back and cab fare home. We got the cab fare.

Once outside, "See there baby, that wuzn' shit, wuz it? I knew all the time we wuz gon' make it. I bet you thought I wuz scaid, didn' you? Shit, I wuzn' scaid one damn minute. I didn' want you to be scaid, thas all."

We left the jail walking, headed for a joint down on the streets. She bought some fried chicken and got herself a bottle. After awhile, the whiskey began to talk and she began telling the other patrons how the sheriff demanded her release "soon as he found out" she'd been arrested.

The next day Emma took me downtown. She stopped on

44

the corner across the street from the Hilton Hotel and kneeled down beside me, "You g'on cross the street now. Watch the cars. Emma'll wait over here for you."

Even with times tough as they were, being a cotton broker, my daddy was always good for at least a twenty. I sat at the hotel drugstore soda fountain like I was a white boy, while she waited across the street.

I had met him before. Emma told me, "Here's yo daddy, boy." They had a big laugh when she said, "G'on over to him baby. Shit, you look jes lak 'em."

After I finished drinking my milkshake and getting the twenty dollar bill stuffed in my pocket, he led me to the hotel door and walked me to the corner. While waiting for the traffic, "Bye son, watch out for the cars now," and gave me a nudge. I ran across the street quickly to hand her the money.

Emma was cleaning the kitchen when Baby Norris stopped by late Sunday afternoon. She hadn't been by for a spell. When they finished their "Whut on earth you been up to's" and "When's the last time you seen so an so," Baby Norris said, "Puss, where's that priddy lil man a' mine? I guess you know he's gon' be my man jes soon as he gits a lil bigger. You might as well tell all them utha hoes I dun staked my claim on 'em cuz he's sho gon' be a heartbreaker onea these days. I'm gon' be the first one to break 'em in. Maybe then I'll have me a man that treats me better'n that sonuvabitch I got."

"Shit," Emma said, "he's jes fo an still got the smell uv milk on his breath. By the time he gits old enuff for you Baby, hell, you'll be on crutches."

Laughing, Baby Norris said, "Thas why I wanna git a head start so's I kin git as much uv it as I kin. I'm so Gotdam tired uv screwin all them old limber-dicked, 'lapidated bastards I jes don' know whut to do. You always lose money fuckin wit 'em cuz you has to lay there an milk th' sonuvabitches for thirty minutes an hope they raise a hard, knowin nine times outta ten th' filthy bastards'll cum in yo fuckin hand!

"Take that shitty ol' man uv mine. Hell, ever once in a while I laks him to take care uv bizness wit me, you know.

45

But I wind up squeezin his dick so long I gits outta the notion. An when he kin git ready, it always bends in the middle an I end up stuffin an crammin it in. Yeah, I'm up to here," motioning underneath her nose, "wit them old farts. All that shit bout I'd ruther be a ol' man's darlin than a young man's fool don' mean shit in my life. I don' want nuthin old but money. An I want that to be crisp!"

"Baby Norris, gal, you still crazy. Hell, I thought Jake wuz really layin it to you the way you fuss over him when I see ya'll together."

"Yeah, thas the truth Puss, but I do that to keep sum uv them licks offa my ass. Do you know that sonuvabitch damn near beat me to death a couple weeks ago?"

"Whut'd he do that for Baby?"

"Aw, shit. He caught me dead to rights. I held out six dollars so I could git me a pair uv them Mary Jane slippers you an me looked at uptown. He found the money I stashed an my ass is still so'. But I kin tell you rat here an now that in bed he ain' shit. Th' muthafucka jes got me scaid uv 'em an he knows it. Say, I been over here damn near a hour. I'm sho thirsty, ain'tcha got nuthin to drank?"

"Yeah Baby, raise up th' corner uv that mattress. It's a bottle under there."

"I found it. Brang two glasses witcha when you cum in here."

"I'll brang you one, but you know I don' drank mine outta no glass. Leave my part in the bottle."

"You gon' drank sum now?"

"Hell yeah, I'm nearly thru. I wuz tryin to git this kitchen cleaned up fo I set down. Gal, jes keep on talkin. I kin hear you. I'll be there in a minute."

"Where's that priddy man uv yourn at? That boy sho got lotsa sense an jes as mannerable as he kin be. I ain' never said nuthin to him that he don't say 'yes mam' an 'no mam' back."

"He oughta be out in the back somewhere. Why don'tcha call him. It's time for him to be comin in anyhow."

"Cum here, you lil priddy thang. Where you been hidin?"

"I ain' hidin Miss Baby Norris. I jes been settin on th' back steps."

"Cum here an give me sum sugar an hug my neck. An you betta quit callin me MISS Baby Norris. Jes leave off that Miss shit. It makes me sound too damn old." Pinching my cheeks, "Don'tcha know I'm waitin on you to grow up an be my sugar daddy?"

She held out her arms and gapped her legs open for me to walk between them. Reluctantly, I did. She grabbed me like an octopus. She hugged and kissed me and even stuck her tongue in my mouth. The way she was smacking and carrying on sounded like I was being eaten up.

Finally, Emma said in a joking tone, "You betta leave that baby alone."

Baby Norris untentacled and pushed me back a little. "You might be actin shy now, but jes wait a few mo years. Yo Mama'll havta git a shotgun to keep them black heifers away. An I'm gon' be one uv 'em!"

They sat on the bed drinking and bullshitting and drinking some more until, "Gotdam Puss, this fuckin whiskey do shit to my brain. I damn near forgot whut I wuz gon' tell you. When I wuz on my way over to the sto' this mornin, I seen onea them work trains sidetracked over by Cotton Street. It wuz three cars an I seen all them Meskins standin round on the outside. I went over an ast onea the white men whut it wuz there for. He say they'd be there for a few days takin up an layin sum mo tracks. Child, I lef there in a hurry to tell my man Jake. Do you know I couldn' git that no good bastard to go over there wit me. Even knowin he wuz gon' take whut I made. He tole me I didn' have no bizness down there fuckin wit them Meskins. Shit, tough as times is now, a dollar's a dollar. Damn who it useta b'long to."

"Thangs been slow roun here an I need some money to git my whiskey stocked back up. Baby Norris, les me an you go down there an make that money, lak we useta."

"Fuck that shit!" Baby Norris exclaimed loudly. "If sump'n happen an Jake fount out I went down there afta he tole me not to, that sonuvabitch'll kill me. Hey, is that the only bottle you got?"

"Yeah," Emma replied, which I knew was a lie. She was

ready for Baby Norris to leave and that was one sure way of doing it.

"Well, it's gittin late, Puss. Guess I best be gittin on fo that damn ol' man o' mine thanks I'm off givin sump'n away. I be seein you gal."

Night had fallen and with it came the late autumn chill. Emma got off the bed and went into the kitchen, returning in her coat and tam. She had one of her sweaters draped across her arm.

"Put this on an cum walk wit me. Baby Norris is gittin to be a squeamish bitch, too scaid to make money. I don' give a damn if a hundred Meskins is in that railroad gang, if they wanna buy somethin, we got somethin to sell. Ain't we, Big Shot?"

"Yes mam, Mama."

"I tole you to stop callin me that!"

"Yes mam, Emma."

She knelt down to my size and handed me her switch blade, "Put this knife in yo pocket an keep it open. We goin down there an make that money."

"Yes'm," I said, and put it in my pocket.

As she turned the kerosene lamp down low, "You cold?"

"No mam, Emma."

We walked out of the house, hand in hand, heading for the tracks. I was frightened at first, but after she told me how important my part was, I was glad she chose me. With every step, she told me over and over what I was to do.

We walked side by side in the darkness. The only sound when she stopped talking was our feet crunching the gravel as we neared the tracks. My short steps were no match for her long, determined strides. We followed the tracks until we reached Cotton Street.

We crossed and stopped about a hundred feet from the long Carson fence running beside the tracks and ending at Cotton Street. It separated the railroad right-of-way from the three warehouses on the other side. Straight ahead were the train cars.

"I want you to stand right here," she said, placing me on the warehouse side of the fence. "Turn aroun an keep yo face turnt to the street. Don' look back. When I cum back

I'm gon' git close to you as I kin. If I call you, don' try to fight 'em, jes put the knife in my hand. I'll git us outta here.''

She began walking toward the cars, but stopped. She turned and asked, "Know why I'm doin this?''

I looked over my shoulder at her, pondering the question. Before I could answer, "For you,'' she said and hurried down the tracks.

I turned my face back to the street, just as she instructed. My heart was trying to pound its way out of my chest. I gripped the knife so tightly my hand was sweating on its cold steel handle. Her feet crunching the gravel grew fainter and fainter. For an instant I quickly glanced around.

I saw her climbing up into the rear of the work train. In a few seconds, I heard loud shouts. I didn't know what they were saying, but I could tell they were shouting acceptance. Still, I gripped the knife tighter and tighter.

After a few minutes, I glanced back long enough to see her and a man walking toward me. She was slightly ahead of him. He must have seen me standing in the shadows because he said something. I don't know if she understood him but I heard her say, "It's awright, thas jes my boy.''

I kept my eyes glued to the dark street; I never looked back. I couldn't hear what she told him, but soon after he left, there came another and another and another and another and another. . . .

I did not want to hear, but I heard. I wished my ears were deaf to all the sounds on earth, except her voice should she call out. My neck ached from trying to choke back the swelling tears; my chest was on fire. I didn't know how long or how many. I only knew the very weak voice calling, "Baby, cum help me.''

I ran to where she lay. The back of her head was resting on one of the rails and her ankles were laying across the other. "Emma, you awright?'' I asked anxiously.

"Yeah,'' she said, struggling to get up. I reached down and began pulling her by the arms. "Cum closer, Baby. There you go,'' she said holding onto my shoulders and pulling herself up. "We gon' make it, ain't we?''

Her legs trembled and her hands shook as she leaned on

49

my shoulders. One of her shoes was off. I stooped over to pick it up and saw the blood coming down the inside of her legs.

"Emma, you got a hanky?"

"Yeah, they's one in my coat pocket."

I got it and began wiping at the blood. "Don' throw it away when you git thru, I need it." I handed her the handkerchief and she put it inside her panties.

Kneeling down, she pulled me close and hugged me tightly. "You Emma's buddy, ain'tcha?"

"Yes'm, Emma."

"Now, buddy, les you an me go party!"

The "party" didn't last but a hot minute. The next day I came in the house, there sat Arthur Johnson with Emma on his lap. He was a bald-headed railroad porter who wore his navy blue uniform even when he was off duty, sporting a big set of "important" keys from his belt.

"Mr. Johnson's yo new daddy an he's gon' live wit us. He laks little boys. So you be nice to Mr. Johnson, an behave yoself, you hear."

"Yes'm."

I couldn't stand him. I had already noticed how he looked at me the other times he came to the house. And those weren't looks of love. Even though he was a top church deacon, he was a cock-hound from way back. He had tricked on my cot many times, and not just with Emma.

The house schedule changed overnight. Whenever he got a lay-over she was up every morning at the crack of dawn to fix his breakfast. I had to serve his coffee. When I lay back down on my cot, he sat at the table staring at me.

One night on the other side of the curtain I heard him telling her about his high standing in the church and, "it jes don' look right when the three uv us be's out together. I don' lak tellin people he's my stepboy." She said she would leave me at the house from now on when they went out.

When she left the house to take care of her tricking-on-the-side business and left me with him, he told her some big lie when she got back. He said I wouldn't behave and "didn' do a thang I tole him." She'd beat the dogshit out of me in the kitchen. After the beatings I passed through the room on my way outside and he poked fun and made ugly faces at me.

He was a sly old bastard. One day while we sat at the table eating, right out of the clear blue sky he told her, "Emma, how on earth kin I set heah an enjoy my meal wit that boy rollin his eyes at me."

Emma slapped me across the mouth and my chair went over backwards. I was dizzy and tasted the blood seeping on my gums. "Git yo muthafuckin half-white ass up off that flo' an take yo Gotdam plate out on the back steps to eat! You the Gotdam reason why I can' keep no man! You run ever one I ever had away with yo peckerwood-lookin ass. You gon' treat Mr. Johnson right! You hear me?"

"Yes'm."

From the back steps I heard her say, "He's gon' mind you or I'll wear all the hide off his ass."

He'd been gone a week when he got his next lay-over. He ate supper and left. Emma left a few minutes later. She was gone about thirty minutes and returned. When he came back, all hell broke loose.

"Where you been MISTER muthafucka?! I know where you been, you Gotdam, sorry, low-down, baldheaded, shit-eatin bastard! Here I am treatin you right, sleepin witcha, feedin yo muthafuckin ass an I ketchcha comin outta Red Sarah's back door!"

He mumbled something and she yelled back, "You jes a muthafuckin lie! Whut th' Gotdam hell wuz you sneakin out the back fo if you wudn' tryin to hide?! An I'm gon' see that bitch too! She knows I don' let no hoe fuck wit my man."

The more she cussed the angrier she got, and started throwing his clothes out the front door. He wasn't saying a word. While she was getting his things in the kitchen, she grabbed the butcher knife lying on the table and broke through the curtain like a mad bull.

When she rushed at him with the knife, his eyes got big as silver dollars. He was trying to get out as fast as he could, but just as he wheeled to run, she whacked him across the cheeks of his ass with the knife. I could hardly wait for Old Arthur Johnson to come running by me outside. When she

51

had started cursing I piled some rocks by the front steps hoping for a shot. I managed to zero one in, right on the back of his shiny black bald head.

4 ||||||||||||||||||||||||| [_____]

Two things our house was never without, dice and men. Old Arthur Johnson was gone, but I knew it wouldn't be long before another took his place. Whenever there was a lull in the action and all was quiet on the southern front, Emma pulled out her old crap blanket. We got down on our knees and she taught me.

"See these burn holes? I always keep 'em spread out to my right. Them holes is my measurin stick an I use ever one uv 'em when I'm shootin for a point. It's a secret, so don' tell nobody?"

"I won't, Emma."

Taking the dice in her hand, "See, when I'm shootin for fo, I roll 'em even wit this first one. An when I'm shootin for five an six, I roll 'em up to these two. Eight's a long-range point, so I roll 'em all the way up to this last hole." After the strategy lesson, she explained how to "gitcha man," what combinations to use.

She bought a pair of pee-wee dice for me to practice with, explaining, "When you learn how to roll them little suckers, you'll have a real good touch when you start shootin big craps lak we use." She taught me how to grip and roll them so that what I set in the middle would stay there. Besides shooting marbles, shooting craps became my favorite game. Now, when I watched the shooters, I knew exactly what was going on. And when the blanket cleared, I practiced.

It was unusual to have such a large crowd on hand in the middle of the week, but the cross-tie loaders had come to town. Their crews were transferred from Beaumont and would be loading railroad ties in Longview for the next few days. Since early morning they'd been at our house drinking and gambling.

Emma had been down on her knees shooting craps all morning. She took a few seconds to look around the blanket at the onlookers who were already broke, "Say." He raised his eyes. "Whut's yo name, baby?"

"George."

"Well George, you look lak a honest man," putting them eyes on him. "Kin I git you to run the game an git my cuts for me so I kin go pee?" Squirming and holding herself, "I'm bout to bust!"

"Sho I will, for a good-lookin woman lak you."

She flashed him a smile, acknowledging the flattery, got up and stretched right in front of him, and headed for the back yard.

I watched him while she was gone. He didn't miss putting a single one of her cuts (a nickle from every bet for the "wear an tear" on the house, blanket, dice, lamp and for running the game) in the cigar box. When she returned to the game, George had cut off more than six dollars.

She kept all the small change and pitched him the green across the blanket, "Here George, take some uv this money to play wit. Maybe it'll make you lucky," she said teasingly.

He scooped up the dollar bills, "I sho thank you Miss Emma, I could use sum luck."

Looking into his eyes, she reached over and patted his hand, "I thank yo luck jes changed." Finding me in the room, "Baby, hand Emma her bottle."

"Yes'm."

She took a BIG swig, with nothing for a chaser, and handed it back to me. "Hand it to George."

"No, I thank you jes th' same, Miss Emma, but I ain' much uv a dranker."

When he refused, "Well, I'll jes be damned! He don' wanna drank wit me. Hand it back here."

54

"Don' take me wrong, Miss Emma. It ain' that I don' wanna drank wit you, SPECIALLY," he said smiling, "but that whiskey will sho tell off on a man when he's got a 300 pound green tie on his shoulder goin up a gang plank in one uv them box cars."

"Suit yoself," she smiled back, saluted him with the bottle, and took another slug.

It didn't take him long to lose the few bucks she had tossed, and he was back to onlooking. There were only three players left in the game, and they were just about broke too. This had been another one of those games where Emma had wiped them out with her Hudson shot. But she wasn't about to quit until the last dollar was in her hand and she heard them sing her favorite song, "Well Emma, you got me! I'm broke!"

Looking up from the blanket at George again, "Say sweet thang, I bet them cross-ties do git pretty heavy. Ain't you tired uv totin 'em, baby?"

She was pouring on the syrup and George was no starnatal fool, "I sho as hell is, Miss Emma."

"Well, kin you cook?"

"As a matter uv fact, Miss Emma, I'm a real good cook."

"Whut kin you cook?"

"Anythang you kin eat."

"Well, maybe you the man I been lookin for. I need a man roun here that kin cook an don' drank." It was her turn to shoot the dice. All the while she was shooting she was talking to him in between her dice verses. "If you tired uv totin 'em, maybe you'd lak to hang roun here wit me awhile an sort uv help me run thangs. An do the cookin. I'll give you part uv whutever we take in. How's that sound?"

"Sounds jus fine wit me, Miss Emma. When does you wont me to start?"

"Soon as you quit callin me MISS Emma."

"Awright Emma, thas a deal."

"Say George, I'm gon' be thru here in a few minutes. Me an my boy ain' had a bite all day. I ain' had time to stop an fix us nuthin. Look aroun in the kitchen an see if you kin rustle up somethin."

He wasn't in the kitchen very long, "Emma, I looked everwhere. I didn' see nuthin in there to cook."

Slightly embarrassed, "Well, don' worry bout it. Here," tossing him a ten from the bills she kept stuffed between the fingers of her left hand, "the store's aroun th' corner, why don'cha go git us somethin."

The game was over. Emma was folding up the crap blanket and I was sweeping away the cigarette butts when he returned. He cooked smothered cabbage, fried pork chops, made a big pan of cornbread, and fixed a peach cobbler. It was the best meal I'd ever eaten. George stayed. Nine months later, my half-sister was born.

Mama Joe lived in a shotgun house half a block down the street. Even though she was sixty years old, she was feisty. Emma and Elzado had met her long ago when they first came to Longview. She was bootlegging back then, and was still plying her trade. Mama Joe even turned a trick now and then, "jes for good luck," she'd say.

It was hard to fathom someone turning a trick with Mama Joe. She was about four feet tall and her bosom was so exaggerated she looked like a bantam chicken. Her head seemed to sit right down on her shoulders, making the hump on her back more visible. To conceal it, she wore middy-collared dresses.

When she came over to our house, she never said more than a few words to me, "How you Whitefolks? Boy, you sho is growin," or "Emma, Whitefolks' hair ain' gittin a bit darker!" If no gambling was going on, she and Emma talked for hours about years gone by. Mama Joe didn't shoot dice, but she loved to play two-bits a game Pitty-Pat.

She usually walked over about once or twice a week, but since she'd found out Emma was pregnant, she was over every day talking to them about the baby. "Lissen Emma, George may not know it, but way back yonder, you member I tole you afta Whitefolks wuz born, if you ever had anutha baby, I wanted it. An you promised me if you had anutha 'un, you'd let me keep it. Didn' you tell me that?"

"Yeah, Mama Joe, I tole you that, but that wuz a long time ago. I can't jes let you have the baby. George got somethin to say bout it. Ain'tcha baby?"

George was a slow talker and Mama Joe seized another opportunity before he answered, "Emma, you an George both know neitha one uv ya'll ain' got no time to mess wit no baby. Since ya'll dun started sellin meals, ya'll keeps a house full uv peoples all the time. When ya'll gon' have time to take care uv it? Emma, ya'll both know I wouldn' let it wont fer nuthin. I'd be good to it an take care uv it, jes lak it wuz mine. Ya'll wouldn' hafta worry bout nuthin. An ya'll kin see it ever day."

Reeking with self-pity, "On account uv my condition, I ain' never been able to have chillun uv my own. I didn' even have no sisters an brothers. Please Emma!" If she came over three times a day, she begged and pleaded with them three times a day.

Long before Emma was due, the cafe part of the business had really picked up. George cooked big pots of chili, stew, chittlins, pinto beans and ham-hocks, and all kinds of greens. Emma helped prepare the meals and I waited tables. Everyday at lunch time, the house was packed with railroad workers, filling station attendants, porters, and others there to get a good, cheap meal.

When they weren't cooking, they were gambling. He was more of a card player than a crap shooter. Not all that good at either. When they were caught up in the kitchen, she had her crap game going and he had another blanket spread out playing cards. I didn't hear much noise on the other side of the curtain now; when they went to bed they were both dog tired. The good thing for me was she was being distracted and wasn't as quick to get the coat-hanger after me.

As Emma's time grew nearer, she became less and less help. George had his hands full. They realized that even with both of them going full blast, it was almost more than they could handle. With a new baby in the house, she would be spending a lot of time taking care of it. They couldn't afford it; George would be left short-handed.

"Baby."

"Yes mam."

"Run down there an tell Mama Joe I said to cum over here."

"Yes'm."

She came right away. "Mama Joe, me an George talked it over an want you to keep the baby for us when it cums. The way thangs is goin, I need to git back on my feet quick as I kin. An for awhile anyway, I don' see myself havin the time to take care uv it. Lissen Mama Joe, you best git one thang straight now, it's only gon' be while it's little. Soon as it gits big enuff where it don' need so much time, I'm gittin my baby back. You understand!?"

Mama Joe was stunned speechless, and only nodded her head. "So when the time cums, I don' want no shit outta you either. You hear whut I said Mama Joe? I'm gittin my baby back!"

Mama Joe agreed with all the terms. She whooped and shouted for joy, jumping in jubilation. "If it's a boy, ya'll kin name him George or whutever, but if it's a girl," she said longingly, "I'm namin her Patsy Sue an callin her Pat for short. I'm goin home rat now an start makin her sum clothes. I already know it's gon' be a lil pissytail gal!" She got to the door, stopped and looked back, "Emma, I betcha a half a pint it's a gal."

"You got a bet, Mama Joe."

When the pains started, George paid Miss Odessa, who lived across the street, to let them use her shotgun house. Emma would have more privacy to deliver in, away from the Saturday night crap game already in progress. George had somebody running the game. He and I kept vigil outside Miss Odessa's house. We got along fairly well. He didn't have much to do with me, nor I with him. We more or less avoided each other, whenever possible.

1936, August 15th, and the mosquitos were driving me crazy singing around my ears before the mid-wife came to the door. "She got heah at zackly 11:59, one minute fo midnite. Ever thang's awright, Mr. George. Didn' have a bit uv trouble an Miss Emma jes fine. I dun got her all cleant up an everthang. Ya'll kin go on in now an see 'em. But try not to 'sturb Miss Emma; she's a might tired."

Once inside the dim lamp-lit room I stepped closer to the bed for a better look. She was lying in Emma's arms, all wrapped up, except for a small part of her face. She was making funny little smacking noises. I told Emma, "She sounds jes lak a little baby puppy.'' George shot me an angry look.

A few days after Pat was born, Emma was back on the job. She and George were both pleased with their decision about Pat. Just like Mama Joe told them earlier, she had the baby clothes ready and waiting. When she brought Pat over for a visit, she was dressed up like a doll. At George's request, ''I don' want that boy uv yo's foolin wit my baby.'' I wasn't allowed to have anything to do with her.

The cafe business continued to grow; their good cooking saw to that. Most of the time customers had to stand outside and wait for a place to sit, especially at noon. They needed a bigger place and George began pushing in that direction.

''Emma, why don' we put mo time in th' cafe? We kin make a lot uv money if we do. You won't need to be gamblin an bootleggin; you kin give that part up an we kin spend mo time wit the baby. Hell, one uv these days, I'd lak to go to church for a change. But livin th' kind uv life we livin, I just wouldn' feel right.''

With ruffled feathers, ''George, anytime you git tired uv th' kind uv life we livin', jes let th' door knob hitcha where th' Good Lord splitcha.''

George persisted more vocally, especially after the brief visits with Pat when she got about four months old. The argument was on as soon as Mama Joe left with Pat in her arms. ''Look Emma! I work jus as hard as you do an jus as long. Whut I'm tryin to git you to understand is, we don' havta be killin oursefs. If you'd quit gamblin so much an stop all that utha shit you do, we both could git sum rest an be wit that baby mo. We kin git us a bigger place an put sum mo tables in it, git us a ol' juke-box, start sellin beer and git outta bootleggin. I know we kin make money runnin a cafe. Emma, how cum you so scaid to give it up? Is this all you wanna do th' rest uv yo life? We ain' got no privacy! There's nigguhs an whitefolks runnin in an outta heah all thru th' night! An that boy uv yo's sleeps right on the utha side uv th' curtain! You may wanna live lak this, but I be damned if I do!''

''I ain' scaid uv nothin! Jes cuz runnin a cafe is yo callin, that don' make it mine. If I tole you once, I tole you fifty fuckin times, I got a good place where I am, an I ain' gon' move!''

"But damnit Emma, it ain' big enuff.''

"It's big enuff for me.''

"Oh, so thas th' way it is!''

Tempers were rising, "Thas EXACTLY th' way it is!''

They were in the kitchen and both were working with butcher knives. Looking at her viciously, George rebuffed, "I know whut's th' matter wit you. You needs a good ass-whuppin! If I git hold uv yo ass, I'm gon' tear this lil house up wit it!''

Facing him and gripping the knife handle more firmly, "George, anytime you feel froggish, jes hop! An if you do, somebody gon' havta burn me loose frum yo ass!'' She was fighting mad, "An furthermo, nigguh, I don' need you!! I wuz makin my livin long fo I met you. I'm the one who took you in! An I don' need no sonuvabitch on earth tellin me whut to do an how to live my life! An nigguh! You bet not lay down an EVEN DREAM you whupped my ass! The last time a nigguh tried that, they found 'em dead wit a bullet in his bosom. ANYtime you feel lak you wanna whup my ass, don'tcha let nuthin stop you. An anutha thang, ain' no Gotdam chains on yo legs an yo feet ain' welded that flo'! When you git ready to leave, leave! One monkey don' stop no show!''

"I jus might do that!''

"Well, do it! George baby, you ain' no *special* nigguh, you jes *anutha* nigguh!''

"If it wudn' for that baby, I'd leave yo ass rat now!''

"Aw, don' hand me that baby bullshit! Ain' no baby never stopped no man frum leavin a woman yet!'' and looked at me.

The next morning I woke up when I heard the front door easing shut. I quickly jumped out of my cot and got dressed for school. I tipped around in the kitchen trying not to disturb them. The crap game had lasted until after four that morning. Emma had been drinking pretty heavy and I knew she would be sleeping late. I got my book satchel from the nail on the wall and tip-toed out the back door, flipping the latch behind me.

60

In the classroom, after we got our wraps put away in the cloak room, took our seats and simmered down, "Good morning, Boys and Girls."

"Good morning, Miz Womack!" we sang back in unison.

"Miz Womack?"

"Yes, Murl Dee?"

"Miz Womack, may I be excused?"

"Not right now Murl Dee. I think you can hold it a little while longer," with a warm smile, "don't you?"

"Yes'm, Miz Womack."

"Alright, boys and girls! Let's get out our pencils and tablets. We're going to work on our writing some more today." Without ever missing a beat, "What's the matter Calvin? Why don't you have your tablet out?"

"I ain' got none."

"Why don't you have one?"

Slumped down in his desk with his head lowered, Calvin was semi-audible, "Mama couldn' buy me none."

"Why that's alright, Calvin. You just sit up straight in your seat, and we'll get you something to write on." She borrowed a sheet of tablet paper from one of the other kids, "All right, Calvin, there you are," placing it on his desk. "What's the matter now?"

"I ain' got no pencil." She went back to her desk and got him one.

With writing behind us, it was on to the alphabet cards where we usually got stuck until recess. Out on the yard, Mrs. Womack kept a close watch over us and had us play together and keep out of the way of the older kids. Seemed like just when the playing got good, the bell rang for us to go inside. Back in the classroom, Mrs. Womack had us going through the daily ritual of singing the alphabet, "AaaaB! CeeeeD! EFGHIJK-Ellaminna-p!"

I'd never noticed before how hefty Emma had gotten after Pat was born, until I looked up and saw her standing in the classroom doorway. I knew something was wrong; I saw it in her eyes. Acknowledging her presence, Mrs. Womack stopped the singing.

"Yes, Miss Emma, may I help you? Come right on in."

"I wanna talk to my boy a minute," scanning over the classroom for me.

Walking past the outer row of desks toward the front, Mrs. Womack pointed me out, "His desk is right over there, Miss Emma."

"Thank you Miz Womack," turning up my aisle.

"Hi Emma!"

"Where's yo book satchel?"

"It's in th' cloak room."

"Go git it!"

"Yes'm." I got it and quickly returned to my seat.

"Hand it here!" snatching it from me. She looked all through it, turning it inside out.

"Where's my Gotdam money?!"

"Whut money Emma?"

She hit me with her balled up fist and knocked me out of my desk, out into the aisle. My nose was oozing blood. The kids in the immediate area scampered out of the way as she flung the empty desks to the side to get to me. All the while, Mrs. Womack was shouting, "No! Miss Emma no! Please, no!"

I was still woozy when she jerked me up by my collar. "Tell me whut you did wit my money fo I kill you!" She hit me again.

"Whut money Emma?!" I cried out.

"Whut money!? The money I put in yo book satchel last night! Whut'd you do wit it!?"

"I didn' do nuthin wit it Emma. I didn' even know it wuz in there. I don' steal frum you Emma!"

"Git yo shit! Miz Womack, I'm takin him home."

She hit and kicked me all the way home, saying, "Last nite when we got thru gamblin an everbody left, instead uv puttin it under my mattress, I hid it in yo book satchel. Wuzn' nobody in th' house but you, me, an George! I wuz aimin to take it out befo you went to school, but I didn'. When I woke up an seen the book satchel gone, I know you had my money. An you gon' tell me whut you dun wit it or I'm gon' stomp it outta you!"

Opening the door to the house and shoving me inside, "Git in there!"

"Emma, I didn' know you put yo money in my satchel. I swear I didn' Emma. I wuz sleep when ya'll quit gamblin.''

She paused and thought for a moment.

"I swear I didn' do it Emma! Didja ask George? Didja look everwhere fur it?''

"Naw, I didn' look nowhere. I know where I put it! In yo book satchel!''

"Les look Emma. You might've put it sumwhere else an forgot it!'' I started looking in all her familiar hiding places, under the mattress, in my jacket pockets, in the shoe box, under the bed, and finally to George's foot locker.

"Emma!'' I hollered through the curtain.

"Whut?! You find my money?''

"Sumbody took George's locker, it's gone!''

She began searching through all the drawers, frantically throwing clothes everywhere. Before long, "All his clothes is gone!'' Standing in the center of the room, amidst the strewn clothes, "That sonuvabitch got me!''

It was back to the two of us again, and it seemed like the roof was caving in. I took the ass-whipping and George took all the money, including the 150 dollars he saw her hide in my book satchel. That money was to get us out of arrears with the whiskey man, and pay for the two cases on order.

But, looking on the bright side, there were no worries about Pat. Mama Joe was taking care of her like she was a little princess. When she heard George had left, she came over to the house and "thanked God" he didn't try to take her away. Regardless of how well Pat was doing with Mama Joe, it didn't change the fact that we were flat broke.

Emma didn't mourn George's vanishing act beyond a long night's drunk. It was time to get into her best clothes and head uptown. She put on her sexiest dress, high heels, and hose. She patted and primped with her hair which was short and parted on the side with large, tapered curls covering each ear. The thirty or so pounds she gained carrying Pat went to the right places in her hourglass figure, emphasizing her already shapely curves. Her long pretty "white girl" legs with thick calves and her big "nigger ass" were eyestoppers.

As she was leaving, "You stay here, I be back afta

63

while." When she returned about an hour later, she pulled off her tam and pitched it on the bed, took off her heels, and busily got ready. "I got some company comin. He'll be here in a few minutes. Watch out the window an lemme know when he gits here." She went behind the curtain into the kitchen to change into her lounge wear.

In a little while a car pulled up in front of the house and stopped. "He's here, Emma," I shouted.

"When he knocks, let 'em in. Tell 'em I'll be out in a minute."

"Yes'm," I said, and opened the door on the first knock.

"Hi, little fellow. Is Emma here?"

"Yessir, cum on in. She be out in a minute."

Emma called out, "Jes have a seat on th' bed. I'll be right out."

"Thas all right Emma. Take yore time. Is this yore boy?"

"Suuuure is. Me an that boy been down the road together, ain't we Baby?"

"I didn't know you had any chilluns."

Stepping from behind the curtain, "There's a whole lotsa thangs you don' know bout me . . . yet," and put them eyes on him. "Baby, you go set out front an if anybody cums by lookin for me, tell 'em I ain' home."

"Yes mam."

In the months that followed, our house became his second home. After that first time, he only came at night. Explaining to Emma, "It's hard to git away frum th' hardware store durin th' day." The night visits soon became a problem when his timing was off. Answering the door to wait on my late night whiskey customers, sometimes it'd be him. Emma already had company; I had to get rid of him, quick!

Whispering to him with the door barely opened, "No sir, she ain' here; she gone. You gotta go now! Ain' nobody here but me."

Trying to peep inside, "Any idea what time she'll be back?"

"No sir. I gotta close the door now. Emma tole me not to open it fo NOBODY."

"Well, tell her I came by, will you?"

"Yessir, I'll tell 'er," and closed the door quickly.

64

On my way past her bed back to the kitchen, "Who in th' hell wuz that? Whut'd they want?"

"They didn' want nuthin Emma."

Emma knew why Elzado had stopped coming to the house; she didn't like George. Elzado was a fast talker who didn' bite her tongue about anything. "I can't stand him. Emma, he's jus fulla shit. I'll be damned if I know whut you seed in him." They cracked up when Elzado quipped, "Must be the cookin." Both of them had spirited senses of humor, and neither got angry when they teased one another, especially about their men.

Now that George had gone, Elzado came regular again. "Emma, you oughta be glad that black bastard left. If it'd been me, I would uv run 'em off long fo now. Say girl, lemme tell you! I stood out on my Gotdam porch this mornin, flaggin cars til my fuckin arm nelly fell off. They kept passin right on by. Shit, ain' hardly nobody trickin no mo! Emma, lemme hold sump'n if you kin spare it."

Whatever money we had in the house, Emma produced it and let Elzado take what she needed, expecting no payback. Elzado didn't care much for gambling, and generally stuck to the basics. She was fairly well content to have some white man "take care" of her and to turn an occasional trick.

Elzado was at the house again, "Emma, I got me a rich, white man now gal! An he don' want me to hit a lick at a snake! All he wants me to do is jes be nice to him ever now an then. Emma gal, he ain' nooo trouble at all! He's old gal, I mean old! Hell, he's over sixty!"

With a deep throaty laugh, Emma asked, "Elzado, if he's old is you make it sound, whut kin he do?"

"Nuthin!" They laughed harder. "He can' do a fuckin thang! He jes laks to play wit it."

"I wish that wuz true wit the one I got. That bastard cums roun two an three times a week, makin sho he gits his money's worth. I can' complain tho. That sonuvabitch sho pulled me outta a hole when George run off. He pays for my whiskey just regular as the man brangs it. That sho takes a load offa my shoulders."

"I know it do gal! Shit! My ol' man's th' same way. I don' havta worry bout no rent, no groceries, no nuthin. An thas

65

th' kinda man I been wantin. Emma, he's the sweetest little ol' thang you ever seen. When he cums over to th' house, he sits off in a corner an sip a little whiskey an sugar water an then he wants to lay down. Don't even take off his clothes! Afta he gits thru pattin on me, he gits up an leaves. Ain't that jus great, Emma?''

The next time the hardware man paid Emma a visit, he told her humorously, ''I'm gonna have to cum up with sump'n different; I just about wore the Legion Hall out. My wife's called there a couple uv times an I wuzn't there.''

''Tell her you out takin care uv bizness,'' Emma joked back.

''I can't, I done used that up too!''

''Well, looks lak you might be in trouble,'' she jazzed.

Elzado had a lot of free time on her hands and was back visiting again. I sat out on the front steps listening to them shoot the shit while sharing a half-pint. I heard her telling Emma she found out Sally B and Bama were living in Dallas, 124 miles away. Soon as the news was exchanged they overwhelmingly agreed, ''Who gives a shit!'' When the car stopped in front of the house, I instinctively hollered inside, ''Emma! Here cum the police!''

The two deputies got out. When they came near the house, I moved off the steps out of their way. They went inside.

''What's yore name gal?''

''Elzado Barnes.''

''Emma, git dressed.'' She was still in her housecoat. ''We're taking both uv ya'll to jail.''

''Whut for?'' Emma asked as she went behind the curtain to change. ''Whut we dun? Ya'll kin see ain' nobody here but me an my sister an my boy. Whutcha takin us in for?''

''Never mind, Emma. Just hurry up in there. All I know is the sheriff wants to talk to ya'll.'' After Emma got dressed they put her and Elzado in the car and took them to jail. This time, my crying didn't help.

I walked to the jail and had to stand on a fruit box to see her through the cell window. She told me the hardware man's wife had been tailing him and went to the sheriff crying, ''Emma, the colored gal over by the railroad tracks, is ruinin my marriage.'' She said they already had a warrant out for Elzado for "swindlin." Her old man's children got suspicious when they detected all the withdrawals he was making at the bank and had been watching him closely too.

"I got money to git us out, so don' worry. Go on back to th' house an stay there."

I left but I didn't go home. I hung around outside the jail. Later that evening I saw several men going in the jail wearing white hoods over their heads. They brought Emma and Elzado out the front door. I hid underneath the tall hedges. I heard Emma begging, "Please, don' take our lives. At least give us a runnin chance!"

After a brief huddle, the men laughingly agreed, "It'd be more fun then runnin rabbits."

One of the hooded men started pushing a few white citizens who had gathered back away. Another held tightly onto Emma and Elzado's arms, while the rest got into their cars. With engines and headlights on, someone yelled from a car, "Turn 'em loose!"

Emma and Elzado started running down the street and passed twenty feet from where I was hiding. I ducked down lower because I didn't want Emma to see me. I figured she would have pulled out of that race to give me a whuppin for not doing what she told me. Some of the spectators began running behind them and got in the way. The "Klu Kluckers" had to slow their cars down, and blew their horns trying to get through the crowd. This helped.

They turned off the main street, cutting through different alleys. I ran with the crowd, and saw them heading for the railroad tracks. Their high-heeled shoes were hampering their running and the cars were catching up. They started running down the tracks. The drivers stopped and turned around, "C'mon!" one shouted, "we kin head 'em off over at the overpass!"

Lucky or not, a train was coming and slowed down a little to pick up any messages from the Y pole. Emma and Elzado hopped it. The train was gone, there was nothing left to see.

I wandered aimlessly for awhile and went home, quickly latched both doors, and lit the lamps. I got the salt box and lay awake all night to throw some on Bloody Bones if he

67

showed up, and listened for a knock and the sound of Emma's voice.

I went to Mama Joe's but she "didn' have no room." I did what Emma told me and stayed at the house until Mr. Booth rented it to somebody else. In lieu of the back rent Emma owed, some men came in a truck and hauled everything away, except the clothes I bundled and took with me.

I never thought she'd be gone so long. I walked the streets and slept under bridges. Dodging the truant officer for not attending school was a full time job.

> *"Mutherless chillun sees a hard time when they muther
>   is gone.*
> *Mutherless chillun sees a hard time when they muther
>   is gone.*
> *They don't have noooo place to go; they jus keep
>   runnin frum door to door.*
> *Mutherless chillun sees a hard time when they muther
>   is gone."*

5 ||||||||||||||||||||||

I was sitting on the bench in front of the Star Cafe when an old gentleman I knew as "Wino" came walking around the corner. He sat down beside me and struck up a conversation. By now, everybody in town knew about Emma and Elzado's "messin wit white men an gittin rid outta town on a rail."

"Has yo mama cum back yet, boy?" he asked in a friendly voice.

"Nawsir, but she be back . . . prob'ly by tomorrow."

"Yeah, well . . . where you stayin since she been gone?"

"At diffunt places."

"Lak where?"

"Lak all kinds uv places."

"Who you been stayin with?"

"Nobody. I don' need to stay wit nobody. I kin take care uv myself."

"I see. Oh, I don' doubt yo word for a minute that you kin take care uv yosef. You a real big, little man. Do you go to school?"

"Oh yessir," I blurted. "I go ever day," fearing he might squeal on me.

"Whut grade you in?"

"The first. You know whut Wino? You sho ast lotsa questions."

"Aw, I'm sorry boy. You right. I didn' mean to pry in yo

bizness. I jus thought you might need a little hep or somethin.''

"Naw, I don' need no hep. Emma'll be back . . . prob'ly she be back in the mornin.''

"Well, she probably will," patronizing me, "but jes in case she don' make it in, an you need a place to stay, you kin cum keep me company an stay in the room wit me. That is, if you don' mind listenin to an old man's ramblins all the time. We could be . . . pals. I git pretty lonesome sometimes without nobody to talk to. I bet you do too. Don'tcha?''

"Sumtimes. But I got me a buddy.''

"You do?''

"Yep, name's Floyd. He's my pal.'' Floyd and I ducked the truant officer together, and stole milk bottles to sell for our picture show money. We would sit up in there all day, sucking on our one cent jawbone breakers, watching the movie over and over until they closed that night.

"Ain't that one uv Miss Bertha's boys?''

"Yep, she's his grandma.''

"I take it ya'll are real good buddies?''

"Yessir! An we don' fight each utha neitha. I'm waitin on 'em right now; we goin do somethin.''

"That sounds excitin. Whut you two boys gon' do?''

"We goin out to the circus grounds an work for us sum free passes so we kin git in to see it.''

Looking down the street, I saw him coming, "Here he cums now. I gotta be goin, Wino.''

"Okay. You 'member whut I tole you. If you change yo mind, I live roun there in the rooming house," pointing, "in the first room on the right next to the back door.''

I gave him a noncommittal smile as I looked back over my shoulder running to meet Floyd.

When I got closer to him, "I hadta tote sum wash water fer Grandma fo I lef.''

"Yeah,'' I said, "I wuz wonderin whut you wuz doin so long.''

Both of us were wearing our TufNut overalls, but the seat of mine was weighted down ten pounds and almost dragging the ground. I had all my valuables and weapons in my back

70

pockets. I carried at least a half dozen big washers for throwing at older boys, rocks and steel ball ammunition for my "nigger shooter," and for close range fighting, I had a railroad spike. Along with my fighting paraphernalia I carried my marbles, spinnerless spinning top, and of course, my protective salt wrapped in a piece of newspaper.

On our way to the circus grounds, "Look Floyd, when we git out there, lemme do th' talkin."

"Whutcha thank they have us be doin?" Floyd asked.

"Prob'ly hepin put up th' tents er somethin. I don' know. But whutever it is, me an you kin do it. An we kin sell us sum milk bottles an get us sum peanuts an stuff."

"Yeah, I'm gon' buy me sum uv dat cotton candy."

"Me too!" We were drooling with anticipation. "Now, 'member," I said as we approached the grounds, "lemme do th' talkin. Okay?"

"Go head! I ain' sayin nuthin."

Circus hands were working all over the place, stretching out the tents and pounding the long anchor stakes into the ground with their huge mallets. I finally saw somebody who didn't look extremely busy. When I did, "Les go ast that man over there."

"You go axe him. You tole me not to say nuthin, 'member?"

"I will," and walked over to him. "Pardon me sir."

"Yeah, what is it?"

"Me an my buddy," looking back at Floyd, "wanna work for sum free passes to th' circus."

"Well, I'm not the man you wanna talk to. See that trailer cabin over yonder? Go knock on the door and talk to that man."

"Thank you."

I beckoned for Floyd to follow. I knocked and the man opened the door. The trailer was up on blocks and when he first looked out, we were so short, he looked right over us. "Yeah, what can I do for youse guys?" looking down at us.

"Mister, me an my buddy here wanna work for sum free passes. An we'll work real hard. Won't we Floyd?"

"Sho will." He was nine, and about a head taller than me. We were so scrawny looking, he thought about it a few

71

seconds before deciding. "Yeah, come to think of it, I can use two more BIG guys like youse two." He opened the cabin door wider, "See that guy over there with his sleeves rolled up and all the tattoos?"

"Yessir."

"Go over there and tell him I said to put youse guys to work. When you's finish, come back by here and I'll give youse your passes."

"See there Floyd," I said smugly, "whut I tell you!"

"Pardon me, mister," I said as we walked up to him.

"Yeah?"

"The man in that trailer said tell you to put us to work so we kin git sum free passes to the circus."

He stopped what he was doing, "Okay, follow me." We did until, "Here," he said handing us two buckets apiece. We followed him again. He stopped at the nozzle of the huge fire hose that lay trickling on the ground. "Okay, I'm goin over there to the fireplug an turn the water up a little." After adjusting the nozzle, "Watch this nozzle an let me know when it's comin out fast enough to fill up your buckets." Using the big wrench atop the fireplug, he slowly opened the valve.

Floyd and I started waving our hands in the air and shouting, "Okay! Okay!"

He returned. "Alright, fill up your buckets and come on, we got some elephant waterin to do."

Water sloshed all over our legs as we hurried to keep up with him, "Do them elefins bite?" Floyd asked in worriment.

"Nawww boy," he said, "elephants don' bite people. Unless, of course, they make 'em mad. You know what REALLY makes elephants mad?"

"Nawsuh," we said.

"When they don' git enough water."

"Well, I sho don' wanna make 'em mad."

"Me neitha."

We could see the elephants standing under the smaller tent, with the sides rolled up about four feet off the ground. It had a large walk-through entrance like a barn and was about thirty feet from the bucket-filling spot. When we walked in under the tent, our mouths flew open and our eyes were filled with the biggest "elefins" in the whole world.

With one of their back legs chained and anchored down with a stake, about a dozen were rowed up on one side of the tent, leaving only a narrow passageway in front of them. The huge monsters swayed back and forth contentedly, picking up bits of hay from the ground and slinging it up on their backs.

Still holding onto our buckets, Floyd and I stood frozen in our tracks. My voice trembled with fear, "Mister, is you sho they won' bite?"

"Nawww, they won't. Here, lemme show you," taking one of Floyd's buckets. He walked up to the first one in line, sat the bucket down in front of it, and began to pat and pet it. "This is Julie," *pat-pat-pat*. "She's a good ole girl. Ain'tcha Julie, baby? Hand me another bucket," he ordered.

I stepped forward to hand him one of mine. He got the empty and handed it back to Floyd. As I reached the bucket out to him, "You sit it down for her," coaxing, "c'mon, sit it down there where she kin get it. She won't hurt you."

I walked closer, set the bucket down, and JUMPED BACK quickly. "I did mine Floyd! You do yours!" I urged, as my heart pulsated with fear and excitement.

"I got to go now," the tattooed man said. Looking down at us, "Think you guys kin handle it?"

"Yessir," we chimed with uncertainty.

Left on our own, we started filling the buckets and packing the water back to the tent. We still jumped way back after we set our four buckets of water down in front of Julie. She emptied a whole bucket with each slurp and reached her long trunk for another. Even after ten trips each, Julie's thirst was still unquenched. Every time Floyd or I tried to walk past her to water one of the other elephants, she stuck out her trunk and blocked our path.

After about thirty minutes of steady toting water to only one elephant, trying not "to make it mad," the five gallon buckets got heavier and heavier. The railroad spike I had in my back pocket became a real nuisance, kicking me in the ass with every step I took. Back at the spigot, waiting for our buckets to fill, "WHEW! Floyd, I'm tired!"

"Me too! Dem bucket hanles dun rubbed a so' on my hands."

"Mines too. The way we goin, we ain' NEVER gon' git all them fuckin elefins watered."

"Sho ain't. This heah circus will be dun cum an gone fo we git thru," Floyd added disgustedly.

"I tell you whut I'm gon' do," I declared. "I'm gon' take that big o' funky elefin one mo drank, an thas all! She kin git mad, scratch her ass till she git glad, for all I care!" We delivered those four buckets to Julie and returned to the spigot. "Floyd, this time les wait till we ketch her lookin off an then run by her," I plotted.

When we tried, Julie saw us and politely stuck out her trunk. Neither of us were brave enough to stoop and run under her road block so we retreated straightway. We set our buckets, as directed, down in front of her. She took her usual four slurps and they were empty once more. Then she playfully sprayed water on the other elephants.

"Look Floyd," I said excitedly, "I got a idea."

"Whut is it?"

"I know how we kin fill 'er up! An all the rest uv 'em too!"

"How?"

"Next time we ketch them men not lookin, les drag that fire hose over here."

"Whut we gon' do wit it?"

"You'll see."

Making certain the coast was clear, we started dragging the hose over to the tent. It reached with plenty to spare. "Okay, Floyd, while I keep a lookout, wrap sum hay roun that nozzle so she won' see it, an ram it in her mouth. Then I'm gon' run turn the water up so . . ."

"Is you crazy? SHIT! I ain' stickin my arm up in no elefin's mouf! You do it an lemme go turn it up."

"Nawww, Floyd. I can't reach her mouth. You the tallest."

"That ain' nuthin, I kin pick you up."

"We ain' got that much time, Floyd. C'mon, wrap sum uv that hay roun it an stick it in there fo sumbody cum."

Grumbling as he concealed the long brass nozzle, "You stick it in the next un's mouf." With the camouflage completed, Floyd cautiously approached Julie, reaching the nozzle up towards her mouth.

"I'm gon' run out to the fireplug an be ready. When you git it in, wave yo hand." Standing at the fireplug, gripping the big wrench, I waited for Floyd to give me the high sign. It took him several frightened attempts before he got Julie to take the hay-covered nozzle. When she did, he waved his hand affirmatively.

I yanked on the wrench so hard I almost went completely around the plug. I had the valve wide open. With the sudden blast of maximum water pressure, the fire hose pitched and jerked as it wiggled on the ground like a huge snake. The water sounded like it was rushing through in big lumps, instantly swelling the hose taut.

I ran back. Floyd was jumping up and down ecstatically. When the full force of water fired through the hose, it shot the nozzle deeper into Julie's mouth. She had a strange look on her face while an elephant-sized tear trickled from one eye. In futile efforts, she coiled and uncoiled her trunk around the hose.

All the while, Floyd and I danced a jig, whooping victoriously. Julie's belly rumbled and shook like an earthquake from the pounding force of gushing water. It got bigger and bigger. She cut loose with a waterfall of piss three hands wide.

We were laughing wildly and forgot all about the workers skittering about. Someone saw us, "Hey! Just what in the hell do you boys think you're doin!?" When he realized what we had done, "Hey! Look at what those crazy-assed boys are doin!" They started running towards us. "Hey! You Gotdam boys, git outta there! Git away from them elephants!"

"Ketch 'em! There they go!" another hollered.

The chase was on. I took the railroad spike out of my back pocket to lighten my load. When Floyd and I reached the road, we left a jetstream of dust behind and didn't slow down until we got to the intersection. He veered one way, heading home; I took off for the railroad tracks.

Fearing the circus folks might call the police on us, I needed a hideout and an alibi. I was almost out of breath as I tip-toed down the rooming house hallway. His door was slightly ajar and I slowly pushed it open. The shabby little room was dusky, except for the daylight I let in. The two curtainless, shadeless windows were completely covered over with newspapers. Wino was lying cross-ways on the bed, snoring loudly. Careful not to wake him, I eased inside and closed the door. I slept on the floor on some quilts and blankets in the corner of his little dollar-fifty-a-week room. Wino was a retired railroad brakeman, with snowy white hair; a weathery, Uncle Remus-looking black man. It was obvious that once he had been a handsome man, but the booze had gotten the best of him.

He cut grass on Nugget Hill for the rich white families who paid him two or three dollars and gave him their left-overs. He didn't eat any of it until he came home and we'd share. To warm the food, we used a charcoal-filled bucket with a little grill on the top. We ate together right out of the pan. Lots of times with one fork because we couldn't find the other one.

He got drunk every night off of cheap fifty-five-cent-a-quart sherry. Sitting around listening to his stories of trips to faraway places and different people he met made me forget she was gone, sometimes. When he was drunk, he had a unique habit of whistling right in the middle of his sentences. I lay on my pallet while he sat on the edge of his bed rambling on and on, and making long whistling noises.

"Well, I'm Alonzo Johnson. I've traveled all over the (whistle) world an I've been in every place in Canada (whistle) an everywhere. I've been frum the golden gates (whistle) uv California to the rocky shores uv (whistle) Maine. I've been to the Empire (whistle) State Buildin an the Statue (whistle) uv Liberty. Seen all kinds uv things. An one thing I learnt (whistle), people's the same everywhere. When you got money (whistle), you got friends for miles around, but when you git (whistle) down an out, ain' no need to look for 'em, cuz (whistle) ain' none uv 'em aroun . . .

76

sususususususus.'' At first, listening to him was mind boggling, but, after staying with him for four years, I could time them to perfection.

I was just like a coyote. I'd get out at night, steal, hustle, and do whatever I could to help keep the household going. In the early dawn hours, I followed the delivery trucks. As fast as they'd put food out in front of the stores, I took all I could carry and ran for the room. I had to get a bunch; we didn't have an icebox. We ate up everything we had at one time, like the natives in the Bush Country.

I probably looked like one too. My hair was long, I was skinny as a rail but tough as a boot, and my eyes were sunk deep in my head. The closest thing I ever got to a bath was swimming in the T&P pond. I didn't bathe, I guess, because Lonzo didn't.

When Emma came back, I thought I was dreaming or had died and gone to heaven. Lying on those raggedy quilts on Lonzo's floor, half-asleep, I heard talking.

"Wake up! It's Emma, I'm back."

I opened my eyes, and there stood Emma and a Mexican. She was much bigger now, close to 200 pounds, but I never saw anything so beautiful in my life. She was all decked out in a glittering, sequin-covered black dress, fur, and had pretty rings on her fingers.

She gave Lonzo fifty dollars for "lookin out" for me. Dividing fifty-five cents into fifty dollars was a lot of sherry! We left in a car with a big shiny bird on the front of the hood. Within her first fifteen words, she asked, "Whut do you think bout this guy? Ain' he good-lookin?"

"Yes mam, Emma," I answered indifferently.

He drove down to the Nickles Hotel, the aristocratic hangout of the "bigtime" hustlers. They'd already been by the room and had clothes lying all over the bed.

"I bought these for you. Go take a bath an try 'em on."

I came out and tried on my new clothes. Nothing fit; everything was too small. "You don' even know whut I look lak."

She angrily threw them in the corner, "Well, fuck it! We'll gitcha sum mo shit!"

In looks maybe, but in principle, she hadn't changed one

bit. She had met Salvador in Mexico and convinced him to sell his bar and come back to Longview with her. Having used up most of his money, she took what was left and set up another gambling, *etcetera* house.

This was the first un-shotgun house I'd ever lived in. It had electricity, three rooms and a kitchen, a well off the back porch, and an outhouse in the back. It was farther from the T&P Station than our other house and didn't tremor as much when the trains went by. Best of all, it was only a half-block from the corner liquor store.

Prohibition was ancient history, and the bootleggers who formerly dispensed homemade moonshine graduated to selling the cheap-packaged whiskey and wine. Emma was no exception. The liquor store man gave a good discount when it was bought by the case, and she doubled her money, reselling it by the half-pints and quarts. So after hours, all day Sundays, and during the games, it was bootlegging as usual. Even when the liquor store was still open, the gamblers would rather pay Emma a little more than to have to leave the game to go get a bottle.

The liquor store was the pulpwood haulers' headquarters. Most of them lived across the Sabine River and came to town after cutting and hauling wood destined for the paper mills. Eighty percent were related either by blood or marriage, and three or four would be part owners in the old, battered trucks. Every evening after work, the huge oak "council" tree at the back of the liquor store was surrounded by the old-model, beat-up, long-railed, pulpwood trucks.

"Them o' pulpwood boys" were noted for hard work and paying their bills, especially their whiskey bills. The white store owner extended them liquor credit freely, cashed their checks, and even loaned them money. All they had to do was sign the book. The haulers marched in and out of the store buying a half-pint at a time.

The cooking and gambling did it. As soon as they finished transacting business at the liquor store, the pulpwood haulers made a beeline for "Big Emma's." Every last one of them loved to gamble and they lined the walls around the crap table as often as possible. Some were there so often it didn't seem like they'd ever left. Big Emma (they named her that) fed them, and won their money.

They walked in heading straight for the kitchen to "jes help yoself." Emma had no set fee for the food, "When you git thru, jes gimme somethin." They emerged as greasy around the mouth as a meatskin, pitched her a "fair price," and bought a half-pint. They gambled and ate at the same time, keeping the dice so slippery Emma had to ofttimes stop the game to drop them into a glass of soapy water.

Just like with the railroad workers, when the pulpwood boys gathered, she sent for Allen. He lived in the Old Field section of town with the same woman he had been living with for years. Sometimes, when I was sent to phone him, his old lady, Lucille, answered, and I gave her the message, "Big Emma said tell 'em to 'cum git suma this money.' "

Allen was a good draw because he kept a pocketful of money all the time and the pulpwood boys wanted to beat him just because he didn't smell like pine resin. He stood out like a show horse in a stable full of mules at the crap table. They had on dirty overalls and he wore his customary tailor-made silk shirts and trousers. Nine times out of ten, the pulpwooders' hopes of beating him was mere wishful thinking.

I'd seen him lots of times at the other house. He ignored me and I did my best to stay out of his way. I liked to watch him gamble. He'd begin to sweat, take out his silk handkerchief, and meticulously place it between his neck and collar. He always rolled up his sleeves so the grime and kitchen grease the pulpwood boys smeared on the blanket nailed to the table top wouldn't get on his cuffs.

He was quick to squabble with them about their crap table etiquette, "Man, don't be puttin that nasty-ass ashtray over heah, gittin all that shit on my shirt! Nasty, stankin, funky-dick muthafucka!"

While Emma was busy running the crap game, Salvador and I manned our designated posts. I covered the back door, handled the whiskey trade, and served as the official runner. Salvador generally sat on the front porch, "out of the way," watching for the police.

Besides the hot tamale man, Salvador was the only other

Mexican I knew of, living in Longview. He kept mostly to himself and didn't participate in the games or on-going hoopla of the gamblers. He drank his Canadian Club whiskey alone. Only occasionally would he take a drink with some of the others, but not before wiping the mouth of the bottle with his sleeve.

Emma was living the life of Riley. There was always a good crowd on hand and she had even rented a nickle jukebox for the crap room. Pat was no distraction. Mama Joe still kept her and had moved just a few houses down the street. Emma had front and back door watchmen, was making lots of money, and whenever Salvador was out of pocket, even turned a trick or two.

It happened again. Only Emma, Allen, and a white gambler called Blackie were left in the game. Emma backed off so Allen and Blackie could go "head to head." She pulled for Allen to take him and sat on pins waiting. When they finished, Allen was the winner.

She woke up all the broke, snoozing players so they could watch. Salvador even left his post when they played head to head, but his interest was not in the game. He didn't like the way Emma looked at Allen or touched his hand. Salvador jealously called him her "sweet man."

The only rule about rolling and setting was, "Go for whatcha know." It was teacher against pupil. Emma sat on the daybed with the crap table pulled up to her; Allen sat at his usual seat directly across the table. They went back and forth for hours, all the while keeping it casual and friendly. Both rolled so smooth and easy that one die seldom stopped more than an inch ahead of the other. Emma had one distinct advantage; she gauged her rolls with the nails tacking the blanket down, just like she used to do with the cigarette burns on her old crap blanket.

Whenever they squared off to duel she did everything to throw him off stride while he was shooting. "Give me anutha drank outta Emma's bottle, Baby. Betcha don' bar it. Shoot 'em!" On and on with the rap. When he got set picking them up, she'd make him put them down, somehow. "Hold 'em up there!" she'd grab his hand and pat it, offer him a drink, and just outright say, "Blue, put them dice down baby."

Frustrated, he'd stop and throw her the dice. "Heah! When you git thru playin wit 'em, give 'em back!"

She'd spit and blow on them, rub them between her thighs to hex the dice, and then toss them back. He'd miss. "Aw, Gotdam! The mule throwed Rucker," she'd say, and could hardly get the top screwed on the bottle fast enough.

They'd been going at it for hours and money-wise, they were about even. Emma called for a time out. "Shit, Blue! Les stop an take a break an have a drank. Ain't you tired?"

"Hell yeah! I gotta git up an stretch my legs a minute. They dun damn near went to sleep."

She pushed the table away, went to the outhouse, checked on Salvador, and returned. "Hand me my bottle baby." Looking around the room, "Resta ya'll WAKE UP! WAKE UP! The house is on fire!"

That perked them up. "Give everbody a drank; pass th' bottle roun when Blue gits thru. Git some water for 'em to chase it wit, them nigguhs ain' useta drankin good whiskey," referring to her personal bottle of "hockey proof" Old Grand Dad. She kept on, "Ya'll wake up now or you might miss somethin."

I certainly didn't need any rousing. I was absorbed and watched every move they made. The others had to ask for the bottle three or four times before I heard them.

After seating herself back on the daybed and pulling the table close, "Blue, you bout ready?"

"Yeah, I'm ready," regaining his seat.

It was her shot. While rubbing the dice on the blanket, with a metal smile, "You know whut, Blue?"

"Whut?"

"I'm goin on an take you lak Grant took Richmond."

"Well, you won't be gittin no cherry. I been busted befo. Quit stallin an shoot the dice!"

"But I'm gon' do it different this time, Blue. I'm gon' make ten straight passes on yo ass fo I miss. Then I'm gon' letcha shoot 'em one mo time, an it's good nite Irene."

After he took his shot and missed, he sang, "You got

me!'' He never beat her. When their game was over, she'd throw him ten or fifteen dollars so he wouldn't leave broke.

They were good gambling friends, but he never-ever slept with her. That's where he drew the line, content with just their gambling friendship developed over the years. It never failed though, when the house cleared and we finished cleaning up, Salvador started his nagging, ''Gotdamme Eemma, you thinkee I'm a Gotdamme suckum, don'tcha? I ain' no fuckin suckum (sucker). I see you make them fuckin goo-goo eyes at you Gotdamme sweet man.''

''Whut the hell you talkin bout, Sabbado?''

''Eemma, you know Gotdamme well what I talkee. Allen, you Gotdamme sweet man. I'm the Gotdamme man to theese fuckin house. I hangee my Gotdamme hat over here, not you fuckin sweet man!'' He was way off base, as ususal. She was tricking with Slim Linzy, definitely not Allen.

Disgusted, ''Aw meskin, fuck you! I'm tired. I don't wanna hear all that shit. Go lay down somewhere.''

''Gotdamme Eemma, didn' I tole for you, you leessen to my voice! I'm the Gotdamme man. . . .''

I was busy as a cat covering up shit keeping a lookout at the back door and selling whiskey to the players. On weekends, Emma's bedroom at the front of the house became the trick room whenever the whores needed it. I had already rented it out twice, and waited for Octavie to get through so I could clean it up quickly. Ida was in the wings.

It was midday Saturday, payday. The crap room was humming. The pulpwood haulers, Allen, two or three crap shooters from across town, and some white railroad workers, all jammed around the table betting hot and heavy. Emma had finished all the cooking earlier and was smack dab in the middle of the action. All the bases were covered. Salvador was at his usual post in the front; I was taking care of all the other house business.

By late afternoon there was a lull in the action because several of the pulpwood haulers, the heaviest losers, left for the liquor store to borrow some money. The white gamblers were gone too. Nobody was shooting craps and the gamblers were just sitting around waiting and bullshitting.

Since there was no game going on, Salvador joined the revelry in the crap room. He stood against the wall drinking and laughing his head off at their "nigger-whitefolks" jokes. They bullshitted about everything, from the way they each looked, to the size of their peckers. Oscar, one of the idle players, especially enjoyed teasing Emma. He said, "Lemme axe you sump'n Big Emma. How on earth didja end up wit a pepper-belly? Frum whut I heard, they screws lak rabbits, ninety miles a minute," he joked. Everybody in the room laughed—except Salvador.

"Fuck you! You black-ass cheeken-shit sonaveech!" Salvador shouted.

"Fuck you back, meskin! If you don' wanna heah whut we talkin bout, carry yo meskin ass on sumwhere else. You stand over dere an laugh yo ass off at everthang sumbody say bout sumbody else, but when sumbody say sump'n bout a meskin, you git mad."

"Leessen you sonaveech, you no talkee to me! I talkee to you! I'm the Gotdamme man to theese house!" moving in Oscar's direction.

Oscar rose quickly from the daybed. Some of the others held them apart. Throughout the momentary fiasco, Allen stayed in his seat at the table, casually playing with the dice. "Say Oscar, let Sabbado alone, man. An you meskin, you oughta take yo ass sumwhere an set down."

Salvador broke the grasp of the restrainers and attacked. He forced Allen into the crap table, jamming it against Emma and hemming her in on the daybed. Salvador had the advantage as they grappled with one another atop the table. Allen was fighting with all his might to get him off but Salvador was fighting equally as hard to retain his position.

One of the two by four legs gave way, and table and all, crashed to the floor. This jarred them apart momentarily. Allen got to his feet first and landed a clean blow to Salvador's face, and he reeled backwards toward the kitchen entrance.

Both were straight up slugging it out in the kitchen. Allen's heavier blows were doing the most damage. He knocked Salvador back seven or eight feet into the icebox.

Emma rushed in but Allen shoved her back through the

doorway and quickly pulled out the .38 long-barreled revolver from his waistband. Before Salvador regained his bearings, BANG! The scent of gunpowder filled the small room.

Still on his feet, Salvador staggered and slumped against the icebox. With blood pouring between his fingers he held his head. "Gotdamme Allen, you sonaveech! You shoot me!"

"An that ain' all, meskin. I'm fixin ta shoot you sum mo!" Like a flash, Salvador ducked and rushed Allen a fraction before he squeezed the trigger. The bullet missed.

He bear-hugged Allen and came out of nowhere with a hunting knife, ripping him from the left shoulder blade all the way down to his hip bone. Allen hit him repeatedly with the gunbarrel and managed to get elbow room for another shot. With his left arm tucked against his wounded side, he raised the .38 to fire again.

The head wound had weakened Salvador and he was about to drop. Allen squeezed the trigger, CLICK! CLICK! . . . CLICK, CLICK, CLICK, CLICK! He wheeled and walked out of the house, heading down the back trail.

Emma followed him out the door, "Blue, you hurt! Don' leave, somebody dun called the ambulance. It'll be here any minute."

He kept walking. Salvador had collapsed on the kitchen floor. She got a towel and attended him until the ambulance arrived. Allen got to the hospital on his own. I heard it took 180 stitches to sew him up. Salvador returned home that night. Miraculously, the bullet ricocheted off his skull and came out near his temple. All he had was a headache and swollen face.

As soon as Salvador recovered from his minor gunshot wound, he started blaming "Eemma" for what happened. "It's all you Gotdamme fault Eemma! You sent off fer you Gotdamme sweet man!" But that was the case no more. Allen no longer honored the calls and quit coming to the house.

Emma and Salvador began fighting like cats and dogs. He soon discovered that when he drank too much he couldn't whip her so he changed the course of things and started faking it. She would still get drunk, and that's when he would make his move.

I was so familiar with the routine I cautioned her not to drink so much, "Emma, you can't fight when you drunk."

Only to get a customary, "Jes hand me my bottle. I don' need you tellin me shit! Hell, I ain' drunk!" Followed by, "You stay outta me an my o' man's bizness! I don' need no help from you!"

Once she got started, the whiskey made her really blow it out, "I ain' scaid uv no muthafucka on earth! Specially Sabbado!" All the while, he sat on the old metal trunk over in the corner of the crap room with his head down, feigning a drunken sleep and taking it all in. "I kin whup a whole cowpen full a' meskins lak him in my underskirt an never show my ass!"

Unfortunately, it didn't hold true when she was drunk. He'd beat the dogshit out of her, but she sternly ordered me not to interfere. Most of the time I left, only to return to find her with a black eye and busted lip.

She put him out of commission for awhile though. They got drunk "together" and went to bed. Salvador waited until she fell asleep. He got up, put his pants on, and went behind the headboard. Reaching his arms through the iron railings, he got a choke-hold around her neck. She woke up struggling and reached her hands through the rails, frantically trying to break the hold. She grabbed the first thing she touched, which happened to be his balls. Using her long fingernails, she ripped his nutsack. When she let go, he fell to the floor, his trouser fly covered with blood. I talked her out of chopping his head (or anything else) off with the hatchet.

I was back in school, but absent most of the time because they fought and stayed drunk so much. When I came home from school one afternoon she told me, "That old white daddy a' yours died."

"We goin to his funeral Emma?"

"Hell naw."

So much for that.

I was practically running the house, and it even spilled over into the crap games. My big chance came after they started arguing while the game was in progress. For fear of the gamblers leaving, Emma put me in charge so they could go in her room and finish the fight.

In many ways, I was better than she was. I had the "rolll" down to a T and controlled the dice better, knew how to gauge them in accordance with the nail-heads, and wasn't drunk. The gamblers didn't hesitate when I took the game over. I had been around them so long, I was viewed as a regular player. Besides, "money's money," young or old. When she sobered up I turned the money I'd won over to her.

Emma was so busy trying to keep the licks off her ass, mine was being spared. When she got whiskey-mean and missed a point on the dice, I still got my "jinky peckerwood-lookin ass" driven from the crap room. But I no longer quivered when she 'buked me; I bit my lip to hold back my seething anger and to keep from lashing out at her.

Their fighting had given the house a bad name; it was losing money. After the police were summoned several times to quell things, the gamblers got scared to come for fear of being arrested themselves. Now, we were lucky to have three or four people at the house on weekends.

It was another Saturday, and I'd been up since early dawn getting things ready, just in case. I scrubbed the floors with Eagle Lye (minus the piss) and cleaned up the crap room from last night's minor activity while she and Salvador were still in their room. With all the preparations taken care of, I left to round up some players. I walked down to the liquor store council tree where the pulpwood haulers were parked, and told them, "There sho is a good game goin at the house."

Two or three interrupted their drinking and said, "When we finish takin care uv bizness, we might cum by." I knew they probably wouldn't.

After leaving them I headed for the Terminal Cafe at the train station to give the same message to any potential players who might be there. I made all my junction rounds to the places where the gamblers hung out before going back home.

I heard the low, muffled scuffling as soon as I stepped up

on the back porch. When I walked through the kitchen and entered the crap room, Salvador had Emma pinned in the corner next to the trunk. He was choking her so hard his hands and arms trembled. The fight had gone out of her and she was barely struggling.

I rushed over and positioned myself where she could see my face. "Emma, you want me to help you?" She couldn't talk, but motioned her eyes up and down for a yes.

We had a pot-bellied, wood burning stove in the crap room, and kept the wood stacked on the back porch. I ran out and got a big stick of the wood, ran back, and hit him just above the ear. He released his hold, and Emma sank to the floor. The first blow stunned him. I got in another before he directed his attention to me. I wanted him to come at me to give her a chance to catch her breath.

As soon as she got herself together she jumped him from behind. Emma wasn't drunk this time, and Salvador was no match for both of us. Fighting savagely, he managed to raise the lid on the old metal trunk where he kept all his tools. I knew about the house's major weapon that was kept inside. He was going for the white-handled hatchet!

Emma slammed the lid down on his arm and sat her 200-plus pounds on top of the trunk. Salvador let out an agonized shriek. When he screamed, Emma looked at me, "Is I got 'em?!" More excitedly, "Tell me, IS I GOT THIS MUTHAFUCKA??!"

"Yes mam, I bleeve you got 'em."

"Don' BLEEVE nuthin. Tell me, is I GOT 'em?"

"You got 'em, Emma!"

"Thas all I wanna know."

Salvador's face grimaced with pain, "Gotdamme Eemma! Git you big ass up! You gonna broke my fuckin arm!"

"You don' say?" and started bouncing up and down as Salvador groaned, "UGHH! ARGHHH!" She was winning one for a change and how sweet it was to be bullyragging him.

"You know whut meskin? I been waitin a long, long time for this day."

"Gotdamme Eemma, you brokeen my fuckin arm!!" he squirmed vainly trying to free his arm.

"I know Gotdam well I am," she said unconcerned "an thas not all I'm gon' do," ordering me, "cum here, Baby."

"Yeah, Emma."

"You think you kin hold this lid down if I git up off it? Be sho now!" she added gravely. "Git up on it an see." I added my skinny 90 pounds on the trunk lid.

Salvador moaned, then cried out, "I no heetcha no mo Eemma! OOOH!"

"Emma!" I said concerned, "I don' thank I kin hold it down settin on it. Lemme stand up so I kin brace my hands on th' ceilin." I stood up and got into position. With my palms pushing against the ceiling, "I kin hold it now, Emma. Git up anytime you ready!"

"Make sho you got it now! I'm fixin to git off."

"I got it," I reassured.

"Be sho now!" as she slowly wiggled off the lid. Looking up at me, "Be sho you got it now! I'm gittin off," she said one more time anxiously.

"Go head an git off Emma. I got it!"

"Okay, I'm gittin ALL the way off," and finally let her feet touch the floor. Satisfied that I had him under control, she taunted, "Awww, Gotdam! Gotcha at last, ain't I. You know whut I'm fixin to do to yo ass meskin? Betcha can't even guess, can ya?" Pausing to look up, "You still got 'em?"

"Yes mam, Emma."

She did her boxing footwork, moving and circling around Salvador.

"Don' turn him loose now!" while she jabbed and shadowboxed, stopping only to put her hands on her hips and shake her "booty" in his face.

Finished with her roadwork, she let him have a fist right in the kisser. "Maybe that'll stop some uv that ol' mouf uv yo's."

Then back to the show, putting her head right down in his face, "Here, hit this muthafucka! Hit this ol' head. I know you wanna hit me. Why don'cha? Oh, don' wanna fight now, huh."

Using her fist like a sledge hammer, she hit him again. "C'mon, hit me back, meskin! You know whut I oughta do? I oughta git that poker an ram it up yo ass. But I know you wouldn' lak that," sarcastically, "so I'm jes gon' give you a good ass whuppin instead. How's that?" POW!! "You still got 'em?"

"I got 'em."

"Why don'cha ball up yo fist an hit me right here where you hit me while ago?" again lowering her head to his. "Here, lemme help you," taking his free hand, "lemme make you a fist."

She balled up his hand and began hitting herself on the head with it, "Black my utha eye, muthafucka. I wantcha to git me good an mad fo I sho nuff start whuppin yo ass!"

She wound her arm up like a pitcher and pommeled blow after blow on top of Salvador's head, using the knuckle side of her fist like a club, only stopping to reaffirm, "You still got 'em?"

She hit him so many times her hand was swelling. "Stop hittin 'em on his head, Emma. You gon' break you damn hand!" I warned.

"Thas awright. I wanna break it on his ol' hard head!"

POW! She pounded him again. "Whew! I dun jesta bout give out whuppin this meskin's ass," adding, "but it sho wuz a lot uv fun, even if I did fuck up my hand. Look at it," she said pitifully, holding it up with her other hand for me to get a better look. It was swollen to twice its size.

"Whut we gon' do wit 'em now, Emma?" I was getting tired of straining to keep the lid down.

"Hold 'em til I git outta the house, then git down an run."

A minute or two later she yelled out, "Anytime! Let the muthafucka go when you git ready!"

I jumped off the trunk and dashed out the back door. Soon as I got outside, "SHHHH! Here I am, over here." She was standing at the corner of the house. "I got some bricks piled up so when that sonuvabitch cums out we kin blast 'em some mo."

Salvador emerged from the house carrying the hatchet, looking for us. When he came around the corner of the house, I let go with an "alley apple" that caught him in the chest. He dropped the hatchet and took off. We had him on the run!

I fired brick after brick as he fled down the street. But with Emma's help, he was on the verge of making a drastic comeback. She was running halfway to him and rolling the bricks like bowling balls.

Every time I zoomed one at him, I had to duck because he stopped running and was returning the fire. Like a short-stop, he scooped up the bricks she rolled and hurled them back at me.

"Damnit, Emma!" I shouted after a near miss, "quit chunkin! You feedin 'em ammunition!"

When she stopped helping, I started winning again. Salvador took off down the street, probably heading for the border. "We got 'em!" she boasted, like she had really blasted him with those bricks.

"Damn, Emma! You gon' git us kilt one uv these days!"

6 ||||||||||||||||||||||||||||||||||| ▭

Even though she had successfully discarded the thorn in her side, the stigma from their stormy relationship lingered stronger than ever. Our white neighbors in the neighborhood, heretofore, had not complained at all about the gambling, boozing, or any of the other things that went on at Big Emma's Place. But with all the hell-raising she and Salvador did, they started calling the police at the slightest disturbance.

Now, practically every time a patrol car came down our street, they stopped by to "look in" on us. The heat was on, and the enterprise steadily declined. Hardly anybody came to the house to gamble any more. Since the success of the bootlegging business largely depended on the gambling crowd, it had to be abandoned. There was no money coming in, and it was back to basics, but with a different twist.

Emma could no longer get all dolled up, go uptown, and come back with a string of tricks following her. She'd gotten too fat. Now, instead of tricks catching her, "we" caught them. I hardly went to school any more and pulled duty on the front porch, alerting her to any potential customer passing by. My stomach always knotted up when I spotted one and summoned her.

It was freezing cold outside, and the lone crepe myrtle in the yard was weighted down with icicles. I woke up early and went over behind Ben E. Keith's produce house to hustle some kindling wood. I had a good fire going in the crap room when Emma came in and joined me.

"BRRrrr! Gotdam, it's colder than a well digger's ass in Butte, Montana!" backing up to the pot-bellied stove. "How long you been up?"

"A pretty long time."

"You ain' goin to school?"

"Nawww, I didn' wanna go."

I neglected to tell her "NEVER no mo." I fought on the way to school and on the way home. Nearly everybody in Longview knew our business, and that included their children. Some kid was always talking bad about Emma and me. "Yo mama laks white mens." "You ain' nuthin but a peckerwood." "You half-white."

I also didn't mention that I beat up Willie Joseph at school with a broom handle for calling her a whore. And that I got a whipping for it and got expelled for three days. She might not have given a damn, but I wasn't taking any "Rayfield chances" (Rayfield would take a chance on anything). I wondered about what it was going to be like for Pat when she started school next year. If they picked on her like they did me, I'd be fighting all the time.

We sat in the crap room gazing, "Emma?"

"Whut?"

"I don' thank no tricks is comin by this mornin. Do you?"

"Never kin tell. Men buy pussy when it's cold, jes lak they do when it's hot. Ain't I got a bottle layin roun somewhere?"

"Yes mam, I know where it's at."

"Go git it."

When I returned with the near pint, I waited for her to take a swig. After she swallowed, "Damn! I kin see now. Thas whut I needed wuz a eye-opener." She was in a decent humor in spite of our wretched condition.

"Emma, since there ain' nuthin doin, tell me bout you an Aunt Elzado sum mo. Where'd ya'll go afta ya'll caught that train?"

She took another drink and cleared her throat, "We rode

92

that muthafucka all the way to Dallis. Did I ever tell you Elzado damn near fell off when we caught it?''

"No mam."

"Hell, for a minute I didn' thank we wuz gon' make it."

"Whut happen?"

"Well, I caught the damn thang pretty good, but when Elzado hopped it, she missed wit one uv her feet. I held her on til it slowed down in Mineola."

Reminiscing, "But we made it. When we got to Dallis, we stayed wit Sally for awhile. Boy, when Bama an Sally told us bout Duck bein dead, I got me a bottle an celebrated. I wisht I knowed where she wuz buried, I'd go shit on her grave! I don' know how Elzado let 'em talk her into stayin. Soon as I made me some money an put a few rags together, I left."

"Then whut?"

"Then I jes went everwhere. If I heard bout a town where money could be made, I went. First place wuz For Wuth. Then," pausing to reflect, "I left there an went to San Tonia, then down to Corpus Christi." Adding, "Thas a pretty place."

"Whut's it lak?"

"Gotta ocean an lotsa people. Then back to San Tonia an on out to El Paso. Since I wuz so close to Mexico, I said whut the fuck, an crossed over. Thas how I met Sabbado. You know the rest uv it." Taking another drink, "You oughta, I dun tole it to you a dozen times."

"Say Emma. I got a idea how I kin help make us sum money."

"Doin whut?"

"Shinin shoes. I could make us a lotta money shinin shoes! Specially when them troop trains stop over at the station. Even when they ain' no troop train, they's always sum soldiers roun the station. I been wantin to do it, I jes hadn' said nuthin to you bout it.

"I saved up enuff money to git whut I need. I kin git two cans uv black, two cans uv brown, an two cans uv tan shoe polish, a brown an black brush, an three shine rags for three dollars at Shiver's. An I kin make a shine box myself. Kin I do it?''

After taking another gulp, ''I don' care. Don't git in the way over there.''

I ran back to Ben E. Keith's produce house and relieved them of two of their sturdiest looking fruit crates. Leaving them on the back porch, I rushed in the house and got the hatchet. After about two steady hours of carpentry, I had beaten those crates apart and put together a good looking shine box. I got one of Salvador's belts and attached it to the box for a shoulder strap.

Only one thing was missing; I had to hustle some paint. The paint store uptown was just the place. They threw paint cans out back, maybe one of them would have enough. I was right, and using a piece of cardboard, painted it green. On the way back, I stopped by Shiver's Drugs and picked up my supplies.

The next day at the train station I made over seven dollars. When the troop trains stopped to let the soldiers take a break, I was right there with my shine box. I even had one twenty dollar day after I learned how to pop those shine rags. I gave all the money to Emma to help make ends meet. Even on the occasional days that I went to school, I took along my shine box. After school, I headed straight for the train station.

In the meanwhile, in an effort to get the gambling going again, Emma started patronizing the police more and more when they stopped by. It didn't take her long to convince them that she knew about all the stealing going on in town.

''Some uv them ol' thievin niggers is always brangin somethin hot by here to sell or hock. I kin git ya'll they names,'' she offered. That is, if they would cut her some slack.

One day an officer came by alone. After he finished tricking and was about to leave, ''Emma, if you hear anything bout that Shiver's Drug Store break-in, you be sure an let me know, now.''

''Oh yessir, Mister Buster, I sho will.''

She had already given them a few tips on some people and was a ''reliable'' snitch. Not only did she snitch on thieves, but also on her gambling and bootlegging competitors. She didn't view it as snitching, ''I'm lookin out for us. Fuck them nigguhs." When things got slow and she figured the crowd was over at so-and-so's house, she'd go call the police and tell them a fight was going on over there, just so the cops would show up and scare everybody away.

The gamblers drifted back, but not in numbers. Most of them still took their chances at one of the other places. Emma never was big on keeping secrets and after the police started coming to our house, everybody knew she was snitching. The gamblers kept on gambling while she talked to the cops in the next room. After the conference and when she returned to the game, a player would ask, "Whut's that all bout, Big Emma? Is they gon' 'rest anybody? Cuz if they is, I'm leavin now!" ready to run.

"Naw," she said, "don' ya'll worry bout nothin. They ain' comin by here to do nuthin but pick up they money." Bragging, "Tell me how many nigguhs' houses could ya'll be gamblin in an the police cum an don' take nobody to jail? Thas one thang ya'll don' havta worry bout at Big Emma's place. Ya'll ain' gon' havta pay no fines."

Word quickly spread and the other bootlegging and gambling operators hated us. Me, because they figured if I knew they were having a game, I would tell Emma and she would call the cops on them. When they saw me coming, "Ya'll betta raise up, heah cums o' Big Emma's boy."

Seems like everyday a different policeman came to the house. When they asked her questions she knew nothing about, she pretended that she did just to stay in their good graces. When this wasn't working, she quickly changed the subject to get them interested in "somethin else."

Now whenever we had a game at the house, there was no need to stand guard at the door. When the police came, I didn't even bother to announce it. They just walked through to the crap room and called her into the other room. I felt as tall as a worm.

School had turned out and I rushed off the campus to get to my shoe shining job. After waiting for the traffic so we could cross over Highway 80, I, along with a hundred other kids, made the mad dash for safety.

I saw the patrol car parked across the highway while we were waiting. When we got to the other side, one of the policemen hollered from his window, "Hey you!" We all stopped and looked quizzically at each other.

"You with the shine box, git over heah!"

The other kids were suuure looking now as I walked up to the car. "Yessir?" I didn't know these two.

"You Big Emma's boy?"

"Yessir."

"Git in, we wanna talk to you."

"Bout whut?" as I crawled into the back seat.

"Bout that shoe polish you got thar," he said as we drove away.

"Whut bout it?" completely dumbfounded.

"Where'd you git it?" the other officer asked.

"At Shiver's Drug Store."

"Thas whut we wanna talk to you bout."

I knew the way to the jailhouse, and we weren't heading in that direction. "Where ya'll takin me?"

"Aw, we jes gonna run out heah a little ways so's we kin talk in private."

After we crossed the Sabine river, they turned off on a side road, stopped the car, "Git out!"

"Look now, you kin save yoreself a whooole lot uv trouble, boy, an us too, if you jes tell us who you got it frum."

"I dun tole ya'll. I bought it at Shiver's Drug Store."

"Lissen boy! Don'tcha be a standin thar lyin to us! We know whar the Gotdam shit cum frum!"

"I'm tellin ya'll the truth! I bought it at the drug store. I paid three dollars for all this stuff, my brushes an rags too."

One of them slapped me across the face and I fell down. "You quit yore lyin, boy! Big Emma dun tole us sum nigguh cum by ya'll's house wit two or three cartons uv polish, an you bought it frum him! Tell us who it wuz!"

The inside of my jaw was bleeding and I started crying, "No sir, I didn', I ain' bought nuthin frum nobody but . . ."

The officer who slapped me reached down and jerked me up. With one hand he held me up so we were face to face. "Boy, I'm tired uv lissenin to you lyin. You heah me?"

I trembled out, "Yessir, but I ain' lyin."

He looked at the other officer, "Big Emma said he wuz

gonna deny ever bit uv it. Boy, you callin yore mama a liar?''

"No sir . . . I mean yessir . . . well . . .''

"Git the belt outta the car pocket.''

While one of them held my face down on the hood, the other dropped my britches and strapped my bare ass.

Pitching and squirming, I twisted my face to one side and cried out, "Ask Mr. Shivers! Ask Mr. Shivers! He'll tell ya'll!!''

After two more licks they decided to go to the drug store. In the back seat, I clutched my shine box in my lap and cried all the way.

"Boy, you hush that shit up back thar. If you're lyin to us, I'm gonna give you a lot worse'n 'at!''

They followed me into the drug store and I pointed out the man who sold me the polish. He confirmed it without hesitation. Satisfied, they left.

When I walked in the house Emma wouldn't look me in the face. She knew.

"Emma, why? You know I didn' buy nuthin frum no nigguh. How cum you tell 'em that an make 'em whup me?''

"Aw, you'll git over it. That wuzn' yo first ass-whuppin an it won' be yo last. G'on outta here an lemme alone!''

I didn't move fast enough to suit her. She grabbed an empty whiskey bottle off the crap table and threw it at me. I ducked, and it shattered against the wall. "I tole you to git yo Gotdam ass on outta here!'' she fumed.

I ran out of the house and stopped when I got to a tree. I pulled the strap off my shoulder and smashed the shine box to smithereens against it, cursing her with each blow. I didn't bother to pick up the polish.

I cried all the way to Miss Bertha's house. I saw Floyd in the yard.

"Hi,'' I shouted.

"Hi.''

"Whutcha doin?''

"Nuthin.''

"Wanna go to the picture show wit me? I'll pay yo way.''

"Yeah! Lemme go axe Grandma.''

97

Miss Bertha gave him permission, and we hit the railroad tracks heading for town. After watching the Tim McCoy movie for the third time and getting so excited when he had a shoot-out with the bad guys, I swallowed my jawbone breaker (round hard candy) and nearly choked to death, the shine box incident faded off somewhere into the back of my mind.

Friday, business as usual; we were getting ready for the weekend. I had taken care of the scrubbing and she was in the kitchen cooking. I was in her room making up the bed and heard a knock on the front door.

I hurried to answer it, "Yessir," I said, unhooking the screen.

He looked at me for a moment or two, "Is this where Miss Emma stay?"

"Yessir."

"Is you her boy?"

"Yessir."

"Is she at home?"

"Yessir, she's here."

"Would you tell her sumbody at the door to see her?"

He wasn't a regular customer. I had never seen the elderly man who looked to be in his seventies before, but he might be a trick. I sure didn't want to let him get away; Emma would kill me.

"You wanna cum in an wait til I go git her?"

"No," he said politely, "I'll jes wait out heah."

I went to the kitchen, "Emma, a man's at the door to see you."

She was busy chopping a cabbage and didn't look up, "Who is it?"

"I don' know. Ain' never seen him befo."

"Whut do he want?"

"He didn' say, he jes ast if you live here an tole me to cum gitcha."

She laid the butcher knife down. "I sho hope it's somebody wit some money," and hurried out of the kitchen. With me right behind, "You sho you don' know who it is?"

"Yes'm."

When she got to the screen, "Yeah, whut do . . . YOU

98

GOTDAM LOW-DOWN SONUVABITCH!!'' She spat venom at the stranger. Clenching her fists so tightly the veins in her hands looked like big macaroni, she screamed, ''WHUT YOU DOIN ON MY PORCH?!! YOU GOTDAM SORRY MUTHAFUCKA YOU!! YOU KILLED MY MAMA!!''

The old man stood with his head lowered, not saying a word.

''WHY, THE VERY IDEA, YOU CUM DRAGGIN YO SORRY ASS UP TO MY FRONT DOOR! YOU MUTHAFUCKA! YOU DON' KNOW WHUT YOU PUT ME THRU IN MY GOTDAM LIFE! YOU TOOK EVERTHANG AWAY FRUM ME!!''

She flung the screen door open, almost knocking him down. His hat fell off and she kicked it off the porch. ''GIT!! YO MUTHAFUCKIN ASS OFF A' MY GOTDAM PORCH!'' shoving him down the steps. ''IF I EVER LAY EYES ON YOU AGIN, I'LL KILL . . . you.'' The tears began pouring down profusely. She cried so hard she could hardly utter, ''You muthafucka you . . .'' She followed him down the street throwing rocks at him.

''Who wuz that, Emma?'' I'd figured it out but asked anyway.

''My ol' chicken-shit daddy. I oughta harked an spit rat in his muthafuckin face!''

She headed straight to her fifth of Old Grand Dad, knocked it halfway, returned to the kitchen and started singing.

Beautiful Hula, down in dream of Honolulu,
Dear I'm feeling so peculiar
Since I first met . . . you
In the moonlight garden fair,
Cupid hearers wandering there
Waiting and dreaming in a garden of roses;
Sometime, in the bright Hawaiian sunshine,
Dear I'm trying to make you all mine
And I'll come back someday
And we'll fly away
My Hawaiian butterfly.

Just as if nothing had happened.

Pat would be starting school in September without a body guard. I hadn't been back since Wallace Clark called me "jailbird" at recess and I knocked out one of his front teeth. He ran and told Mr. Mason, who promised me a whipping when we returned to the classroom.

After we were seated, Mr. Mason called me up to his desk. Dangling the wide razor strap in his hand menacingly, he ordered, "Bend over boy! I'm gon' break you up frum all this fightin." Everybody was quiet and the loud WHACK! WHACK! echoings of the strap on my butt filled the room.

The stinging pains grew and I bit deeper into my lip. I wasn't going to cry with all those kids looking at me. This seemed to infuriate Mr. Mason, who was determined to make me cry out. Each time he hit me, he tip-toed for more leverage. After about a dozen hard licks, "Git on back to yo seat. Soon as I rest my arm, I'm gon' give you sum more."

All the kids snickered. I sat at my desk and took the boy scout pocketknife out of my overalls and opened the big blade. He summoned me for an encore. When I bent over this time I gigged him in the thigh and fled. I told Emma I wasn't "never" going back to school. She didn't ask why, "If you wanna grow up wit no schoolin lak me, thas yo bizness."

Gambling had fallen off during the past weekend due to several raids at different joints around town. The new sheriff was trying to put everyone out of business. Emma was feeling the crunch too, and her fleeting usefulness no longer excluded her from the top ten list.

Tricks had been pretty slow over the past few days too. "Knubby," one of Emma's regulars, hadn't been around yet, and I was sitting on the front porch watching for him. He was a one-handed white man who always wore the same old khaki pants and shirt. I couldn't believe Emma let him touch her with that knub. Just the thought of it gave me the "all-overs" (shudders). If we missed him, he kept going around the block and coming back by until one of us flagged him down.

I saw my pal, Floyd, walk around the corner. He had a

big, shit-eating grin on his face and I thought he was looking more like a monkey everyday. He came up on the porch and sat down beside me. Handing me the box he was carrying, he said, "Hi."

"Hi," I said, examining the box, "whut is it?"

"Open it an see."

I ripped at the cellophane tape and my mouth flew open. Two pearl handled, nickel-plated, Gene Autry cap pistols with a braided holster!

"You kin have 'em," showing his monkey grin.

"Where'd you git 'em?"

"I bought 'em."

"They sho must uv cost lots," as I fumbled with the buckle adjustment.

"They did, but I don' care. I got heaps uv money."

With the cap pistols strapped on and practicing my quick draw, "How much you got?"

He ran his hand into his pocket and pulled out a wad of bills.

"Damn, Floyd! Where'd you git all that money?"

"Thas awright where I got it frum, I got it. An I got sum mo hid."

I ran into the kitchen, "Emma, kin I go to th' picture show with Floyd? Look whut he bought me." Adding, "He got a whole lotsa money . . ." Her eyes lit up like a slot machine.

"Where'd he git all that money?"

"I don' know. He won' tell me."

"Where is he?"

"Waitin on the porch."

She began drying her hands and heading for the front door.

"Floyd, baby, cum on in the house," she said holding the screen open. "Let Big Emma see all that money you got."

Floyd, acting more like a five year old than fifteen, was grinning from ear to ear as he showed her the roll of bills.

"Big Emma got somethin she wanna show you, Floyd, honey." Looking at me, "You go on back out on the porch." When I heard the door to her room close, my heart sank. I knew the rest.

Ten or fifteen minutes later, Floyd came out, still buttoning his overalls with sweat rolling off his forehead, "You ready to go to th' show?"

"Naw! G'on. I ain' goin," I said angrily and brushed past him into the house. I stopped at Emma's doorway, just looking at her and trembling all over.

"Don'tcha be standin there turnin that peckerwood nose up at me! Money's money."

I stormed out the back door and ended up at the T&P pond. With my feet in the water, I sat watching the dragonflies skitter across the top, wondering how they kept from sinking. I unbuckled my holster belt and threw the whole thing at them damn skiddy-hoppers.

I found out later Floyd took the money from the grocery store where he worked as a porter. The manager left the safe open and Floyd just helped himself. He called the police and, except for what Emma took Floyd for, got most of it back. He wouldn't press charges and was quite satisfied with the ass-whipping Miss Bertha gave him in the presence of the police. The manager even let Floyd keep his job; but, he sure lost his picture show pal.

Over the past month, the weekend gambling had been running hot and cold. The police were raiding other places pretty regularly, and the crowds had drifted back our way. This was a live weekend; the house was full. I went to the liquor store earlier and got a case of wine and half-pints on credit, and was busy selling it.

Emma was surrounded at the crap table, constantly taking big swigs out of "her" bottle. She was missing a lot of cuts out of the bets because she was arguing and bragging with the gamblers.

During one of my passes through the crap room, I heard Herman telling her, "Naw you don', Big Emma. You don' wanna be fuckin wit me. No way, shape, form, or fashion."

"Shit nigguh!" she snarled back, "I had my own brother killed. Whut makes you think I won' fuck wit you?"

Whenever she got whiskey mean and told somebody that, it made me cringe and usually a hush fell over the game. This time was no exception. After the brief silence, another player spoke up, "Say Big Emma, ya'll cut out all the shit. I ain' won a bet since ya'll been jaw-jekin."

I was with a customer when Emma called, "Baby, cum here when you git thru."

I nudged past the gamblers standing around the table, "Yeah, Emma?"

"These Gotdam nigguhs dun gathered up all the change outta the game an crammed it in they pockets. Run down an git me a rolla nickels," handing me the two dollars. "An don't you tarry! I need 'em."

I left running for the liquor store and headed back at full speed. Streaking past the outhouse on the back trail, my hand hit my thigh and the roll of nickels sailed into the darkness. I put on the brakes and ran back to the spot where I thought the roll landed.

I spent what seemed like an hour crawling around and uprooting every blade of johnson grass. Two of the gamblers leaving the game saw me crawling around and Hawk Shaw asked, "Whutcha doin, man?"

"I lost a rolla nickels."

They volunteered to help. Before long Hawk Shaw said, "Cum on man. We gotta go. We can't find nuthin, dark as it is out heah."

I kept on looking for a while longer, but gave up. I suspected Hawk Shaw found the nickels when he abruptly withdrew his services.

I went into the crap room and walked to the table. Emma glanced up, "Where's my change? Hand it here!" Not getting the nickels, she looked up again, "Whut you dun?"

I squeezed out, "Emma, I lost th' nickels."

Busy placing a bet, she didn't hear me and demanded, "Hand me my Gotdam change!"

"Emma, I lost th' nickels, I wuz comin aroun the trail runnin an my hand . . ."

"You jinky peckerwood muthafucka!" She pushed the table back and came at me. When she got within striking distance, she hit me in the mouth with her fist, knocking me in the corner by the juke box. I slunk to the floor. My tongue quickly detected the loose front tooth.

Emma sat down on the daybed and pulled the table back up to her. Casually asking, "Whose shot is it, baby?"

Still dazed, I stood up and wobbled into my room, grabbed my navy jacket and left.

7 ||||||||||||||||||||||| ▭

I cut behind Ben E. Keith's and stayed on the tracks until I
got to the trestle and sat down underneath. When the freight
train, waiting back at the station, blew its clearance whistle,
I got ready. The big engine spun its wheels to get a starting
grip to pull the long line of box cars.

It started rumbling slowly in my direction. Crouching in
the weeds beside the tracks until the engine lumbered past, I
waited until about twenty cars went by, picked out an empty
one, and hopped aboard.

I learned about catching trains from Lonzo. In his
drunken stupors he had talked about hoboing and being a
brakeman, until he would keel over backwards, asleep.

He told me what the whistles meant, which end of the car
to catch, all the brakeman hand signals, about the signal
lights, how to brace the gondola from the inside so nobody
could lock it from the outside, how to read the destination
markings on the sides of the cars and oil tankers, how to ride
the rails (riding underneath the box car on two rods), which
way to face when on top, how to make a train slow down,
how to stop it, etcetera, etcetera, etcetera.

When the freight came to a stop I jumped out of the car
and made a dash for the underbrush. The "knob-knockers"
were already walking down the tracks inspecting the long
string of cars while the train waited. After the passenger
train whizzed by, the freight whistle sounded for clearance

up ahead, the signal lights went from red to green, and it slowly started pulling off.

I left my hiding place and jumped back on. When it was running fast again, I fell asleep. I woke up and looked out of the open door and saw signs along the highway indicating Little Rock wasn't far away. While the train was stopped in the Little Rock freight yard, I got off to hustle some grub, made my way to the highway, and started walking. I wandered about a mile from the freight yard and came to a small country store. Approaching the entrance, I wondered what to buy with the thirty-five cents I had in my pocket. I settled for a dime's worth of bologna, a dime's worth of block cheese, and a nickel box of crackers. After paying I asked for an empty jug that I could fill with water.

I ran back to the underbrush near the tracks, ate, and waited. Watching from my hiding place, I saw them switch engines. This was as far as old Texas & Pacific (T&P) was going; a Cotton Belt engine was hooked on. When the engineerman blew the whistle for take off, I climbed aboard. I had no idea where the train was headed and didn't care, just as long as it was far, far away from Longview.

Lonzo didn't lie when he told me the Cotton Belt was the fastest freight line. The train was going much faster now, like it had to be somewhere and was already late. Every time it neared a railroad crossing, the engineerman started the old whistle to moaning and I rushed to stand in the open doorway to wave at the car passengers as we streaked by.

It side-tracked for a few minutes in Memphis to let another train have the right-of-way, and took off again. Knoxville, Richmond, and on to Baltimore. I had to do some hustling in a hurry. That cheese, bologna, and crackers had long since disappeared, and my belly talked in growls.

I looked pretty grimy when I stepped inside the small cafe in the colored part of town and took a seat at the counter. There wasn't a thing on the homemade menu tacked to the wall I could get for a dime. I ordered a 25¢ hamburger "to eat here" and bought a package of pigskins to munch on while I waited. The cook brought the hamburger and sat it down in front of me and went back to the kitchen. He'd collect for it after I finished. I caught him not looking, wrapped the hamburger in the napkin, and hit the door running. He came to the door shouting something, but I was long gone.

I bummed around town, sleeping here and there until I started hanging around Miss Lizzie's Place, running errands. She had six rooms upstairs, and rented them out for transient trade. With servicemen everywhere, her rooms were rarely unoccupied. I worked my way from errand boy to cleaning up the rooms behind the whores. For this, she paid me five dollars a week and board, and anything I could hustle, short of stealing from her military trade.

Miss Lizzie's Place was safe because she actually did pay the police to let her operate her bawdy house. They only came by to collect their dough. With that in mind, I kept a crap game going out in the back yard after I got off work and kept all the neighborhood boys broke. Sometimes, my little crap game attracted grown-ups. They'd shoot for nickels and dimes with us for awhile, but then invariably raise the stakes. That's when I really "rolled" the craps.

After losing more than expected in what started out as a nickel and dime kid crap game, one of the men would ask, "Where'd you learn how to shoot craps lak that boy?"

"I don' KNOW how to shoot 'em sir, I'm jes lucky."

With some good jeans and tennis shoes, a new multi-bladed pocketknife, and some jingle in my pockets, it was time to move on. I still hadn't seen any of the places and things in Lonzo's stories. I walked to the freight yard, hopped a train, and headed on up the Eastern Seaboard: Trenton, Newark, and finally New York City.

It didn't take long for my money to run out. I started shining shoes in Grand Central Station by day and sleeping at one of Father Divine's flop houses. Each night the rows of cots in the flop house were filled with derelicts, drunkards, and the run of the mill down-and-outers. The shelter also provided one meal a day. When passing through the chow line we were required to say, "Peace Father," before receiving a helping. Occasionally, Father Divine, a black preacher (followed by an entourage of "angels"—all pretty white women), paid a visit to the facility, in the flesh.

I was so busy trying to survive I almost forgot about the Empire State Building and the Statue of Liberty. After about a year, I came to realize that New York City was full of very private people who could care less. I could hardly wait until winter was over so I could get back to hoboing. Soon as the weather broke, I headed west. It was late spring and the railroad dicks were chasing me all over the Chicago freight yards. The train I caught in Akron was loaded with military equipment. Fearing possible sabotage, railroad security was strenuous. Extra precautions were taken to keep the hobos off. I had to sneak back that night to catch one.

Just this side of Omaha, the train stopped and I headed for the bushes, following my nose to the smell of brewing coffee. Walking into the clearing I saw five colored hobos crouched around the fire.

"Hi," I said.

Two or three nodded their heads.

"How bout a shot uv ya'll's java?"

"Sho boy, c'mon an hep yosef." After I filled a tin can from the gallon bucket brewing in the middle of the fire, "Where you cumin frum boy?"

"Chicago," adding, "I was lucky to git outta there, them dicks run me all over the place."

"Yeah," another said, "they pretty rough now on account uv the war. Where you headed?"

"West."

"Where west?"

"Jes west."

"Good thang you is, cuz it sho be hard hoboin thru the South. They gotta dick name Texas Slim wekin twix Fort Worth an East Texas thas been throwin hobos off lef an right."

"Yeah, I heard bout 'em," one of the others said, "but he jes one man. They got sum places down South where a nigguh bet not show his face. Whitefolks hate nigguhs so bad in Lollibell, Miss-sippy the train don' go thru fas enuff fo me! I gits off an runs thru town, an re-ketchs it on the outskirts."

Everybody laughed at that one. "Ya'll be laughin," he said more seriously, "but I ain' lyin, man. One time I wuz hongry an got off in a lil ol' one-hoss town in Miss-sippy an started walkin down the road an kept noticin how the whitefolks wuz lookin at me when they driv by. I met one walkin an axed 'em, Suh, kin you tell me where the colored folks hang out in this town?

"He looked at me lak I wuz crazy or sump'n, pointin off in the distance, 'See that tree down yonder, boy?' I tole 'em yessuh. 'Thas where they all hang out when we ketchs 'em.' I sped up an fo I got outta town I saw a sign say, 'NIGGUHS-ef you kin read-RUN. Ef you kin't read-RUN ANYHOW!' Thas when I struck up a fas trot."

I made it to Omaha, and joined up with a travelling carny. When it left Omaha, we headed back mid-west. We made Kansas, Missouri, Oklahoma, Nebraska, southern Illinois, crossing the Mississippi River and Old Big Muddy at least a dozen times. I did everything from hawking for the side shows to operating the concessions. I stayed with the Smith Brothers Show almost two years, and indeed, saw some of the places Lonzo had told me about.

The Huckleberry Finn in me gave call and I headed west once more. I caught a freight out of Illinois and left the carny behind. After a change of trains in St. Louis and another in Kansas City, I made connections with the Denver Line. I climbed up inside the empty cattle car and squatted down in a corner. It was dark as a sack of black cats. The only light came when a flickering light poked its way through the open door. The train had been running and "hollerin" steadily for what seemed about two hours.

There wasn't much to see in the darkness outside except the green signal lights alongside the tracks. By watching the ground as it zoomed by, I could tell the "monkey-motion" on that old engine was really churning and the green lights beckoned "c'mon."

I pulled some of the ankle-deep, loose hay up under me to soften the hard floor. My belly said it was time to knock out that last can of sardines I had in my back pocket. I took out my all-purpose hobo pocketknife and began opening them up.

A flash from a passing car's headlights shot through and I saw movement at the other end. My heart almost jumped out of my chest as I squinted to make sure I saw what I thought I saw.

The harder I looked, the clearer the outline became. The shadowy figure sat up and started brushing off the hay. I closed the can opener, opened the big blade, and slid the knife just underneath my sleeve.

Standing up and walking over to the doorway, a tall man harked and spat out the door several times. In a gruff voice, "I saw you when you got on way back yonder. Got any idee where we at?"

"Nope."

He walked toward me and stopped a few feet away, his body wavering. "How bout a taste uv them sardines?" He was so close I smelled the booze from his clothes.

"I jes got enuff for mysef," all the while easing the knife into my hand.

"Oh yeah? Well, we'll see about that!"

He lunged and I let him have the full force of the blade. He doubled up in pain, clutching his groin and cursing. He backed away toward the open door. I leaped and threw my shoulder against him as hard as I could. Out the door he went. He rolled and tumbled into the weeds. I watched until the caboose passed the spot I last saw him. After that, I hardly slept the rest of the trip to California.

At night, the Golden Gate Bridge was everything Lonzo said it was, "It looks lak a diamond (whistle) neckalis stretched cross the (whistle) ocean."

I had learned how to pick pockets while travelling with the Smith Brothers Show so the Alameda Race Track became one of my regular stomping grounds. Armed with a brand new single-edged razor blade, I stood at the rail. When the horses came into the far turn and headed for home, the excitement grew. While the men jumped up and down rooting for their horses to win, I cut their back pockets with the blade.

When I made one of my better cuts the billfold almost dropped into my hand. By the time the horses crossed the finish line, I could collect two or three billfolds.

There were eight races today. That meant mucho crowds.

When the races started, I went to work. I had a feeling it would be a good day at the tracks.

During the third race, while pretending to watch, I accidentally cut the wrong pocket of the guy next to me. He let out a painful yell. He looked at me and pointed his finger, hollering "I've been cut! This guy's tryin' to rob me!"

I took off through the crowd, shouting and pointing up ahead, "Hey somebody, stop that guy! Stop that guy!" My race track pick-pocketing had to be abandoned. The one thing I didn't want was to get busted, and so far, I'd been extremely lucky.

Lady Luck was still on my side. An older woman, Gladys, living at the same rooming house, took note of my worldly ways and youthful good looks. One day she commented on "what pretty eyes" I had. Learning from Emma what to say and how to say it, I took her advice, "Don' be no fool. If a woman got somethin else to gi' ya sides pussy, take it."

Gladys placed me under her everloving wing. All I had to do was provide her with loving and let her show me off. She provided the rest. Attractive at thirty-five, she was a recent divorcee whose old man was pretty well off. She took him to the cleaners and was living there until her house was ready. When Gladys moved, I moved in with her.

I'd been around whores all my life and viewed women either as trickees or potential tricks. I stayed with her over a year, not "hittin a lick at a snake," as Aunt Elzado would say, until the call of the wild hit me again. While she lay sleeping, I got up and put on my travelling clothes, took half the money from her purse, and eased out the door.

I caught a freight to L.A. Working at odd jobs got boring; I became restless and decided to head for home. I hooked a freight and took off for Texas. I made good connections in Phoenix and Tucson. I took the Missouri Pacific (MOPAC) out of El Paso going East. Changing trains in Dallas I hopped my first diesel driven train, the Cotton Belt Route. I realized after I settled down in the box car that the Cotton Belt didn't go to Longview, close as it went was Tyler, thirty-two miles away.

It was midday when the train stopped in Tyler. I hurried

111

out of the freight yard and found my way to a joint in the colored part of town. In a matter of hours I was in a fight and in jail for "assault with intent to kill." When I went before the judge he gave me a choice, "army or jail."

With a lot of help from the recruiting officer who looked over my shoulder and guided my hand to enough correct answers on the entry test, two days later I was in Fort Riley, Kansas. After basic training and breaking everybody in the barracks shooting craps in the shower stalls, I got my first furlough and caught the Greyhound for Longview.

Instead of taking a cab from the bus station, I gambled that she hadn't moved and decided to walk the six blocks. I felt like a million bucks. My adrenalin was pumping and I could hardly wait for them to see me in my soldier suit. At five-foot-eight, and a solid one hundred forty-two pounds, I was a svelte welterweight, muscular, with a good set of shoulders and a smooth, confident gait. My bootcamp haircut had grown out a little and tiny dark-brown curls covered my head. With the cotton broker's hazel eyes and anglo facial features, I was often mistaken for Italian or Puerto Rican. I was asked many times "what" I was, placing me in a position to choose for the occasion. I crossed the line back and forth and drank the wines of many vineyards.

After covering the five blocks to the "junction," my old neighborhood, I walked into the corner liquor store. I was surprised not to see any of the pulpwood trucks parked in the rear until I looked at my watch. It was only two-thirty, and too early.

"Hi, Mr. Milton," I greeted.

"Hi. What'll it be?" Taking a better look, "Say, ain't you Big Emma's boy?"

"Thas right."

Reaching his hand out to shake mine, "Damn, boy. It's good to see you. How've you been?"

"Jes fine."

"Well," he said, "you sure ain't the scrawny little kid you used to be. Looks like the service agrees with you. What'll you be havin today?"

"Lemme have two quarts uv hockeyproof Old Grand Dad."

"Bet you gittin this for Big Emma, ain'cha?" he said while reaching on the shelf.

"Yeah. Do she still live up the street?"

"Yep, same place," rubbing his chin, "seems like I recall her an Pat in earlier. Yep, they wuz," he said with certainty. "They wuz gittin ready for the weekend," winking his eye. "Be needin anything else?"

"Naw, thas all for now."

After tabulating the adding machine, "That'll be twelve dollars and sixty cents."

I paid him and stuffed the two bottles into my duffle bag. "Be seein you, Mr. Milton."

"Take care now, cum back in to see me."

"I will."

With only a half block to go, I stopped to wipe the dust off my spit-shined paratrooper boots, fix my cap, and square my shoulders. I could see the house. It looked pretty good with a fresh coat of white paint. It even had a new front porch.

Pat and another girl were playing in the front yard. I walked right up on them before either looked up. Pat saw me and let out a squeal.

"Oh! Bubba, it's you!" throwing her arms around my neck.

"It's me alright." Holding her away from me, "Damn, lemme take a look atcha. You nearly tall as me! I can't believe how you growed up so fast. Whut you doin over here?" I asked.

"I live here."

"Oh you do? Where's Mama Joe?"

"She died three years ago."

"She did?"

"Yeah, when she got sick she wouldn' go to the hospital at first, lak I tried to git her to. When she did go, it wuz too late. I been here wit Mama ever since."

Looking around at her friend, "Girl, I'm sorry. I'm so glad to see him I forgot. Bubba, this is my friend, Betty Carol. She live next door."

"How you, Betty Carol?"

She almost blushed right down through the ground. "Hi," she managed, then got the young girl giggles.

Pat admonished her teasingly, "Betty Carol, stop actin so crazy, girl."

"Where's Emma?" I asked.

"In the house. Betty Carol, wait for me. I'm goin in the house wit Bubba. I be back in a minute."

"Awright."

Walking toward the steps, "Bubba, boy you suure look good." Snickering, "Didja see the way Betty Carol wuz checkin you out?"

Chuckling, "Yeah, I saw her."

"How cum you didn' let us know you wuz comin?"

"I wanted to surprise ya'll."

I dropped my duffle bag in the hall and followed Pat through my old room into the crap room. Emma wasn't at her usual station. Jake was running the game.

"She mus be in the kitchen," Pat surmised.

The ten or fifteen players gathered around the crap table hardly noticed us passing through to the kitchen. She wasn't there either.

"She mus be in her bedroom, Bubba."

When we walked back out of the crap room into my old room, Pat paused, "I got yo room."

"I kin see that." I said jokingly, "Looks lak a girl's room. But how do you sleep with all the noise in the crap room?"

"Same way you useta. I close the door an go to bed."

"That ain't the way I did it."

"How'd you do it then?"

"I didn' go to bed til the game was over."

"Well, I can't stay up lak that. Mama makes me go to bed."

Stopping in the hall to get the bottles out of my duffle bag, "Say," I whispered, "why don'cha go on back an play with Betty Carol. I wanna go in by myself an really surprise her."

"Okay," she whispered back, "but don'cha go off nowhere."

"I won't," I assured her.

She tipped down the hall and I knocked on the door, "C'mon, it ain' locked."

I pushed the door open; she was lying across the bed. Without looking to see who it was, "Whut is it?"

I didn't answer. She turned her head toward me, wiping away the tears, "Well, I'll be!" She rushed to hug me. "Damn! Let Emma gitta good look atcha." Excitedly, "Do Pat know you here?"

"Yeah, I talked to her out in the yard."

"Damn, you sho look good in yo uniform, look lak it wuz melted an poured on you." Exclaiming as she squeezed my arms, "An muscles too."

Smiling back, "Yeah, I got a few."

"Sit down, sit down," she said leading me toward the bed. "I can't git over how good you look!"

"Sorry I can't say the same for you," unoffensively.

"Yeah, I know." Seeing the two sacks in my hands, "Whut'd you brang me?"

"Aw, I stopped by the liquor store an picked up two O.G.D.s."

"Well, bust one. I kin sho use a good drank right bout now."

"What's th' matter?" I broke the seal and passed it to her.

"Whut's th' matter?!" She took a swig and wiped her mouth, "Pat didn' tell you?"

"Tell me what?"

Her eyes quickly refilled with tears, "Blue's dead."

"What? When?" I said in amazement, handing my handkerchief to her.

After drying her eyes, honking her nose, and another long snort, "Two days ago. Died right out there on the front porch, bless his heart." Vainly biting her lip to stop the flow of tears, "He wuz tryin his best to make it back to Emma."

Astonished, "On the front porch?" I repeated more for myself than her. "How'd it happen?"

"Wuzn' long afta you left, an Blue started comin to the house agin. Thangs picked up afta the war an he wuz over here much as he wuz at home. When the game wuz over an everbody wuz gone, I got out my bottle an me an him would

115

jes sit an talk. We'd been doin that for a long time. Finally got roun to sayin we still loved each utha. We jes sorta left it hangin, cuz neitha uv us didn' have no ready answers for whut we oughta do bout it.

"Wednesday I had a house full uv folks. The round-house bunch got paid off, an I sent for Blue. We gambled all night, on into the next mornin. Both uv us wuz so damn tired when the game wuz over, we cum in here an jes fell out cross the bed an went to sleep. I woke up bout 'leven o'clock, eased off the bed, an went in the kitchen.

"I wuz almost thru cookin by the time he got up an made it back to the crap room." Reminiscing, "He looked so pretty wit his clothes all rumpled up . . . an needin a shave. We knocked out all the Old Grand Dad the nite befo so all I had for a eye-opener wuz a fifth uv vodka. I got him a glass an put the bottle on the table. We killed it in bout a hour. I dished us up a plate an we set at the crap table eatin an talkin.

"We made up our minds we wuz goin back together. When he said thas whut he wanted to do, I couldn' keep my hands off him. My mouf wuz greasy, but I kissed him any-how, got grease all on his silk shirt. He didn' give a damn, I hadn' seen Blue that happy in a long time. He said it wuzn' no use to keep puttin it off, soon as we got thru eatin he wuz goin home to git his clothes.

"We walked an hugged up to the door. When the taxi cum, he kissed me an said, 'I be back afta while.' Afta he left, you could hear me singin frum here to the courthouse. Pat wuz next door playin wit Betty Carol an I didn' know whut to do wit myself. I wuz goin crazy waitin.

"I filled up my wash tubs an started washin clothes. That Pat keeps me washin all the time, but she's sho a big help. I bet I made a dozen trips lookin out the door to see if he wuz comin. I thought he must be havin hell gettin away frum his old lady.

"I wuz out on the back porch washin an thought I heard somethin, but wuzn' sho. All uv a sudden, I had a real funny feelin, lak spiders crawlin all over me. I cum thru the house runnin. When I got to the screen an seen him layin on his side I thought he wuz takin a nap.

116

"I walked on the porch an knelt down 'side 'em, 'Blue! Blue! Whut's the matter baby? C'mon, wake up, Blue. Let Emma help you in the house.' Bless his sweet heart, he was holdin his pretty clothes in his arms. I turnt him over on his back an saw my baby's face . . . my heart . . . seem lak it jes shut down . . . lak it wuzn' gon' beat no mo. I set down an lifted his head up an put it in my lap. I . . . didn' know . . . whut else to do," her head drooped with each agonized word. The rush of tears splattered off the near empty bottle cradled in her lap.

With a deep sigh, "I don' know how long I set there rockin an holdin him fo the ambulance cum. Don't even know who called 'em."

"Whut killed 'em?" I asked dumbfounded.

"The doctor said afta he dun one uv them thangs on 'em . . . er . . ."

"Autopsy?"

"Yeah, he say that vodka jes recooked them cabbage an hamhocks in his stomach. That acid spread thru 'em so fast it made 'em deathly sick an helpless. The doctor say it wuz 'acute indigestion.' I tole him I drunk an et the same thang Blue did, an that I drunk mosta that vodka myself. He tole me everbody's system ain't the same. He say Blue would probably be alive today if he jes stuck his finger down his throat. Bless his heart he was jes too sick to do it."

"Damn," she said wiping her tears and reaching for the bottle. After a big gulp, "Whut time is it, Baby?"

Looking at the Bulova I'd won in the barracks latrine, "Ten after fo."

"Shit! I didn' know it wuz that late. I wuz spose to be at the undertakers at three," she said and stood up.

"Who got the body?"

"Nobody but the best, Swifty."

"When's the funeral?"

"Well, I don' know right now. They got in touch wit his sister in California an I'm waitin on her to git here."

"You think she comin?"

"Aw yeah, she'll be here. You wanna go down there to see 'em wit me?"

"Have they got 'em laid out?"

"Naw, he ain' dressed yet. Swifty's got 'em back in the cold room," she said looking in the mirror and fixing the tam on her head.

"I'll wait til he gits some clothes on. 'Sides, I wanna spend some time with Pat."

"Suit yoself, Baby, I gotta go." Leaving out the front door, "Why don'cha git us anutha bottle while I'm gone?"

I looked out the window and saw Pat on the porch by herself. I went out and sat down on the steps. She came over and sat beside me. "Thas kinda weird bout Allen, ain't it?"

"Yeah, sho wuz. I wuz over to Betty Carol's house when it happen. Mama be down to that undertaker parlor fo or five times, jes lookin at 'em. Tried to git me to go down there wit her. I said NO WAY. I'm scaid uv dead peoples. You scaid uv 'em, Bubba?"

"Naw, but I don' wanna see none buck naked. How long do she generally stay down there?"

"No tellin. Sumtimes a pretty long time."

"Say, what all do you do roun the house?"

"Aw, I help wit the cleanin-up an cookin, watch for the police, run errands, stuff lak that."

"You do go to school, don'cha?"

"Sho, Bubba. I'm in the sixth grade, least I will be when it starts agin."

"Do you lak it?"

"I hate it."

"I felt the same way when I was goin. But you need some so you kin git a job when you grown."

"Aw, I know Bubba, but I still hate it. I wisht I didn' hafta go at all. By the way, I heard bout whutcha dun to that teacher."

"Do the kids pick on you?"

"Naw, they know I'll tell my big brother on 'em if they do," she kidded.

"Do you ever hear anything from George?"

"Not since Christmas when he sent me them two old funny-lookin sweaters. Look lak he bought 'em for sumbody's grandma, 'steada me."

"Where's he at?"

"California, sumwhere. Bubba where all you been? I mean, fo you got in the Army."

"Lotsa places. New York, Baltimore, Philadelphia, just about all the midwest states, California, Little Rock, you name it."

"How'd you git to all them places?"

"Hoboed. Lemme ask you somethin, do you git many whuppins?"

"Nawww, Mama ain' never whupped me. She cuss me out sumtimes, but thas bout all."

"Well, if she ever tries to, you run."

"Don' worry, I will. I know how she is when she gits to drankin. Thas when I stay outta her way."

"Nonea them old crap nigguhs don' mess with you do they?"

"Nawww, if Mama wuz to ketch one uv 'em meddlin me she'd run his ass way frum here."

"Don' make no difference. Jes keep yo mind where yo ass is. You a big girl now. So watch yo step, know what I mean?"

"I know whut you mean, Bubba. I am."

The taxi pulled up; Emma was back. "Les talk some mo later, okay?"

"Okay, Bubba."

Emma stopped in the yard, "You been in the game yet?"

"Nawww, I was waitin on you to come back."

"Well, I'm back an jesta bout ready. Whut you an Pat been doin?"

"Just sittin out here talkin."

"Didja go down to the liquor store?"

"Not yet."

Walking down the street, "Where in the world you been all this time?"

"All over."

"How?"

"Hoboin mosta the time, 'cept when I was travellin with a carnival."

"A carnival? Whut on earth . . . ?"

"Aw, I used to stick my head through a hole an let 'em chunk balls at me."

Since I was buying, I thought about it a few seconds, and decided I didn't want to be running back and forth to the liquor store all night. "Mr. Milton, why don'cha let us have two."

"That'll be 12.60, and let's see, half of that would come to 6.30. Emma, yours is on the house, an I'm sorry to hear bout Blue." Shaking his head, "Too bad."

"Thank you, Mr. Milton," she said.

"Think nothin of it. Hell, Blue was all right."

"Thanks agin for the bottle. C'mon Baby, we betta git on back fo Jake pockets ALL my Gotdam money."

"Ya'll hurry back now."

"Awww, I'll BE back," Emma emphasized, "an if anybody cum by here lookin fo 'somethin,' be sho an tell 'em where Big Emma's at."

"I'll suuure do it."

When we walked up on the porch, Emma said, "Pat, it's still early. Why don'cha go see if Betty Carol kin play?" That was right down Pat's alley and she left running. Emma stopped by her room, hid one of the quarts underneath her mattress, and we headed for the crap room.

We waited at the table for the current shooter to "fall off," (finish his turn). When he did, "Jake, I'll take it now."

The disruption of moving the table to let Jake out and her in afforded a piss break for some of the crowd, and left their spaces up for grabs. I positioned myself at the table across from Emma. While she squared up the cut money with Jake, three more gamblers left the table and were on the prowl in the kitchen.

One of them came back to the door, "Big Emma?"

"Yeah, baby. Whut is it?"

"When you cook these beans an pig feets an stuff?"

"Yestiddy. It's good. Find ya'll some pots an warm up anythang ya'll kin find. Help ya'll's self."

Talking low, pretending not to want those in the kitchen to hear, "I wuz thankin bout grabbin me onea them feet afta while, but I kin forgit it now. Them long-moufed wolves'll eat up ever last thang in there 'ceptin my pots an pans."

The gamblers around the crap table began laughing at her

120

and she really put on a show. "When these nigguhs git hongry, they even eats up all the lard out the bucket. They crawls roun under the kitchen table worse'n them roaches an finds the sack uv Irish potatoes, eats 'em, skins an all."

One of the kitcheneers overheard. "We heah you talkin bout us in there, Big Emma," he said and laughed.

"Naw, I wudn' baby. Not me. You know Big Emma wouldn' do a thang lak that. Don' pay me no mind. Jes go right ahead an help ya'll's self."

"You needn' worry, we is."

"Ya'll know whut I did?" she asked, speaking low again. "I went down to Kerns Bakery an bought twenty-seven loaves uv day-old bread, cum back an cooked a big pot uv neck bones," she paused to take a swig, "five pounds uv 'em. An a fo pound sacka Navy beans. Alla ya'll dun et my cookin an know I love hot pepper."

The listeners nodded and she continued, "I don' cook without it. I cut up at least a dozen fresh cayennes an crumbled a half pack uv the dried ones. I said I'm jes gon' see. Them fuckin beans an neck bones wuz so hot you couldn' stand close to the pots. Did that stop 'em? Why, hell naw. I bleeve these nigguhs' moufs is made outta iron. They'll eat wood . . . anythang." She could make a dog laugh when she started hurrahing.

Snickering at herself, she kept on, "Some uv them nigguhs got broke, went to ramblin roun in the kitchen an found them beans an neck bones. Shit, they et the meat an chewed them bones up into sawdust. An jes turnt them beans up an drunk 'em lak lemonade. An et up them twenty-seven loaves uv bread an cum back in here wit sweat pourin off 'em. I tole Ollie he sho bet not shit in them woods an start no fire!"

When the laughter subsided a wee bit, Percy said, "She ain' lyin, I wuz one uv 'em. Man, I tell you, them wuz the hottest muthafuckas I ever tried to eat. Only way we could half way cool our moufs off wuz wit that bread. Shit man, I betcha I drunk up two buckets uv water, look lak steam wuz comin outta my ears."

Emma interrupted the break in the action folly, "Hey, ya'll in the kitchen, brang ya'll's plates on in here. We kin

121

make room.'' They came marching out, plates in hands. ''Ya'll move roun a lil bit baby, an let 'em git in here. Jake, look out the back an see if them nigguhs is thru peein. Tell 'em quit playin wit they selfs an git on back in here.

''You nigguhs eatin, keep ya'll's plates outta the way so the dice won' hit 'em. An baby, fo ya'll shoot, don't wipe ya'll's greasy hands on my blanket neitha. Use that dish rag hangin in the kitchen. Whose shot is it?'' She still didn't miss a beat.

It was Percy's shot, three shooters ahead of me. My turn came, ''Twenty, I shoot.''

Randall faded me, ''Shoot 'em.''

Emma watched closely as I picked them up. She saw me set the dice. I had never developed her famous Hudson shot but had my own style of concealing my setting motion. Locking the two aces in the middle ''on the come out'' (first roll) prevented me from rolling eleven (winner) but, it eliminated the possibility, providing I controlled them, of rolling two, three, or twelve (craps). With the two aces in the middle, I provided myself the chance to roll four-trey seven, and five-deuce seven, both winners. If that didn't happen, I'd catch a point (four, five, six, eight, nine or ten).

I gave the fake shake and rolled them across the blanket. Five for a point. ''I bet I bar it for twenty.''

The fader Randall called, ''Bet.''

Looking around the table for more, ''Bar it on you Claude, for this twenty.''

Claude called the bet.

The bar points (four, five, nine, and ten) are cakewalks if you know the combinations and can roll the dice so they tumble in the same direction. As I placed my bets, I quickly surveyed the position of the dice on the table, anticipating the combination for five. I joined them together smoothly, placing the trey from one in the middle against the deuce from the other. This rules out missing five with the four-trey seven or five-deuce seven. (Both losers after you catch a point.)

The only seven left I could roll is six-ace, and if I miss five with the six-ace seven, that's the bar. (You don't win or lose the side bets—you ''draw down.'') I lose the ''fade''

122

(what I shot originally) but I break even on the side bets. When shooting for any of the "bar points" (four, five, nine, or ten) the six-ace seven is a key factor. If I miss a bar point, that's the seven to do it with.

But, if I roll five again before I roll the six-ace seven, that's a winner all around. With a trey and a deuce locked in the middle, two sevens are eliminated, and the only one left is the bar. With the 3-2 combination in the middle, I have two ways to roll five, 4-1 and 3-2, two to one odds in my favor.

For the moment, I couldn't think of any place on earth I'd rather be than across the crap table from Big Emma, with five for a point. I loved to bet on it and shoot for it. Double checking around the table to make sure all my bets were covered, I started into motion.

Emma reached across the table and blocked my arm's path. "Jes hold whutcha got, Baby," referring to the 3-2 combination I held locked in the middle, "an let Emma try to git a bet on. Thirty dollars he bar it. Bar five for thirty!"

I was poised and waiting, I KNEW I was going to make five, never giving a thought to the six-ace seven. Somebody covered her bet and I went into motion once more. I was going to show her just how fuckin good I really was, and that I didn't need the tacks in the blanket for yardsticks. I knew the rolling distance for each point by memory.

Emma was right, I had developed a sensitive touch from all the years of practicing with my pee-wees. That's the size I cut my eye teeth on, nowadays the size most commonly used. I held the two small dice between my index and little fingers, cupping them against my palm with the two middle fingers, using my thumb for concealment and added balance. This allowed the dice to be only slightly ajar when shaking.

My "fake shake" merely clucked the dice against each other. What's in the middle, stays in the middle. With a guiding follow-through with my thumb at the time of release, I let go.

They took off across the blanket side by side like a pair of Dalmatians. At the crack of my "whip" (snapped my finger), "Oh Fantail Fannie!" They stopped right in front of Emma on 4-1.

"Five!" she exclaimed. "He jumped it!" (Making the point on the first roll.)

That struck a cord. Randall wanted to fade again, "Whatcha shootin?"

"Shoot the forty," I replied.

"I gotcha," counting his money down on the table, "let 'em take wings an fly."

Emma bet "I do" again.

I rolled four-trey seven on the come out, a winner.

"Damn!" Randall said. After picking up the dice and blowing on them for good luck, "Let 'em shoot agin, I'll fade anybody three times." Knocking the dice over in my direction, "Shake up an brang 'em on."

I picked them up, locking the two aces in the middle, "I'm shakin 'em," holding the dice over to his ear. "I know you hear that, they sound like a nest uv rattlesnakes." I sent them sailing again, caught eight for a point. Damned near all the gamblers at the table wanted to bet against me on eight.

When I finished covering all the side bets, I had close to two hundred dollars riding on eight. Emma had sixty dollars saying that I would make it. I made six rolls and hit it with two 4's. I had their noses wide open.

Two or three different ones said, "Let 'em shoot, I got 'em." All to no avail, Randall still had the choice since he'd been fading me from the beginning.

"Whatcha shootin now?" Randall asked.

"Forty."

"I'm gon' fade you one mo time, then the devil kin. Shoot 'em."

I caught six for a point and made it after a few rolls. Big Herman faded me for thirty dollars; I rolled another seven on the come out. Next roll, I caught four for a point and loaded up on bets again. Second roll, I made it with 3-1.

That one stung. Walter said, "Damn! This nigguh ain' missed nuthin."

Emma bet with me every time; I made nine straight passes before I fell off. When the dice got back to my turn again, I rolled three sevens on the come out, caught four for a point twice, and made it with trey-ace both times. The players began to draw back, folding their arms.

Ralph spoke up, "Hell, suma ya'll fade 'em, I jes had 'em."

I couldn't get faded.

This caused a stand-still in the action until Emma brought out her bottle. "Here Baby," handing it to me, "take a drank an pass it roun to these po devils. Ya'll gitcha a swallow uv that good whiskey." Barnstorming, "Take the rags outta ya'll's asses an gamble. Tell ya'll whut. I ain' gon' shoot no mo, I'm jes gon' back up an side bet." Giving me the green light, "Go head Baby, do yo stuff."

I tried again to get faded, "Forty dollars I shoot."

They stirred uneasily. In order to get any more action, I knew I would have to resort to proposition gambling, commonly known as "sucker bettin." I picked a point on the dice (four, five, six, eight, nine or ten) and bet that I would roll it a certain way. If I rolled it any other way, or rolled ANY seven in the process, I lost.

"Awright," I said, "I know ya'll waitin on somethin dead. Insteada forty dollars I shoot, forty dollars the dice make fo with two deuces."

"Shit," Jake said, putting his money down, "I'll jump off a airplane to bet ginst that. I don' care if you is Big Emma's boy. Shoot 'em," he said confidently.

Emma knew that either I was crazy to make such a bet, or I really knew how to shoot the shit out of a pair of craps. I slowed around, rubbing on the dice, waiting for her to place her bet. She was hesitating because she would NEVER make such a bet. "Forty mo he do," she announced; Walter quickly covered her bet.

Making four with two deuces sounded gloomy until I did away with one of the fours and set the 3-1 in the middle with the two deuces on the bottom. With this combination in the middle, the only seven left is 5-2 and a hurting four, 3-1. Narrowing the odds from four to one against to two to one against. Good, consistent rolling and a bit of luck makes it about even.

I knew the distance I could roll the dice before they'd start to run ahead of one another, and had a mental picture of how far they should roll to allow the two deuces on the bottom enough turns to settle on the top. I used to practice this shot by sticking the dice together with a little dab of spit. That way, I could see how far they'd roll before breaking apart.

Control is the key. Releasing them with just the right push and dash of follow-through so that before they reached the predetermined distance they'd put on the brakes, like Tim McCoy's horse sliding to a halt. I did it three times in a row, doubling the bet each time. Emma did the same thing betting on the side.

"Damn Emma! This nigguh's worse'n Wizard Ganzi," Jake exclaimed. "An that nigguh kin throw a pair uv craps clean cross the roof uv a house an tell you whut they gon' land on on the utha side!"

"He's a chip off the old block. I taught him everthang he know," she said proudly. "Shit, me an that boy been down the road together, ain't we Baby?"

"Yeah, Emma."

What an honor to even be mentioned in the same crap-shooting breath with Wizard Ganzi, a craps master who could "shoot the dots off" a pair of dice. He put so much "English" on them you could hear them humming when they zoomed down the blanket and stopped on the right numbers, as if being pulled by invisible strings. Even Emma didn't fade Ganzi. Whenever he came to our house, he had to bet the "straight make" on all bar points. Hardly anybody who knew him would bet against him.

Jake broke the interlude, "Say, Big Emma, ain'cha got anutha bottle stashed sumwhere? Many licks this nigguh dun hit me, I could drank a gallon."

Acie joined in, "Hell yeah, Emma. Go git da bottle." Looking around at the others, "Ain' ya'll tired?" They nodded their heads in agreement. He added, "I didn' hafta axe ya'll if you wuz broke."

Emma told Acie, "Stick yo head inside the door an see if Pat's still up."

After doing so, "Guess not, Big Emma. Ain' no light on in dere."

"Well, tip-toe on thru. Go in my room an look under my mattress an git it."

126

The game was over. I finished counting my money and had won $640. I tossed Emma a hundred for the "wear an tear." The rest of the night we just sat around bullshitting. I asked about Lonzo, "I wanna see 'em befo I go back, an buy 'em a drink."

PeeWee said, "Lonzo been dead over fo years."

"Damn," I said, "everybody I hear about is dead."

"Yeah," said PeeWee, "they been drappin lak flies."

Walter said, "Slim Linzy dead too."

"How'd HE die?" I asked.

"Accident. Slip an fell goin up the gang-plank into one uv them box cars wit a cross tie on his shoulder. Fell on his neck an broke it."

"I'll be damn!" I said. "An he'd been loadin 'em a thousand years. I used to like to watch Slim eat fish an gamble. When he got about half-drunk, he'd lean back against that wall, put one uv Emma's fried perch in his mouth an close his eyes."

Everybody was laughing at my kind remembrances. "He wouldn' leave nothin but the skeleton. Whenever his shot came, he'd open his eyes right on cue. Emma'd wind up cussin 'em out for 'fish greasin' the dice if he made a point an she had him faded." Looking over to the wall, "That was his favorite spot over there."

"Yeah," Emma said, "jes lak that wuz Blue's favorite spot you in."

"Say Big Emma, tell us that toast you say all the time fo this bottle run out," Jake requested.

"Okay," in toast gesture she held the bottle up over the center of the table,

"Whiskey, oh whiskey Gotdam yo soul,
You caused me to spend both silver and gold.
We wrestled and tussled and you throwed me in the ditch,
But I'm gon' try you one mo time,
You red-eyed sonuvabitch. Snakeshit."

And the whiskey took a long trip down her throat.

The next day, Sunday, Allen's sister arrived. She came to the house in a taxi. After they finished hugging and greeting, she told Emma, "I went straight to Lucille's. Didn't take her long to send me to you," she kidded.

127

"You shoulda cum here in the first place."

"Well, I would have but her and Allen's address was on the telegram. Before I go any further, let me apologize for not bein here sooner. I had a little difficulty puttin the travelling money together on such short notice," she said, embarrassed.

"I understand," Emma commented.

Being seated, "Emma gal, tell me what on earth happened to my brother?"

"Blue died right out there on the front porch . . ."

Effie cried through the whole story. Shaking her head in disbelief, "Oh, my God. What a shame," she bemoaned.

As I sat in the room listening to them talk, I could definitely see the resemblance of this fiftyish lady to Allen. They had the same deep black coffee-grounds complexion, maybe she was juuuust a shade lighter, and very similar facial features, nose, mouth, and smile. There would be no mistaking them as sister and brother. Except for sounding like a white woman with a heavy California accent, even their voice tones were alike.

The conversation took a direction that let me know they went back a long way together when Effie asked, "Emma, don't tell me this is that pretty baby all grown up."

"Thas him."

"Gee, it just doesn't seem like I've been gone that long. When me and James moved to California, he wasn't more than two years old. How old are you now, young man?"

To sound old as I could, "Goin on nineteen."

"Effie, I got a girl too." Asking me, "Baby, didja see Pat out there anywhere?"

"Yeah, she's over at Betty Carol's playin."

"Oh, that's alright Emma. Don't take her away from her friend. I've got to be goin pretty soon so I can take a bath and clean myself up some. How old is your daughter?"

"She'll be twelve this comin August. You got any?"

"Naw, I haven't been so blessed."

"Have you got any place to stay?"

"Oh, yes. I stopped and got a room at the hotel on my way over here. Emma, this is as good a time as any to talk business, and if I don't ask, I won't know. Who's handlin the arrangements, you or Lucille?''

"I am, I'm takin care uv everthang."

"How is Lucille taking all this? I mean, you handlin everything an all.''

"How she takes it is her bizness, I'm still his legal wife. Everthang he had, he lef it to me.''

"Did he have insurance coverage?''

"Yeah.''

"Is it enough to cover everything? I have to ask you because I hadn' heard from either Allen or Lucille in over three years. So, I don't know nothin about nothin.''

"Effie, don' worry. He left enuff an I'm puttin it all on Blue. When the insurance man handed me the check for 3500 dollars, I took it straight to Swifty an tole 'em to give Blue a full 3500 dollars worth.''

"Well," Effie said, "that sure takes a load off my mind, cause money-wise, there isn't a thing I can do. I've been in financial trials every since James died a year and a half ago. It's not easy for a woman my age to find work that pays a decent wage. I've been barely able to make it. Everything's so terribly expensive. When do you plan to have the funeral?''

"Whut about tomorrow? I know Blue's ready to git outta that cold storage. An you probably wanna be gettin on back soon as you kin, don'cha?''

"Well, yes. I only have enough money to stay a couple of days.''

"Awright, we'll have it tomorrow then. All I gotta do is let the preacher know.''

"Where at?''

"Gallilee Baptist Church at 2:30. You know where it is, don'cha? Same place it wuz when you lef.''

"Yes Emma, I remember. Emma, you're so sweet to be doin all this. Is there anything I can do?''

"Naw, Effie. He wuz my man, I'll do it.''

"Are you expectin a large crowd of people to attend? Reason I asked, there isn't much notification time.''

"There'll be a few.''

I was asked to call Effie a taxi. I ran around to the cafe to use the outside pay phone and returned quickly.

Standing and smoothing down her dress, "Emma gal, except for the extra pounds, you haven't changed a bit."

"You ain' neitha, Effie," pause, " 'cept for 'the extra pounds.' "

"After I take a bath and rest a little bit, I'm goin over to the funeral home and sit with brother awhile."

"You can't do that yet, Effie. Swifty got some stuff smeared all over 'em to keep 'em lookin fresh for the funeral. I know Blue'll be glad to git that shit off."

When the cab arrived, "Well, Emma, I'm goin to my hotel room and cry some more. I still can't believe it, the only brother I had."

"Yeah, I know. He wuz one uv a kind."

"Okay, Emma, I'll be seein you, and nice seein you too young man."

"Nice meetin you, Miss Effie."

Soon as Effie's cab pulled off, "Damn, I got a lot uv thangs to do," Emma said. "Baby, I hate to bother you agin, but will you go call me a cab? I didn' wanna ride in that one wit her. I wuz tired uv listenin to her shit. All that slut wuz interested in wuz if it wuz gon' cost her anything."

I had to explain to the taxi dispatcher that, "Yes, one came, picked up a passenger, and now we want another one." It came shortly, and Emma hightailed it.

Swifty came to the house and picked up the "family" (Emma, Pat, and me) the next day at two o'clock in the company limo. The church was located in Allen's neck of the woods, the "Old Field," a predominately colored neighborhood. Swifty, all decked out in "tie an tails," spats and white gloves, escorted us.

It was packed! I found out later that Emma had paid somebody to drive around where the street hustlers hung out, blaring the time and place of his funeral over a loudspeaker. The street people heeded the call, dressed up in their finery, and turned out *en masse* to bid farewell to one of their own.

Following Swifty down the aisle, he led us to the front bench in the church. Emma took the first seat, then me, then

Pat. A short while later, Swifty escorted Effie to her seat beside Pat. Lucille, eyes straight ahead, sat on the front bench across the aisle.

Even with all the church windows and doors open, the early summer afternoon had the church steaming hot. People fanned themselves frantically. The soft, low playing of the organist was almost drowned out by the appraising "ooohs" and "aaahs" from the spectators as the casket was rolled down the aisle.

When Swifty and his attendants rolled it past our aisle and placed it in front of our bench, I could understand their exclamations. The expensive, mouse-gray casket, adorned with full-length high-polished stainless steel handles, was a show stopper. The eggshell, fluffed, crepe lining matched perfectly with the spray of white carnations that lay on the top. It was a stylish, befitting send-off, symbolic of his flair for imported hats and tailor-made clothes.

I don't know if Emma bought all the flowers, but the front was full. Emma leaned over, "Ain't that casket a knockout? Swifty say it's stainless steel and won't leak—wudn' nuthin too good for Blue. These nigguhs'll be talkin bout this funeral for next twenny years," she whispered just before the music stopped.

The preacher positioned himself behind the pulpit, read a long verse from Isaiah and commented, "The Lord giveth and the Lord taketh away. The Lord blessed Allen Sample with forty-five years on this earth and decided it was time to take him on home. Allen Sample has paid the debt we all got to pay."

He turned things over to Swifty, who walked up front to escort the immediate family to the casket. Effie was first, lingering awhile and weeping. Swifty assisted her back. Pat had agreed earlier to go up with me, but when the time came she wouldn't budge.

I looked at him. Except for the mingling gray hair and longer sideburns, his appearance hadn't changed much since I'd seen him last. The collar of his white silk shirt meticulously folded back over the top of his steel gray suit collar. The way Emma said she liked to see him wear it.

Swifty reached for Emma's arm to assist her. She

snatched it away from him, "I don't need nobody to help me git to Blue." Rising slowly and smoothing down her black chiffon dress, she cast a "Blue always b'longed to me" look at Lucille.

Immediately she reached over into the casket and began straightening his clothes and cooing to him. "Here I am agin, baby," the tears streaming down her face. "Looks lak this is the last time I'm gon' git ta see you." You could hear a pin drop. "Emma's dun cum far as she kin go. I loved you hard as I could Blue . . . you knows that," bending over in the casket and placing a kiss on his lips. "I'm sho gon' miss you, but Emma'll ketch up wit you agin someday, . . . somewhere down the line." She kissed him again, wiped her tears off his face, and came back to her place on the bench.

After a few moments of silence, Swifty raised his hands. The others rose and started filing past the casket. Every time a hustler passed the casket, he or she dropped a dollar bill in it.

I leaned over and whispered to Emma, "Why are they doin that?"

"Thas the way hustlers do good hustlers."

After everybody passed the casket and viewed the body, just before Swifty closed the lid, I rushed up and put in my crumpled dollar bill.

On our way back from the burial, "Let us out right here, Swifty," Emma told him as we passed the corner liquor store. He made a U-turn, pulling to a stop under the canopy in the driveway. We got out, Emma walked around to Swifty's side, "Thanks, Swifty. You sho done a good job on Blue."

"Thank you, Miz Emma. If I kin be uv service to you in any way, now or in the future, please mam, don't hesitate to call."

"Yeah, well, I ain' plannin on callin you agin no time soon." Flashing his ever-ready smile, he thanked her again and drove away. After Emma told Mr. Milton all about what a "good funeral" Allen had, we took our two quarts and left.

When we walked up in the yard, Sweetie, Ralph, Jake,

Acie, and some of the other regulars, still dressed in their funeral rigs, waited on the porch. "Pat," Emma told her, "go pull yo Sunday dress off an put somethin else on."

"Damn," she said to the players on the porch, "ya'll sho got back in a hurry."

"We didn' go out to the graveyard, we cum on straight frum the churchhouse," Jake responded. "Big Emma," Jake continued, "we been talkin bout it, an I wanna tell you sump'n, baby. You sho had Blue put away." The others nodded their heads in agreement. "He look so natural," Jake added.

"Yeah," Sweetie said, "they say o' Swifty sho know his stuff."

Leading the way into the house, she stopped in the hall, "Here, Jake," handing him the dice from her purse. "Ya'll go head an git started. I gotta duck somewhere an pee."

Emma speeded up, rushing through the house, headed for the outhouse in back. The other eight of us scurried for favorite spots around the crap table. By the time she returned, the game was well underway. She took over.

Nobody would fade me when my shot came. I passed my turn to the next shooter and started betting on the side. I had the same feelings she did about that, "I'd ruther be shootin at a bird than have the bird shootin at me."

She opened up one of the O.G.D. bottles, drank a big swallow, and passed it around. By early evening, I was just twenty dollars ahead. The "Wizard Ganzi" label they hung on me stuck like glue. Still nobody would fade me and I was losing incentive in a game of "fade, but can't shoot."

Emma didn't have her mind on the game, AT ALL. She was losing, and drinking that 100 proof like it was water. The pace of the game slowed down, matching the tempo of Emma's lack of interest and enthusiasm. "Say, Big Emma, whutcha got to eat?" Sweetie asked.

"Nuthin."

"Well, hell. When you gon' cook sump'n?" he asked with customary expectations.

"Is you nigguhs ALWAYS hongry?" she asked semi-aggravated.

"Yeah!" Acie and PeeWee chimed.

Emma loved to cook and I knew she would get up and do it; she always did. It was part of the plan I'd seen her carry out for years. She never missed a trick and one of her mottos was, "When they git to drankin, feed 'em." Some would go to sleep and before the night was over, if somebody else didn't beat her to it, she turned their pockets inside out.

Nobody was betting anything, Walter was "playing" with the dice on the table. Looking up at the ceiling, he said, "Les see, I been over heah all day, when's the last time I et?" rubbing his chin, feigning to remember.

"Awright, awright! I'll git up an cook somethin in a minute. My bottle's empty, an I ain' goin NOWHERE til I git another drank."

Walter ran his hand in his back pocket and pulled out a three-quarters-full pint of Gordon's Gin. Reaching it to her after uncapping it, "Big Emma, I know this ain' yo drank, but you sho welcome to sum uv it." Adding, "Ain' nobody drunk out uv it but me."

"Hand it here," taking the bottle and turning it up. After she drank, it was half empty. "Percy, you the closest to the kitchen. Step in there baby an see if you kin find Big Emma a piece uv lemon, an brang the salt box."

"Okay, Big Emma."

He came back with it and she salted the lemon, took a big suck-lick, frowned, and told Walter, "Now, hand me that bad-tastin muthafucka agin. I'm ready for its ass now." When she took that next slug of gin, I said to myself, *pull ya'll's hats down tight, we goin round some mighty steep curves.*

"Jake, I'm gon' leave my dice wit you. If ya'll wanna play some mo', go head. But be sho an git my cuts. Ya'll lemme out," as she pushed and we pulled the table back. "Baby," talking to me as she passed by, "go out there an see if you kin find Pat. Tell her I said cum on in here an help me."

I walked out on the front porch, not seeing her, "Paaat! Paaat!" She came running out of what seemed to be her second home.

"Whatcha want Bubba?"

"Emma wants you to come in the kitchen an help her."

134

"Oh, awright," she said angrily. Stomping up on the porch, "Ever time we git to playin good, she calls me."

I followed her back through the house and stopped at the crap table to rejoin the "jaw-jekin" session. I listened to my fill of bull and went in the kitchen. "How ya'll comin in here?" I was getting hungry too.

Emma didn't say a word as she cut up the two fryers. I knew why Pat wasn't talking, she was still mad. I stood watching until Emma looked around and asked, "Whut time you got?"

"Eight forty-five."

"Go down to the liquor store an git me anutha bottle fo it close."

I said jokingly, "Emma, git somebody else to go. I don' work here no mo."

She turned away from the table to face me, glaring that hateful stare that used to send shivers up and down my spine. Gripping the butcher knife tighter, "Why you Gotdam half-white sonuvabitch! Don'cha talk back to me! You do whut I tell you! If it wudn' for yo muthafuckin ass, Blue . . ."

"I'm goin back in the crap room," turning to walk away.

She grabbed my arm and spun me back around, "Don't walk yo pecker . . ."

The anger swept through me so suddenly I didn't have time to bite my lip. Retaliating, "Don't you put yo muthafuckin hands on me . . ."

Pat screamed, "Bubba, no!"

The explosive blow to her jaw carried her 200-plus pounds crashing into the refrigerator. She crumpled to the floor.

"Don't never call me that no mo!" Trembling, fist clenched, "If you do . . . I'll kill you. It wasn' my fuckin fault!"

I brushed past the onlookers in the doorway, got my duffle bag, stormed out of the house, and headed for the bus station. I felt like I had just committed the most shameful act of my life and didn't try to hold back the tears.

BREAK TIME
I broke restrictions, "All new personnel are restricted to

135

the base for thirty days prior to eligibility for passes to town,'' the same day I arrived at Fort Bliss, my new base. Soon as I was located in my quarters and the corporal left, I left. I walked off the base, caught a taxi, and went to downtown El Paso. After reporting back three days later and getting my ass chewed out, I caught extra duty for thirty days cleaning the latrines. And re-restricted, this time, to the company area. ''One thing you better learn quick Private Sample, I'm not gonna put up with no horseshit,'' my CO told me.

It took a week to get my gambling-bootlegging operations in full swing. I kept a hut full of drinkers and would-be gamblers nightly. My hut was the hottest spot in the company area. During the day, as soon as latrine inspection was over, I'd run a half mile to the off-limits liquor store, pick up four gallons of cheap wine, and resell it to the players for two bucks a half-canteen full. When it wasn't my shot, and I took my time and measured it right, I could pour twelve half-canteens from the $3.50 a gallon wine. Since we were using my blanket in my hut with my dice, I cut the game for ''wear an tear.''

Even Sergeant Top, the company First Sergeant, joined in the crap games when he had to pull weekend duty. He was a good bettor but didn't know how to gamble. On more than one occasion, he left my hut owing me as much as eight hundred dollars. Usually, he paid it back during the crap game. But the times when he couldn't or didn't pay up when due, I didn't pressure him. One hand washes the other; he covered for me at roll call and kept my name off the KP and guard duty rosters.

Five days prior to expiration of my area restriction period, I won 1700 smackeroos! All that money started, as the old folks used to say, ''burnin a hole'' in my pockets. I sneaked out of the area, hailed a cab and hooked it for town. Top took care of me long as he could, but after eighteen days, had no choice but to declare me AWOL.

On the twentieth day, I got arrested by the locals in El Paso for fighting in a bar. After checking with the base and being instructed to ''hold,'' the locals turned me over to the two MPs. Top, with twenty-four years in the service and practically running the company, used his pull to persuade the CO to push for only a Summary Court-martial and thirty days in the stockade.

Rejoining the company after I pulled my sentence, I picked up with my gambling-bootlegging operations right where I left off. Less than a month after I was released from the stockade, I won big again. I took off AWOL and went to Juarez, Mexico, got with a woman, bought some civilian clothes, and was shacking up. I'd been AWOL for twenty-seven days and didn't try to hide. I knew the MPs couldn't touch me in Mexico.

However, some of my compadres in my company saw me at the same bar several times and told Top. He came to Juarez and waited around in the bar until I finally showed up. "Sample," he said, "I can help you if you come back with me now. But man, if you fuck around over here three more days, you're gonna be up for a General which means at least ninety days in the stockade, and possibly a BCD (Bad Conduct Discharge). If the CO recommends a General Court-martial for you, there won't be much I can do."

He pleaded with me to go back with him, but I steadfastly refused, "Top, I ain' goin back with you. Tell you what I'll do, I'll come back tomorrow."

After much dickering, "Okay, Sample," he conceded, "I think I can hold things off one more day, but git your butt back tomorrow," he warned.

As fate would have it, I got arrested that night in Mexico for assaulting a police officer and put in their no-top jail. I escaped, and three days after I promised Top I'd be there, I showed up at the base. I got a Special Court-martial, the middle rung on the military courts' ladder, and was sentenced to sixty days in the stockade. I'd hardly begun serving my sentence, before I broke a fellow stockade inmate's face, and got thrown in solitary for assault and battery.

With one Summary, and two Special Court-martials under my belt, two-and-a-half years later I had 150 days "bad-time" (lost time in the stockade) to make up before I could get discharged. But, with a lot of help from Top when the time came, I managed to somehow slide out of there with a good discharge.

In 1952, not quite six months after being discharged, I was standing before a judge, ''I sentence you, Albert Sample, to two years in the State Pen'' for burglary . . .

III

Racehoss

8 ||||||||||||||||||||||||||||||

When we treat a man as he is, we make him worse than he is. When we treat him as if he is already what he potentially could be, we make him what he should be.
Goethe

. . . and violated parole.

I was sent back to serve the six months remaining on the two years. In 1956, I was sentenced to twenty years for Robbery to run concurrent with the thirty I got for Robbery by Assault. My mind was racing as the transfer truck, "Black Betty," slowly backed inside the gates of Retrieve, one of the twelve prison units comprising the Texas Prison System.

This was it, "the burnin hell," the place that "gits yo heart right" I heard so much about when I served time at the Clemens Unit. Retrieve, formerly an all-white prison unit, had been repopulated a few years previously with the worst, most incorrigible black cons that were in the prison system. Most were multi-recidivists serving heavy-duty sentences. That measly two years I pulled on Clemens was just a drop in the bucket compared to this new thirty year package I was breaking the seal on.

While unloading off the back of the black van, I looked up and saw the numbers inscribed above the red brick archway. 1934 leaped out at me. This widow-maker was born during the depression just like me. What a coincidence, I thought, that was the same year I got "busted" for the first time when Emma went to jail for bootlegging. Going to jail was fun and games back then, but as I stepped into this bastard world of the prison system, I knew growing up with

Emma and the time I served on Clemens was just bootcamp for what I was facing now.

Inside the building, there were four separate "tanks" on the lower level and one on the upper level across from the inside picket post. It was late morning and the field hands were still outside working. The tanks were empty, except for the building tenders.

The guard who brought the six of us in hollered up to the inside picket guard, "Boss, open up them Number 3 and 2 tanks. Put half uv these nigguhs in each one uv 'em."

The picket guard threw the levers opening the tank doors, "Awright, you first three nigguhs," pointing us out, "git in that Number 3 tank. Rest uv you git across the hall in Number 2." After we were inside the Number 3 tank, the picket guard hollered, "Got three new 'uns comin in Ol' Bull!"

As the building tender walked toward the front of the tank, the long piece of chain hanging from his belt rattled noticeably. "Got 'em, Boss," Bull hollered while the door was clicking shut. He told us our bunk and locker numbers, what time we'd be fed, and when the lights went out. Then he laid down the tank "laws," "Ain' gon' be no loud talk an no two nigguhs settin on no one bunk. Don' nobody git offa yo bunk at nite afta count time til you holler alley boss, an gits a OK."

When he said that "alley boss" part, it reminded me of the time I was five and had a bad cold. Emma carefully measured out two spoonfuls of castor oil into a cup with a little squeezed orange juice. As I was putting the cup up to my mouth, I pleaded with her not to make me take it. Just the smell was making me nauseous. She told me I'd better drink it and forget about the smell.

I turned the cup up and swallowed it, but it wouldn't stay down. I immediately vomited all over the kitchen floor. She grabbed me by my hair and pressed the butcher knife she used to half the orange against my throat. She held it so tight it cut the skin.

"Pick up that bottle and drank ever bit uv it, an you bet not waste a drop. If you utter, I'll pull yo Gotdam, peck-

142

erwood head off!" I gulped down the rest of it. She ordered me to get on my cot and "stay there."

In a very short time I needed to go to the outhouse. Since I wasn't supposed to get up, I hollered into the kitchen, "Emma, kin I go outside to do-do, please mam?" My life hadn't changed much. Here I was having to get permission to take a shit again.

I tuned back in to hear Bull saying, "When dey rangs dat bell, be ready ta git ya'll's asses outta dis tank."

The tank had three double deck rows of bunks, with twenty bunks each, and one with twenty-five. Bars that ran from the floor to the ceiling separated Number 3 tank from the one adjacent to it, Number 4. At the front of the tank was an old-fashioned barber chair with silver painted lockers lining the front wall. In the back was a six-sprinkler shower stall, a urinal, a long, eight-faucet face basin which doubled as the tank's drinking fountain. And a row of eight doorless commodes (with those old-timey wooden seats regulating the flushing) faced the front of the tank.

About thirty minutes later, the field workers came in for lunch. They were wet and muddy. Our clean, white clothes tattle-taled we were new arrivals. Some made snide remarks as they rushed for the back to wash up, "Ya'll won' be so priddy an white after dat bell rangs."

Within a few minutes, the picket guard pulled the tank door levers and Bull hollered, "Les go eat!"

The Number 3 and 4 tank (eastside) cons single filed into the messhall along with the cons from the westside tanks (Number 1 and 2). I quickly scanned the messhall hoping to see someone I knew, but didn't. After passing the steam tables, we sat eight cons to a table. While we ate, the building tenders slowly walked up and down the aisles—overseeing. No talking allowed, and fifteen minutes to eat.

When the messhall emptied and we returned to the tanks, the picket guard hollered down, "All you ol' new nigguhs, cum on up to the front," as he opened the Number 2 and 3 tank doors. The six of us stepped out into the area underneath the inside picket. The captain who was waiting there ordered us to line up against the wall. He sized us up and I knew my light complexion made me stand out like a sore thumb against the blackdrop of the other five.

He told the first two men who were both bigger than me, "Ketch that Number 3 hoe, and you ketch that Number 5." I learned on Clemens that the higher the squad number, the better off you were. Judging my size against theirs, I figured I'd probably be put in Number 7 or 6 at least. I was in Number 12 utility squad on Clemens, mending fences, putting in culverts, and had never done field work.

I was next, "You ain't all that big," he said stepping in front of me, "but you wuz big enuff to rob them folks. Got you sum big time this time, didn' you?"

"Yes suh."

"Well, I'm gonna put yore yaller ass where you kin start doin sum uv it. When that Number 1 hoe cums out, you ketch it."

Back on the tank one of the cons said, "Man, Cap'n Smooth put you in a bad-d-d muthafucka! All them nigguhs is wild. An the lead row nigguh they got, Ol' Road Runner, runs wide-open all day long. An Boss Deadeye is a sho nuff number one driver. You betta be ready to hit th' door runnin!"

The turnout bell sounded. I tensed.

"Lemme have 'em, Boss," shouted Cap'n Smooth, who stood at the back door.

"Number 1!" the inside picket boss hollered down, opening all of the lower tank doors.

The Number 1 hoe squad cons from all four tanks ran at full speed down the hall like a herd of buffalos. Bosses on horseback were waiting as we fled out the back door.

Cap'n Smooth counted us and hollered, "Got twenty-seven uv 'em, Boss."

The boss with the patch over his eye rode up behind us and answered loudly, "Thas right! Ol' Road Runner, ya'll git sum grubbin hoes an shovels."

As we left the hoe rack, running behind Road Runner, Boss Deadeye rode at our heels, yelling, "Gitcha Gotdam asses offa this yard an on that turnrow," narrow roads that separate the acres in the field. "Go Head!"

It didn't take much to figure out why they called the lead

144

row man "Ol' Road Runner." He was tall, skinny, and extremely long-legged. He walked so fast the rest of us ran and trotted to keep up with him. His long "drag step" with his feet never leaving the ground made him look like he was walking on a pair of skis.

We must have walked and run five miles down that muddy road behind him. The muscles in my legs cramped and the new brogans were killing my feet.

By the time we reached the "bottoms," my shirt was wringing wet. Road Runner never broke stride until we reached the place to "catch in." I was glad to get there, just so I could stop running.

Boss Deadeye stopped his horse and started yelling, "You nigguhs ketch in heah an start diggin up them tree stumps. Git ever bit uv them roots outta thar."

I started shoveling dirt like a salamander around one of the huge stumps. Even with one eye, Boss Deadeye quickly spotted my shovel-handling ineptitude.

"Ol' new nigguh, cum heah!"

I stopped digging and dropped my shovel. I walked to within ten feet of where he sat astride his horse, and pulled off my flop-down hat. EVERYBODY knew this "rule." I learned that much on Clemens.

"Where you cum from nigguh?"

"I'm frum Longview, Boss."

His next question, "Whut color is yore ol' mammy?"

Before I knew it, I told him she was white and my daddy was a colored man. I saw it in his one eye, he didn't like my answer AT ALL. Angered, he spat tobacco juice at me.

"You know whut nigguh? You mind me uv a big pile uv yaller shit." Some of the cons in the squad started snickering. "Frum now on, I'm gonna call you Ol' Shit-Colored Nigguh. When I call you that, you betta answer me." Leaning forward in his saddle, "Do you unnerstand that nigguh?"

"Yes suh, Boss, but that ain' my name." The cons stopped snickering and giggling, and a hush fell over the squad.

"Why you Gotdam impudent, shit-colored mawdicker!" He spurred his horse and tried repeatedly to hit me with the

145

knotted end of the big rope tied to the horn of his saddle. Avoiding him and his horse, we went around and around. Finally, he gave up.

Thoroughly aggravated, "Gitcha Gotdam ass back over yonder an git ta wek!"

Later, a con began to sing in the squad working next to ours. Another con urged him on, "Blow it outcha soul nigguh." As the singing grew louder, I realized the cons in the next squad were cutting trees and hitting their axes in rhythm with the song. I listened to them and kept on digging.

We dug stumps and we dug stumps until, "Dere it is, it's in da air!" Cap'n Smooth, who sat on a horse up ahead, had raised his hat, signalling that the work day was over. We rushed to line up behind Road Runner for the long run back to the building. I was on the back row in the squad right under the nostrils of Deadeye's horse. Each time he snorted, he blew cold slobber on my back. Seems like I was running in slow motion.

Boss Deadeye yelled, "You nigguhs betta git on to that house. Go Head!" Road Runner laid his ears back and took off. He left us struggling to catch up as we trotted wearily behind him with the other seven squads behind us.

On the yard, we stopped by the hoe-rack to put away our tools, then took off again for the backgate. Boss Deadeye rode over to the outside picket and dismounted. He hung his pistol and shotgun on a hook tied to the end of a rope and the backgate picket boss pulled his weapons up into the picket. We stood at the backgate entrance behind Road Runner, eagerly awaiting the signal from Boss Deadeye to "go head."

Instead, he walked over to the side of the squad, evil-eyed me, and said, "Ol' Shit-Colored Nigguh, cum heah."

I didn't move. Cap'n Smooth came out of the small building beside the backgate. Deadeye walked toward him, "Cap'n, I got a ornery ol' nigguh in my squad that laks to play deaf." Then he yelled, "Ol' new nigguh, git yore Gotdam ass over heah."

I stepped out and the rest of my squad went through the backgate. Cap'n Smooth told me, "Stand over yonder," pointing toward the other side of the backgate. I was the first con cut out that evening.

Waiting by the gate, I saw all the other squads. Each one stopped at the backgate and waited for the ''go head.'' They rushed through, stopped midway in the yard, stripped, and were searched. By the time the last squad went through, five of us were standing outside the fence waiting.

After the backgate boss searched us and we had our clothes back on, Cap'n Smooth marched us into the building hallway. He yelled up to the inside picket boss, ''Hand me down five pairs uv cuffs, Boss.''

When my turn came, Cap'n Smooth took my right wrist and clamped the cuff on tight-tight. Then he backed me up against the iron bars that separated the messhall from the inner hall. With one cuff clamped on my right wrist and my back against the bars, he took the unclosed cuff and looped it through the bars above my head. Then he told me to fold my left arm above my head while he clamped on the other cuff. When he finished, I was left hanging with my toes barely touching the floor.

After an hour, a couple of the cuff hangers started groaning. I bit my lip to keep from crying out too. I thought about what that lying boss told the captain, ''All this nigguh's dun all day long is look up in the sky an count birds. Cap'n, I had to beg this nigguh to git him to go to wek.'' The pains shot through my arms; I dug my teeth deeper into my bottom lip until I tasted the blood inside my mouth.

When the bell rang for supper, none of those who made it in would even look at us as they filed past to enter the messhall. They looked straight ahead. As I listened to their spoons scraping the tin pans behind me, I thought about those big, thumbtack-sized butter beans I passed over at lunch and wished I hadn't.

After ''count time,'' nine o'clock, the lights were dimmed inside the tanks and the hours crept by. I sure had to piss, but the con hanging next to me told me, ''We git to piss when they let us down. If you piss in yo britches, thas anutha hour.''

''How long will they leave us hung up here?'' I asked.

"They lets us down in time to eat an git ready to go to work."

Along about hour six, one of the hangers began moaning louder and louder, violently jerking and pulling against his cuffs. He frantically wiggled and twisted his body around until he was facing the bars. Using his foot to push against them, he reared back, pitching, straining, and pulling as hard as he could. Realizing he couldn't get loose, he bit into his wrists as if they were two chocolate eclairs, growling and gnawing away like a coon with its foot caught in a steel trap.

The blood-splattered con hanging next to him pulled as far away as he could, hollered and yelled for the picket boss.

Looking down from his perch, the picket boss ordered the turnkey, "Run git a bucket an dash sum water on them two crazy nigguhs down on the end."

The dousing worked; he quit mutilating his wrists and contented himself to moaning and groaning out the night like the rest of us.

Finally, the dim lights were turned back to bright. The picket guard handed down the cuff keys to the turnkey, who unlocked us from the bars. After the cuffs were removed, my swollen wrists throbbed like a bad toothache.

The picket boss opened the door to my tank and I headed straight for the back to take a piss and get a drink. I barely sat on my bunk before one of the building tenders shouted, "Les go eat." That walk to the messhall past the bars I had just hung on all night wasn't fast enough for me. I didn't want to look at that place of pain either. As I passed the steam table, I pointed to every food item on it.

Oh my God, here we go again, I said to myself when the turnout bell rang. "Lemme have 'em, Boss."

"Number 1!"

We tore down the hall. The last man out the door got kicked in the ass by Cap'n Smooth. "Got twenty-seven uv 'em, Boss!"

"Thas right Cap'n." Then, "Go Head! Git offa this Gotdam yard!"

We were low-flying as we followed Road Runner down the turnrow. How could he possibly be in such a big hurry to get back to digging stumps? Every stride keeping up with him was torturous. When we reached the edge of the bottoms, it was like following a bloodhound. He headed straight through the woods to the same stumps we were digging around yesterday.

We started working. The other cons in the squad shied away. They surmised that I was on the boss's shit list after yesterday's episode. I dug around a stump by myself and managed to dig it out. I got in a hole with a crew and started digging. Nobody said a word as we dug and dug.

There was a slight drizzle when we left the building. Now, icy pellets dropped. Thirty minutes later, Cap'n Smooth knocked us off. When we got to the turnrow, Boss Deadeye made us take our brogans off so we wouldn't "be awearin 'em out in the mud."

The slick turnrows were like walking on wet glass. While we slid and half-fell across the mud, that damned Road Runner with his barefooted ass was making two ski tracks straight down the middle of the turnrow. In order to stay in the middle of the turnrow, I walked in his tracks.

This time, after the strip-search, I made it back to the tank. Once inside the building, we tried to crowd through the tank door at the same time. The two on-duty building tenders yelled, "You nigguhs, throw dem muddy clothes on dese sheets" which they had spread on the floor in the front of the tank. "Don' ya'll be slangin dat fuckin mud all ovah dis Gotdam flo!"

I was so cold all I wanted was to get to the shower. I had so much mud clogged between my toes, my feet looked like I was wearing a pair of grayish-black flippers. So far, coming in the building first was the only good thing about being in the Number 1 squad. After the shower, I quickly went to my bunk and put on the dry clothes the building tenders had placed on it. Picking up and delivering the field workers' clothes from the laundry was one of their main duties.

The hard walking and shovel had my body aching all over. My palms and feet had blisters stacked on top of blisters. After I ate, it was back to my bunk. For the first time since I arrived yesterday morning, I saw the full deck, all eighty-five of us together. I recognized the ten Number 1 squad members in the tank, but saw no other familiar faces.

The tank was beginning to sound like the Cotton Club in Longview on Saturday night. Cons were laughing, bull-shitting, grabassing, and acting like they were having the time of their lives. None of them even looked tired, and I was near exhaustion. Hanging on the cuffs all night took it out of me. I heard some guys bragging about who was the fastest worker, and who had the toughest bosses. The field work and the bosses were the general topic of most of the conversations.

The tank activities got into full swing. Several radios, each on a different station, were blaring. Some cons were setting up cigarette rolling operations; some were getting out their cards and dominos. Dice shooting wasn't allowed because "nigguhs git too loud shootin dice." A few cons were diligently striking and blowing out wooden matches to glue together to make lamps and jewelry chests, leaving the air with a heavy smell of phosphor.

Everybody seemed to have an outlet. Some guys were reading the Bible, while others wrote. The con in the bunk across from mine was using a tin snuff can, with holes punched in the top, to scrape and sand the calluses on his feet. Three separate quartets were singing in the back near the commodes, and one con was sitting on the ledge above the commodes beating "Bongos"—tin buckets.

Two or three card games were in progress on the back bottom bunks, out of the sight of the inside picket guard. They played for cigarettes and Buglar tobacco in lieu of money. I sure wanted to get in a game; but, since I had no cigarettes to gamble with, I couldn't.

I got in the shave line at the front of the tank. "Ol' Crip," the barber, was built like a question mark with a hump on his back. One leg was shorter than the other, causing him to limp and walk like the hunchback of Notre Dame.

He shaved cons and squabbled incessantly when too many got on the waiting bench. He acted irritated with each "customer" who sat down in the barber chair, and swished his razor like Zorro. When a freshly shaved con got up out

150

of that chair, he was both bloody and lucky. Nobody dared squak with Crip while he had a razor so close.

My turn came. Reluctantly, I eased into the chair and lay motionless when he let the chair back, and said not a mumbling word while he ripped his dull razor across my face. After that, I knew I had to make preparations to get my own shaving gear, but quick! I went to the back of the tank and splashed some water on my face. There were no mirrors, but I didn't need one to know that I, too, displayed Crip's battle scars.

All of our heads were clean as cue balls. I had been scalped right before I left the Walls in Huntsville and sure hated to think of Crip with those Triple "O" clippers on my head. Those hickeys and scars on the bald heads in the tank were reminders of his heavy hand.

Besides a razor, I needed a toothbrush and a box of soda. Hoboing around, I learned to make it with the bare basics. I knew the only way I was going to scuffle up on some cigarettes to buy my toilet articles was to get in a card game, somehow. I knew how to "deal" cards almost as well as I could "roll" the dice.

I sat down on one of the back bunks to watch the card game and was sitting there about an hour when one of the building tenders called out, "Ol' Kotch Tom, cum on up to the front!"

He looked around at me and said, "Hey man, stop my hand for me til I cum back." He was gone about half an hour, and when he returned, he commented, "The bosses didn' want nuthin, jes fuckin wit me."

I had won eighteen packs of cigarettes in his absence, and he gave me half. That was my start. When the game broke up about fifteen minutes before the chow bell rang, I was a winner again with twelve "decks of squares," three packs of Buglar, and five sacks of Bull Durham. When I got off the con's bunk that I'd been gambling on, I felt obliged to give him a couple of packs for "wear an tear."

After returning from supper, I got in the commissary line when the picket boss called it out. Even though I had no cho-cho book (script coupon book used in place of cash with denominations of one, five, ten, twenty-five, and fifty cents issued to those cons whose relatives sent money for them to the Inmate Trust Fund) I was in a position to barter at the commissary. I swapped one pack for a toothbrush, two for a razor and blades, and three for a lock for my locker.

When I got back to the tank, I asked Kotch Tom how I could scrounge a box of baking soda. He told me, "See Big Filet Mignon when he cums in from the kitchen." With a name like that, it wasn't hard to spot him, and I put in my order and paid him a pack.

The call went out, "Ya'll git on 'em. Count time." I got on my bunk and awaited my first bunk count time on "the burnin hell." The lieutenant rushed into the tank counting two rows at a time as he walked briskly down one alleyway and up another. Big George, the other day building-tender, was supposedly counting right behind him. After they made the final turn in the last rows of bunks, Big George had a confused look on his face.

When they reached the front of the tank, the lieutenant hollered up to the inside picket guard, "Eighty-four uv 'em, Boss." The guard acknowledged that he was right, and added that one was in the hospital. Big George looked relieved. The lieutenant entered into Number 4 tank, repeating the process, and across the hall into Number 1 and 2 tanks.

Then he went upstairs. Number 5 tank upstairs, eastside, housed the trusties, cons with "jobs" who work without supervision. The auditorium, westside, bunked fifteen white cons. We remained quiet and on our bunks until the head count was over. "Count's clear!" came the shout, after the lieutenant, inside picket, and turnkey completed their calculations. All 415 of us, the figure I saw on the count board located on the wall at the bottom of the stairs, were accounted for.

The switch was thrown to dim the lights in the tanks to about a 20-watt bulb's worth. Activities were at a standstill and we settled in for the night. It was hard to fall asleep and I had to piss anyway, "Alley Boss," I hollered. Several seconds later, I got his OK. I walked about midway down the alley, and heard a catcall whistle. I turned my head and looked straight into the eyes of the whistler.

"What you got on yo mind, man?" I asked him.

He grinned, and said belligerently, "Whut diffunce do it make?"

Forty, the "night alley," night building-tender, was in back cleaning up, and overheard our conversation. He yelled up the alley, "Ya'll betta git down on dat bullshit. An Ol' Rag you betta take yo ass to sleep an let dat new nigguh 'lone."

I continued on my way toward the back. He whistled again, I didn't stop. I knew my future in the tank was on the line. I walked over to the row of commodes and picked up half of one of the broken wooden seat lids. I concealed it beside my leg and walked back up the aisle. When I was even with his bunk, I smashed him on the head with the edged side.

He hollered like a stuck pig and struggled to get out of my reach. I hit him with the flat side, right above his ear. That lick sounded like somebody fired a .22 pistol in the tank. He fled down the alley to the back with me in hot pursuit.

Forty rushed up to us and blocked my pathway, "Say man," he said without malice, "don' hit 'em no mo. Lemme hannel it."

I stopped. Forty went over to Rag and looked at his head. Then he hollered up to the picket boss, "Got one comin out, Boss. Needs to go up to the hosspital an see Doc Cateye." Forty followed him to the front of the tank.

When they got to the door, the boss looked down from his lofty perch, "Gotdam, Ol' Forty, whut happened to that ol' nigguh?"

"Wudn' nuthin, Boss. He jes had a nightmare an fell off his bunk."

Seeing all the blood on Rag's head, the boss, apparently an ol' timer on the job, quipped, "I thought that nigguh slept on one uv them bottom bunks."

"Yes suh, Boss, he do."

"He musta dreamt he fell off a fuckin skyscrapah," the boss said as Rag made his way upstairs to the hospital.

The next morning, the sleet was still coming down and we didn't turn out. As soon as we returned from breakfast, the card and domino games got started pronto. Kotch Tom was busy in the back setting up a card game on one of the back bunks.

Two or three cons were at the face basin mixing up their Magic Shaving Powder. They spread the hair remover on their faces instead of using a razor. After that stinking, blue gook dried on, they shaved it off with tongue depressors. The tank smelled like everybody had farted at once. They probably felt the same way I did about Crip's razor.

While I sat on my bunk trying to catch a name here and there, the tank door opened to let Big Filet Mignon back in after his breakfast shift. A little later, he walked over and handed me the box of soda. I went to the back and brushed my teeth, then got my cigarettes out and got in one of the card games.

I was deeply involved in the game when Big George yelled out, "All you ol' thangs, cum on up heah to da front an unlock dese lockers. Git ready fo shakedown!"

There was a mad scramble to the front of the tank and the sound of unlocking locks could be heard throughout. I asked a con, "How long do it take?"

"Long as dey wants it ta take," adding, "it give da bosses sump'n ta do when we lays-in."

Big George did a follow-up, "Don' ya'll take nuthin outta dis tank to dat messhall, 'ceptin yo ass, the clothes on yo back, an yo brogues."

As we filed out of the tank, I saw that "everybody" was there. All the field bosses, the captain, lieutenant, and dog sergeant were standing underneath the picket waiting for us to empty out. The captain split the bosses up into two groups. One group took the westside tanks and the other took the eastside. The captain and lieutenant went upstairs to "check out" the auditorium where the white cons lived and the dog sergeant took the trusty tank.

The 300-plus of us lower tank inhabitants filed into the messhall and took our seats at the tables. All the cons were there, except the trusties still out working and the whites. We sat quietly as the banging of the lockers and bosses' voices filled the messhall like hollow sounds coming from an empty barn. The bosses carried on a lot of bullshit with each other and seemed to enjoy ransacking the tanks.

154

Two bosses remained in the messhall with us, walking up and down the small aisles that separated the tables. Watching. Every so often, a con was called out; he wouldn't return. Instead, he stood underneath the inside picket until the shakedown was completed. After a good three hours, the order came from the captain for us to re-enter the tanks. By this time, at least twenty cons were standing under the picket.

We stripped in the messhall, and slowly filed into the area underneath the picket where the bosses waited to squeeze-search our shirt and pants, and inspect our brogans, before we went back into the tanks. After the clothes search, it was the "bend over and spread yore cheeks" part. Some of the comments those bosses made were rib splitters and I could hardly keep from laughing as I waited my turn.

"Hey, Boss, take a look at this un. This ol' nigguh's asshole looks lak a burnt out stump."

Another said, "Looks lak this heah nigguh had a complete overhaul, cause all his bushins, rangs, an inserts is amissin. Big as this nigguh's asshole is, I betcha he couldn' shit in a number three washtub."

My turn came, "Well, looka heah, heahs onea them white nigguhs!" one said looking at one of the older bosses. "Boss Harper is this heah onea them nigguh babies uv yourn?" He kept on, "Say, has Boss Harper evah tole ya'll bout how many nigguh gals he's dun screwed? An how many uv 'em he knocked up?"

Another said, "As a matter uv fact, if I recollect, it wuz fifteen uv 'em." They were all laughing and teasing him so much that little attention was given to me as I bent over.

We filed past the two cardboard boxes filled with contraband sitting under the inside picket. While we were busy dressing, back inside the tank, the warden, "Big Devil" as he was called by the cons, held court in the hallway. He made each con reach into the boxes of confiscated items and pick out what belonged to him. Sometimes it was crude-looking knives made out of spoons and forks, clubs, chains, lengths of iron pipe, hand-drawn fuck books, or a scrapbook of female mannequins from mail-order catalogs.

Each was sentenced according to the importance Big

Devil placed on the contraband item. Those with the weapons got the lighter punishment, and were made to stand on the soda water boxes (wooden cases) for several hours. Those with the forbidden jack-off materials were sentenced to hang on the cuffs all night long.

Kotch Tom was one of those who got the cuffs. They found a photograph of a white woman in his locker. I later learned that it was a picture of his wife and that he was doing a life sentence for killing a white bus driver in Houston. The way I heard it was he had boarded a bus in Fifth Ward, a predominately black ghetto, with his German wife whom he met and married while in the Army overseas. The bus driver allegedly stopped the bus, and demanded that he not sit in the seat next to the white woman. When Kotch Tom told him she was his wife, the bus driver slapped him. Kotch Tom pulled out a pocketknife and stabbed him to death.

As count time neared, Crip and Big George gathered up their mops, brooms, and buckets from the back, signalling that it was time to get on our bunks so they could clean up. They had soapsuds a foot deep all over the tank floor. One was spreading it with a mop while the other was following behind scrubbing with a scrub broom. In twenty minutes, they had water-hosed the entire brick floor and herded all the suds down a six-inch drain in the center of the tank floor.

Each time the inside picket boss, the cons nick-named "Wise-em-up," paused to look down into the tanks, he'd holler down, "You ol' wild-ass'd nigguhs betta git down on it! Suma you ol' sorry-ass'd thangs gonna hafta talk ta that warden in the mornin." He did that periodically with each tank, whether it was quiet or not. Two or three cons were in the back using the commodes, "Awright, suma you ol' wild-ass'd nigguhs keep on millin roun back there an yore gonna hafta talk to that warden in the mornin."

After count time I finally dozed off, only to be awakened by a bone-chilling scream. Earlier that day I had overheard Big George and one of the new cons, who rode down on Black Betty with me, having some words. I heard the new con tell him, "I don' play that shit."

Big George walked up on him while he was sitting on one of the commodes and hit him across the back with the piece of chain he wore on his belt. After the scream, Big George shouted, ''Git yo Gotdam ass up under onea dem bunks fo I kill you!''

Hearing the commotion, Boss Wise-em-up hollered down his customary threat. Big George yelled up to him, ''Brangin one out, Boss. I got onea dem smart nigguhs in heah.''

Wise-em-up let the victim out of the tank and made him sit in the hall under the picket for the rest of the night. His groaning joined with the others who were being punished out in the hallway.

Shortly after wake-up time, the doors under the picket, which led from the guard's barber shop, were opened by the turnkey. The captain came through. He walked over to the new con, who stood up and showed the chain marks on his back. The inside picket shifts had changed, Boss ''Humpy'' was on duty. He told Cap'n Smooth that he had been told this con created a disturbance on the tank and Big George had to put him out. Since it involved a building tender, no questions were asked.

Cap'n Smooth told the turnkey to get a soda water box. He ordered the con to get up on it. After a couple of tries and falling off, the captain told him he'd put him in the pisser if he didn't get his ''goat-smellin ass up on that soda water box an stay there.'' Finally, the con was able to maintain his balance on the upright box and began serving out his official punishment. Those hanging on the cuffs were let go so they could eat and catch out.

Each passing month I was doing better and better keeping up with Road Runner on the turnrow and learning how to ''wek.'' When we weren't cutting down trees, underbrushing in the woods, and grubbing stumps, we were on the yard using wedges to bust logs for the furnaces. Then to the muddy garden, crawling on our knees picking the half-frozen spinach. Road Runner could crawl damned near as fast as he could walk. His knees must have been made out of stone because he never complained like the rest of us.

When it was too wet and cold for these jobs we got our aggies and headed for Oyster Creek, which ran right through the middle of Retrieve, to flatweed along the creek banks.

157

There was always some con in the squad who got out into the cold water to hoe all the weeds. Seeing this, Boss Deadeye would holler for the rest of us to do the same and start riding his horse all along the bank, crowding us up to make sure that we got knee deep out into the cold water.

When we finished the Oyster Creek banks, it was on to the shit ditches and all the shit they caused. It usually took a week to clean the two sewer ditches that snaked their way from one side of the prison unit to the other. Squads worked on both sides of a ditch, hoeing everything on the way down to the middle of the shit stream, and pulled the muddy grass and weeds back up the slope to spread it out on the turnrow to dry.

It never failed, when two squads met in the bottom of the ditch face to face and started splashing shit on one another, the battle started. After the fighting, everybody left the ditch covered. We'd get back in line beside each other and stink it through the day. The bosses drove and pushed us relentlessly to get finished. They hated to ride behind us, "Ya'll's goat-smellin asses is stagnatin these hosses." True or not, the horses were their unruliest when we worked the shit ditches; but, so were we.

Even as grueling as the work was in the squad, I'd rather do it than work in the kitchen. They worked seven days a week, rain or shine. The kitchen flunkies were the first ones out in the mornings and the last ones to get back in the tanks at night. Between meals, they hosed down and scrubbed the messhall.

News quickly circulated in the tank one Sunday afternoon that Big Filet Mignon got busted. He could slip those pork chop and steak sandwiches off the guard's stove and out of the kitchen right under the guard's nose. He wrapped them in some dish rags and tied the bundle to his nutsack. No guard was going to feel underneath there when frisking the flunkies and cooks.

It happened right before the evening meal. We were having baked ham for supper, but the meal was held up because one of the hams was missing. Big Filet Mignon had swiped one from the oven, took it back to the vegetable room, and hid it in one of the vegetable bins to let it cool.

When it cooled to his liking, he deboned it, propped it up on a table, and made love to it—pineapple rings and all! He got carried away, and began calling it affectionate names out loud, "Oh! Bessie May, you sweet thang. Oh! Bessie May, tell me it's good to you. Oh, baby-eeeee!"

Cap'n Foots, the mess steward, and some of the kitchen crew heard him and went to investigate. They said Cap'n Foots walked right up behind him while he was "humpin' dat ham."

Cap'n Foots brought him out of the kitchen and stood him under the inside picket to await Big Devil's arrival for sentencing. After word filtered through the tanks why he was busted, we threw cups of hot water, and even our brogans through the bars at him. Everybody was furious with him for making us potential second-hand dick suckers.

The inside picket guard hollered for the captain, "Cap'n, Cap'n, you betta cum move this rotten bastard away frum under this picket afore sum uv these ol' nigguhs knock hell outta him."

When Big Devil arrived, he and Cap'n Foots took Big Filet Mignon back through the kitchen, headed for the pisser. Big Devil cursed him every step of the way, "Why you Gotdam low-down sonuvabitch! I'll bet you been afuckin that meat ever since you been heah! Ain'cha?"

"Naw, suh, Warden. I swears thas th' first time I ever dun it."

"Shet yore Gotdam lyin mouth, you rotten bastard!" Smack!

Big Filet Mignon stayed in solitary overnight and was shipped away on Black Betty the very next day. Nobody touched the ham that evening. He taught us a lesson—don't eat the fuckin ham.

9 ||||||||||||||||||||||| ▭

Ol' Doc Cateye, serving 460 years, had been running the hospital "forever." However, recently he had inherited a medical officer who was hired on with the rank of lieutenant to take over the helm. Lieutenant Maulden spent a few years in the Navy and supposedly worked in the ship's sick bay. His experience and training must have been superb since he acted well-prepared for the tremendous responsibility now resting upon his narrow shoulders.

The hospital upstairs at the rear of the trusty tank consisted of four bunks which were rarely occupied. It required near death to lie on one of those bunks. Besides Doc Cateye, Lieutenant Maulden would also supervise the convict dentist, Ol' Nolan. Now that he commanded his own hospital and medical staff, Lieutenant Maulden was finally in the upper echelons of medical practitioners.

Lieutenant Maulden stood about 5'6", was forty-plus years old, had a fat beer belly, and wore his britches anchored down off the low part of his hips. There was so much slack in the seat that his pockets waved when he walked. When Lieutenant Maulden listened to a con's ailment, he was very cautious not to stand too close. He'd stare at the con through the bars in a trance-like state while smoking his pipe. Every so often, he'd kick out a puff of smoke and nod his head. When the con finished, the lieutenant would give his diagnosis in long, rambling medical terminology.

Regardless of the illness, the medication was always the same. If the problem was from the waist upward, Maulden prescribed aspirins. If it was from the waist down, he prescribed Doc Cateye's "jet juice"—a special concoction of castor oil, mineral oil, epsom salts, a little sugar, a little dab of quinine, and either grape or strawberry food coloring.

Doc Cateye had convinced Lieutenant Maulden, the warden, and half the convict population that his nostrum really worked, and could cure everything from the flu to epilepsy. After drinking a cupful, the con spent the rest of that day or night on the commode. We all knew not to drink it when going to the field because there's no way the bosses would let anybody stop working ten times a day.

Every night after we finished supper, the medical duet appeared at the tank doors and hollered out, "medicine line!" It sounded like they were racing to see who could say it first. Cateye carried the little medicine tray and kept it neatly arranged with cotton balls, aspirin, methylate and mercurochrome bottles. He also had Whitfield ointment, which cons put on the calluses of their feet. They had to be careful because that ointment burned like acid.

Lieutenant Maulden watched over Doc Cateye like a resident physician as Cateye issued the medication through the bars. And did Cateye ever resent his new intern status! After all, he'd only been the "Doc" for a measly twenty-one years before he became the lieutenant's assistant.

Occasionally, when Cateye would be busily waiting on two or three patients at the same time, the lieutenant shook out a couple of aspirins or whatever and handed it out. He certainly didn't want any of us to think he minded touching fingers with a black con as he handed out the medication. To him a "patient is a patient, regardless of race, creed, color, religion, or national origin."

Only thing contradictory to his equality stand was the way he treated the fifteen white "hide-away" cons. They went directly to the hospital to receive their medication, instead of having it poked through the bars to them. And they didn't need a 102-degree temperature to get a lay-in either. All they had to do was say they were sick; their word was good enough for him.

The black cons didn't want the lieutenant handing them medication from Doc Cateye's little tray any more, anyway. He had scared most of them away. Unwittingly, Lieutenant Maulden almost single-handedly broke up all the homosexual activities on the entire camp. Hospital business suddenly picked up, but even then, Doc Cateye came up with the prognosis for the epidemic.

The breakout occurred because of Maulden's inability to differentiate the Whitfield ointment from the petroleum jelly. Granted, they are both alike in clearness, but they certainly smell different. Of course, Lieutenant Maulden wouldn't smell the jars because it might appear that he didn't know his medicine. Except for smelling, it is difficult to tell them apart, especially for the trained, infallible, medical eye of Maulden.

He inadvertently gave some cons the Whitfield ointment instead of the requested petroleum jelly. Needless to say, all the cons in the tank and the inside picket boss knew for certain some screwing was going on in Number 3 tank that night. One of the Whitfield ointment recipients, Ol' Mus-Havit, had gotten with his partner and paired off under a bunk. That ointment got hot and all of a sudden a loud howl was heard, "Whew! Say man, git up offa me! My ass is on fire! Oh! Gotdam!!"

They came out from underneath the bunk like two mad bulls. The culprits were put out of the tank by the building tenders and the inside picket boss made them sit under the picket all night without allowing either to wash it off. I bet they would have been glad to sit in something wet and cool, even the stinking shit ditches.

With two bars on his shirt collar now, Captain Maulden ventured downstairs to the tanks without Doc Cateye at his side. He must have thought there was a need for him to come down alone every so often to establish that he was the man with the fuzzy balls and not Doc Cateye. He wanted the cons to get used to the idea that everything having to do with medication, lay-ins, or the hospital in general had to be coordinated through him and him alone.

It seems the Classification Committee made another terrible miscalculation when they sent a "gnat liver" (young), first offender to serve his measly two-year sentence at the burnin' hell. There weren't many young cons on our camp, and even fewer serving under ten years, unless they had screwed up on one of the other camps. If that was the case, they were reassigned to Retrieve to help rid them of whatever "adjustment problems" they were experiencing. However, they were already pretty tough cookies by the time they got here.

Yet, here the new con stood pitifully, like the Pope in the middle of hell. When Black Betty dropped him off at the backgate, the boss brought him in the building and stood him underneath the picket to await his tank assignment. The building tenders crowded up to the bars, hung on them like apes, shouting obscenities at the "new one."

They acted like a bunch of dogs over a bitch in heat. Their clamoring worsened when Cap'n Smooth showed up.

One started begging, "Please Cap'n, put him on my tank. If ya'll put 'em in heah wit me, I swear I'll pick a bale a day."

Then another, "Cap'n, you knows I been heah a long time, pleeze Cap'n, hav mercy. Pleeze, lemme have 'em."

Still another, "Cap'n, if ya'll put 'em in heah, ya'll sho won' have no troubles wit dat nigguh. I keep it so slick 'twixt his legs he won' be able ta walk fur runnin'," he remarked blatantly.

"You nigguhs dry up them ol' mouths an git back away frum them bars! You sonsabitches ack lak you ain' never had no boar pussy befo. Hell, this heah ain't the first little ol' mare nigguh ya'll dun seed." He continued, "I ain' gonna tell you sonsabitches no more ta git down on that ol' head runnin'!"

After they quieted down a little, Cap'n Smooth asked the new con, "Nigguh, if I wuz to letcha choose the tank you want frum one to fo, which'un you'd choose?"

Mumbling, "It don' make no difference."

Sarcastically, "You mean it don't matter who fucks you in yore ass?"

In a voice reeked with fear, "Captain Sir, I ain' no punk, sir. I jes wanna do my time an git away frum here."

"Hey, ya'll heah that? This nigguh claims he ain' no

163

galboy. Whatta you thank about that, Ol' Trigger Bill? You b'leeve this little ol' nigguh's tellin me the truth?''

Trigger Bill was the building tender on Number 2 tank begging to have the new con put in with him. After being singled out, he looked down and started shuffling his feet and grinning like a mule eating briars. "I don' know, Cap'n, suh," he said sheepishly, "jes whutevah ya'll say."

"Tell you whut I'm gonna do, since you ain' no bigger'n a piss ant an wouldn' last long as a fart in a windstorm in that field, I'm gonna put yore scrawny little ass in the kitchen. Now, I hafta pick a tank fur you since I can't gitcha to do it." Turning to the bar apes, "I'll put this little ol' nigguh on the nigguh's tank whut cums up wit the best name fer 'em."

The vultures began hollering out name after name. "Betty Grable, name 'em Betty Grable, Cap'n." That got a sharp stare from Cap'n Smooth.

"Name 'em Sweet Meat, Cap'n," another shouted.

"Cap'n, bein dat ya'll dun put 'em in da kitchen, name 'em Ol' Dumplin," Bull rendered.

Cap'n Smooth liked that name, so "Ol' Dumplin" it was. The picket boss threw the lever and the door opened. Clutching onto his few personal belongings tightly, Dumplin noticeably flinched when the big steel door slammed shut behind him.

Bull, nicknamed for his brawny wide chest and big arms, was an imposing figure as he stood waiting. The two daggers and trace chain hanging from his homemade belt were an awesome sight. No sooner had the door closed, Bull quickly made his move.

"You kin put yo stuff in my locker so nobody won' steal it. An you kin use anythang in it. I'm gon' hep you til you git settled in."

Next, Bull got permission from the picket boss to go to the laundry to get some sheets for the new con. All a building tender had to do to get out of the tank was ask. They received preferential treatment and were privileged to possess overt weapons. They were the policemen of the tanks. Under the guise of enforcing the "rules," their brutal behavior was tolerated by the officials. Their gang rapes, beatings and harassment of weaker cons were ignored and their ver-

164

sions of "what" happened in the tanks were readily accepted.

Bull used his power position, promised to pay cigarettes, or whatever, and soon returned from the laundry with a mattress cover, pillow case, and *two* neatly starched and pressed sheets. Unlike the rest of us, Dumplin would be sleeping on a sheet instead of the stiff, ducking mattress cover.

"I'm gon' look out fer you," as he slow-eyed Dumplin's physique. "If any uv dese nigguhs fuck witcha, you jes lemme know." Lavishing his concerns, "Betta put yo brogues on cuz dey's gon' call you in a few minutes so you kin go ta wek in dat kitchen."

Just like he suggested, Dumplin sat on Bull's bunk and changed from his free world shoes to his brogans. He followed Bull's lead like a lamb being led to the slaughter. Bull was a pro when it came to conning new cons.

It wasn't long before the call came from Cap'n Foots, "Boss, lemme have that new nigguh outta there."

The boss opened the door, "Ol' Bull, gimme that new nigguh. That Cap'n wants 'em in th' kitchen."

When Dumplin stepped out, Bull stepped out behind him and hollered up to the picket boss, "Comin out wit 'em Boss, I needs ta see da Cap'n."

He said this to back up what he'd been shooting Dumplin about being heavy with Foots and talking to him in his behalf. Cap'n Foots sent the new con on to the kitchen before asking Bull what he wanted.

Bull knew that was the way it would go down and had timed it perfectly. Dumplin was gone now, and wouldn't hear him tell Cap'n Foots, "Cap'n, suh, we's outta toilet paper."

As soon as Dumplin finished his shift in the kitchen and came back in the tank, Bull met him at the door and led him to his bunk in the back. Bull sat down beside him and began making his demands for pay back.

"Man, I thought me an you wuz awright, that you wuz my friend. I ain' doin but two years an I don' wanna git involved in no stuff lak that."

Bull got more aggressive, "Muthafucka, you dun smoked up my tight rolls, et up my stuff, used my fuckin locker, an

I'm even out dere gittin down tu da man fer yo ass. Whut you mean you ain' gon' do nuthin? Nigguh, jes fer dat, you gon' suck my dick!''

With no forewarning, Bull punched him in the eye, knocking him clear over to the next row of bunks. Before Dumplin could get up, Bull's brogan caught him in the short ribs, preventing any outcry. Bull fiercely stomped him while Big George blocked the alleyway so the picket boss couldn't see. They didn't want to involve him as a witness, that way if any inquiry was made, it was their word against Dumplin's.

After Bull tired of his kicking assault, he got some water from the basin, dashed it on Dumplin's face, and jerked him up by his shirt collar. ''Nigguh, you gon' suck my dick!'' he bellowed while pulling out his prick and forcing it into Dumplin's bloody mouth.

Nearly every night after Dumplin pulled his shift, Bull lay on his bunk in the back and forced Dumplin to play with his pecker until he raised a hard. Then he'd make Dumplin suck him off while anybody in the tank who wanted to, looked on. After work one night, Dumplin came back to the tank, and took his shower as Bull waited for him. Dumplin went up front and put his toilet articles into his locker, obediently returning to Bull's bunk to begin the nightly ritual.

The same scene had been played so often that most of the cons now paid little or no attention to it. He played with Bull's pecker until it got good and hard. All of a sudden, Bull let out a bloodcurdling yell. His long, black peter was lying on the floor in the alleyway, and looked like it was breathing. Dumplin cut it off with a razor blade.

Bull went running up the alleyway toward the front of the tank hollering every step of the way. He climbed up on the bars to get the attention of the picket boss who was pacing around in the picket, cracking and eating pecans. ''Boss, Boss! Hep me! Dat nigguh dun cut my dick off!''

Boss Humpy angrily yelled back, ''Nigguh, gitcha Gotdam ass down offa them bars, an quit askeetin 'at blood in heah all over this fuckin flo!''

''Boss! Lookit whut dat crazy nigguh dun ta me!''

''Hell, nigguh, I don' wanna look at it. Now, I dun tole

166

you to gitcha Gotdam ass down frum heah! I don' give a damn if he chopped yore nuts off! Aim that Gotdam thang th' utha way!'' Trying to coax him down, ''Ef ya git down frum thar, I'll call fer Cap'n Maulden.''

After Bull descended, Boss Humpy hollered across to the hospital, ''Cap'n Maulden, you an Ol' Cateye betta cum on down heah. I got a ol' nigguh wit his dick cut off. Cap'n, kin ya'll hurry? This sonuvabitch is ableedin all over everthang.''

Ol' Bull damn near bled to death before they arrived and took him upstairs. He left a trail of blood behind as they went. A trail the turnkey hurried to erase with his mop. From the hospital, we heard Bull's hollering, ''Lawd! Ham mercy, Jesus! Oh Lawd! Oooh! Jesus! Jesus! Jesus! OOOH! Cap'n, ham mercy!''

It took awhile for the ''healers'' to get him quiet. An hour had passed before Captain Maulden and Doc Cateye reappeared at the tank door. Proudly displaying his blood-splattered doctor's smock, Captain Maulden called out, ''Ol' Forty, will you cum on up here to the front? I need to talk with you a minute.''

Forty was the only building tender on the eastside tanks who treated everybody pretty decently. He didn't participate in the gang beatings and wasn't viewed by the cons as a bona fide member of the goon squad. He got punished many times because the other goons bad-mouthed him to the warden. About all he liked to do was gamble. So when Cap'n Maulden called him to the front, he interrupted Forty's card playing.

''Yassuh, Cap'n?'' with a frown on his face.

''Ol' Forty, I suppose you know what happened awhile ago to Ol' Bull.''

''Yassuh.''

After shooting up a puff of smoke from his pipe, ''Well, what I need to ask you is this, ahem,'' clearing his throat, ''you wouldn't happen to know if Ol' Bull's penis is still layin roun back there, wouldja?''

''His whut, Cap'n?'' glancing at Doc Cateye.

''Reason I'm askin is I, we, might be able to save it for that ol' boy.''

167

"Yassuh, I reckon it's still back dere sumwhere, Cap'n. Ain' nobody moved it as I knows uv." True. We were just stepping over and around the nasty-looking thing and laughing.

"Well, I tell you what I want you to do. Go on back there and git it and bring it up here so me and Cateye can have a look at it. We just might be able to save it, but we gotta work fast. I'd hate to see that ol' boy go through the resta his life without a stick to fight with."

"Cap'n, suh, I ain' tryin ta be smart witcha or nuthin, but Cap'n suh, I been in heah over sixteen calendars an ain' nobody never tole me ta go fetch anutha nigguh's dick."

Doc Cateye toyed nervously with his stethoscope as he watched the captain continue to hog the spotlight. "Now, Ol' Forty," Cap'n Maulden continued, "I admit this might be a bit unusual, but it ain't every day that some nig—" pause, "poor fellow, goes an gits his life-line whacked off. How'd you feel if it was yours laying back there? Just think about it, Ol' Forty. Let's work together on this thing. Now, go on back there an git it so we can have a look. Don't force me to pull rank on you," he urged.

"Yassuh," Forty yielded.

Forty was cussing under his breath as he sullenly walked down the aisle. He went to the back where the mops and brooms were kept. He got a broom and began sweeping the severed sex organ up the alley. More than once it rolled underneath a bunk and he had to get down on his knees to reach it with the broom. He was having difficulty keeping Bull's lollipop rolling in the right direction.

After a lengthy ordeal, he rolled Bull's gritty prick up to the bars. While the healers bent down to scrutinize the seven- or eight-inch piece of meat, Forty leaned on his broom and looked off into the distance, totally unconcerned.

Cap'n Maulden broke the silence, "Roll it over for me, would you Ol' Forty?" Looking at his able-bodied assistant, "What do you think? Think we can make it work?"

Cateye, still making his own medical observation, said in his high-pitched Southern drawl, "Well Cap'n, I don' rightly know, might be worth a try."

"Gotdam, that ol' boy sure was blessed! Here Cateye,

take a look at it through this magnifyin glass.'' When Cateye finished, Cap'n Maulden asked, ''You wanna look at it, Ol' Forty?'' offering him the magnifying glass.

''No suh!'' Forty quickly rejected.

''I'll bet he had a lot of fun with that thing.''

''Yassuh, Cap'n,'' Forty agreed, ''I 'magine he did. But it's sho over now,'' he quipped with a telling smile.

After much deliberation, ''Tell you what Cateye, why don'tcha run back upstairs an take another good look at the other end of this thing, an see what you think.''

Cateye hurriedly ran upstairs. Before long, he was skipping steps as he came back down quickly. ''Cap'n, I don' thank whut you got in mind is gon' wek atall.''

''Why not? Why won't it work?!''

Cateye went on, ''Well, Cap'n, the utha end uv Ol' Bull's dic . . . , 'scuse me Cap'n, penis, shrunk lak a vine afta we sewed it up. But this part heah is still so big an hard, I doubt if we kin match 'em back. Sides, it's too heavy.''

Cap'n Maulden's face flushed and clearly registered disappointment. He wasn't going to get to practice his surgical skills on Ol' Bull's pecker replant.

As the two stood up and shook their heads in dismay, Forty interrupted, ''Er . . . , pardon me, Cap'n, suh. Now dat ya'll ain' gon' use dis dead peter, whut ya'll want me ta do wit it?''

''Well, tell you what, Ol' Forty. Just take it on back there and git rid of the damned thing.'' Cap'n Maulden's last action before closing the matter was to snap his fingers in disgust, ''Damn! It's a damn shame, that's what it is, a damn shame.'' As he turned and walked back up the stairs, he sighed, ''What a waste.''

Forty began sweeping Bull's ''remains'' down the alleyway. When he reached his destination, he got the dustpan from behind the big green trash barrel and swept Ol' Bull's once precious cargo onto it. Walking carefully so he wouldn't spill it, Forty dropped the contents into the commode, mashed his foot down on the lid, and SWOOSH! Away it went, off to the shit ditches enroute to Oyster Creek.

The next day Black Betty came, and a neutered Bull was

169

transferred to the Walls Unit to the "sho nuff" hospital. He didn't return after that. We heard a few years later he made parole. He certainly left prison with a lot less than he came in with.

As for Dumplin, Big Devil decided he should do his two-year sentence "flat." This meant instead of getting out in the normal fourteen months and twelve days, the equivalent of two years with good time, he would serve the full two calendar years. After the de-dickatashun, even though his mouth may still have been dirty, Dumplin could pull his shift in the kitchen, return to the tank, and get on his bunk without anybody bothering him. Not even a little bit! He had earned his right to sleep in hell.

My body had toughened to the work. I could do the different jobs well enough to keep up and the cons in the squad had accepted my presence. I was a bona fide hoe-carrying, shit-ditch fighter. Boss Deadeye even let up a little. After I got cursed out about it, I learned not to look at him when he removed his patch to wipe the sweat away with his bandanna. He got angry when any of us caught a glimpse of his "dead" eye.

When we cut trees in the bottoms that lay along the banks of the big Brazos River, we sounded like a bunch of woodpeckers. We dug the blades of our axes into the trunks of the huge sweetgum trees while the bosses sat lazily on their mounts. Both men and horses were half-dozing in the warm, wintry sun creeping down through the dense tall timbers. Their tranquil nodding allowed the tree-cutting foursomes to take turns standing behind the trees for a few minutes rest, while the other three cutters in their crews kept up the lick.

Those old bosses had been listening to the sound of those axes for so long, they could almost tell when all the axes weren't hitting. The horses were no dummies either. They knew how to get out of the way when one of those big trees was falling. Of course, sometimes we did get lucky when a horse and boss were napping so serenely neither reacted quickly enough to avoid getting brush-whipped by a falling tree everybody "forgot" to yell "TIM-BERRRR" for.

Huge brush fires were burning all along the massive clearing we left behind. We continued plodding through the dense underbrush native to the Brazos River bottoms, felling tree after tree. After the axe teams cut down "enuff" trees and the brush pullers finished their tree-trimming work, the axe teams pulled back and began cutting the trees into sections for the sawmill. Whenever Big Louzanna got on a fallen tree, he took the butt cut, the largest part of the tree trunk. He and three other cutters perched themselves atop the thirty footer and began chopping away at each section.

A couple of squads away, Little Alfonso, a lifer, started up a river song, "Black Betty's in the bottoms, let yo hammer rang. Black Betty's in the bottoms, let yo hammer rang." Little by little we began to join in. Our axe licks harmonized more and more as we cut with a steady rhythm to the beat of the song. "Black Betty's in the bottoms, let yo hammer rang, let yo hammer, hammer rang. Great God Amighty! Let yo hammer rang. They ain' gon' be no jackin" (brushing chips out of the way before continuing to cut the tree down—used as a rest break) "til we heah the butt cuts crackin."

By now, I knew the work songs and sang along with the two hundred con choir. We echoed back, "Let yo hammer, hammer rang, great God Amigh—ty! Let yo hammer rang."

"I wanna drank o' water."

"Let yo hammer, hammer rang."

"I want a drank o' water."

"Let yo ham—mer rang."

"I don' wanna drank it."

"Let yo ham-mer rang."

"I wanna spit it on my hammer, cause my hammer's strikin fi—re!"

All of us sang and cut in a frenzy to keep up with the beat. Working much faster now, we had a steady flow of chips flying as we chisled deeper and deeper into those about to become logs.

Over all the chopping and singing, Big Louzanna cut loose with "Roberta" and "Loucindy," slowing everything down. His BOOMING, heavy baritone voice completely drowned Lil Alfonso's lead. By the time he let go with the second heavy moan, "Oh! Roberta! Roberta!

won'cha cum by heah," the choir switched over and joined in with him. Humming and moaning the background, we slowed our axes to half the previous pace to keep beat with Big Louzanna's axe and began to "rock" in the bottoms.

"I got a woman in Georgia, an I got a woman in Alabam. Dey both jes as sweet as dey kin be. Sweet as dey kin be. But neitha one uv 'em will ever see po me," he led.

"See po me, see po me."

"But dat woman in Alabam, hot ta mighty Gotdam."

"Hot ta mighty Gotdam, hot ta mighty Gotdam. Sweet lak blackberry jam."

He sang the lead with such melancholy it almost brought tears to my eyes. Then he'd go right into "Loucindy."

"Oooh! Loucindy! Loucindy! won'cha cum by heah. Oooh! Loucindy, won'cha cum by heah. An let me rock you mama whilst yo man ain' heah."

"Hot ta mighty God knows, hot ta mighty God knows."

"Now I ain' never been ta Houston, but I been tole. Never been ta Houston, but I been tole . . . The women in dat Houston town got sum sweet jelly roll."

"Sweet jelly roll! Dey got sum sweet jelly roll!"

"Dey say dat when dey walks, dey reels an rocks behinddd! Now ain' that enuff ta worry a convict's mindddd?"

"A convict's mind."

"Oh, Loucindy! won'cha cum by heah, an let me rock you mama whilst yo man ain' heah. It rangs lak silver an it shines lak gold."

"Rangs lak silver an it shines lak gold."

"But th' price uv my hammer ain' never been tole."

"Ain' never been tole."

We all sang the last stanza together,

"So les raisem up together, an then drop 'em on downnnn! Dey can' tell the diffunce when the sun goes downnn! Dey can' tell the diffunce when the sun goes downn."

Singing very low now, we faded out,

"When th' sun goes down. When th' sun goes down. When th' sun goes downnn . . ."

Every axe was hitting in rhythm. Boss Deadeye sat on his

172

horse contented. "When them ol' nigguhs is sangin, everthang's awright." With his shotgun laid across his arm, he listened as we sang and sang.

10 ||||||||||||||||||||||

Spring had sprung. Oh, spring! And with it, Boss Deadeye's field of agitation bloomed. "You Gotdam, shit-eatin sonsabitches! Move them Gotdam rows on away frum heah! Gotdam rotten-ass'd bastards, wanna jes drag them ol' asses roun. Don't wanna do no wek. But I tell you mawdickers one damn thang, ya'll Gotdam sho won't eat no seppa tonite. Ya'll Gotdam sho gonna miss that ol' hog an bread. Jes cum on back heah ever Gotdam onea ya'll, an ketch in on the end uv them rows an start 'em over agin.

"Aw, I know you sonsabitches wanna go down thru thar buck-jumpin an leavin halfa them Gotdam weeds! I spose you rotten bastards is leavin that fuckin grass fer me ta git! I wants 'fo stalks ta a hill,' " (thinning the row—leaving four cotton stalks to a group a hoe blade apart). "An I wants ever fuckin blade uv grass out uv that man's cotton. Not sum uv it, ever fuckin blade uv it!"

Then he singled out a slower worker. "Aw, I know you don' wanna do nuthin 'sociated wit wek. You got yore fuckin mind on that ol' nappy-head, snuff-drippin whore you lef out thar in that free world. Ain' no needa thankin bout her cuz sum utha mule-dicted nigguh's bogged up ta his belly in her rat now. As she damn sho ain' thankin bout yore rotten black ass. Aw, I know you don' lak it bout sum utha nigguh fuckin yore ol' whore. I might even drap by her house this Sadday nite mysef."

On and on, "I know you wanna hit that Gotdam Brazie. Well, I tell you whut, why don'cha hit it. I ain' lookin atcha. This ol' raggedy shotgun ain' even loaded. Hell, only reason I tote it is so I kin fan away suma these Gotdam gnats. Go Head!"

Knowing we were hot and thirsty, "Water nigguh!! Brang me sum water." We could hear the ice rattling in the gallon syrup bucket each time Water Boy Brown hopped over the freshly chopped cotton rows. After he drank, rinsed his mouth and spat water on the ground, Boss Deadeye dismounted and poured it down. The horse pissed too.

He got the kerosene-soaked rag from his saddle bag and wiped around the horse's eyes and underneath his belly to help keep away the gnats, flies, and mosquitoes. When he completed his pissing and horse-wiping ritual, he got back in the saddle and picked up his agitating rhetoric right where he left off. All day long, everyday.

Spring was almost over and so was cotton chopping time. Hallelujah! The next phase in the work cycle was picking the white gold. I never picked cotton; this would be my first time.

I kept hearing the cons in the tank talking about the hog law so much until one night I asked Beer Belly, who was in the Number 4 squad, what it meant. He was a talker, and began his explanation by saying that Cap'n Smooth decided who made it through the backgate every evening based on how much cotton each picked that day. The weights were recorded in the Hog Law book. If a con didn't pick "enuff" he didn't eat. Besides missing the evening meal, the con hung on the cuffs or spent time in the pisser.

He told me cons try everything to beat the Hog Law during cotton picking season, "Dey piss on th' ground, make big mudballs an cover 'em wit cotton an throw 'em in dey sacks. One time a nigguh even weighed up Big Devil's dog in his sack," chuckling. "He let 'em out on th' way to th' dump sheets." He went on to say Cap'n Smooth even based his decision to punish on the condition of the cotton. If it was "dirty" it was the cuffs. A mudball brought an ass whipping and the pisser.

From what Beer Belly said, cotton was picked on an average in the "bull" squads, Numbers 1, 2, and 3. "Ta keep frum gittin punished, you hafta stay within fifty pouns uv whutever th' highest weight in th' squad wuz fer dat day. Dey puts th' high rollers, best pickers, in dem three squads. Dey even sews three extra foots onto dey cotton sacks so dey kin hole mo." I damn sure wasn't a high roller and began to worry about the Hog Law book.

"You know whut? We be sendin so much cotton to dat gin over at th' Ramsey camp, dey runs outta storage space an dey send word back by the truck drivers ta tell us ta hold up fer awhile. Thas when we git sum rest. Sumtimes we set rat down on our sacks in the middle uv th' fields fer nelly a hour ta give th' gin a chance ta ketch back up wit us." He went on to say Numbers 4, 5, and 6 squads didn't have to pick as much as Numbers 1, 2, and 3. And the "pull-do's," older cons with a physical disability i.e., a finger missing, a limp, in Numbers 7 and 8 have to pick less than all the squads. Adding, "Don' be fooled cuz suma dem ol' fuckers kin pick a whole lotsa cotton.

"Durin pickin time, we weks seven days a week. We gits a short half on Sunday, knocks off roun three. You sho do hafta watch yo cotton, cuz dem nigguhs'll sho try ta steal it. Dey have mo fights out dere bout dat den a liddle bit. Specially when we leaves our sacks on th' ends ta come in ta eat. When we git back, nigguhs start grabbin th' fullest lookin sacks dey kin find. Cap'n Smooth say, 'ain' no such thang as a nigguh whut can' pick cotton—an a whole bunch uv it.'

"An man, dey haves dat field s'rounded! Dat high rider" (additional field guard who doesn't have a squad) "be settin off over yonder wit dat 30-30, an th' dog sergeant brangs fo packs" (four dogs to a pack) "uv dem ol' skinny houns to th' fields 'stead uv th' usual two packs. Dem dogs an th' dog boys who hannle 'em be layin off to th' side under a tree in th' cool, jes waitin fer sum nigguh ta run off. Dem ol' dogs is so po, don' look lak dey could run fifty foots. Hell, all dey feeds 'em is milk an conebread, but dem bastards'll run a nigguh long as Luke run John."

Beer Belly hardly paused to catch his breath. "Dey got one name Ol' Rattler who got two open-face crowns on his front teefs, a reward fer trackin down convicts. One time dey wuz runnin a nigguh, an all th' rest uv dem ol' dogs had give up on th' trail. But Ol' Rattler wouldn' quit. He kep on sniffin fer two days an nites. Th' track led 'em to th' airport. When Ol' Rattler got dere, he sot rat down in th' middle uv th' runway, looked up in th' air howlin, an pointed to th' sky wit one uv his front foots. Dey checked whut airplant jes lef, when it landed in Memphus an dat nigguh stepped off, dey grabbed him an brung his ass back. So don' even thank bout leavin cuz dey ain' bout ta lose no nigguhs cum cotton pickin time. We needs all the hep we got.''

After he finished his tall dog tale, I asked, ''Can you pick good?''

''I picks enuff ta make it thru the backgate. I can't 'ford not to,'' he joked while patting his big belly. ''But thas awright, you needn' worry. You'll git use to it.''

''I hope so.''

''You be surprised how much dem miss-meal cramps make a nigguh's cotton weights go up.''

The constant humming of sewing machines operated by the night laundry crew could be heard all through the night. They were sewing on the three-foot extension to Numbers 1, 2, and 3 squads' sacks. As I lay on my bunk with my hands folded underneath my head, I became very anxious anticipating the morrow's coming. When the dim ceiling lights gave way to the glare of the 100-watt bulbs, it was still pitch black outside.

''Chow time, les go eat!'' Eating savagely, we rushed to finish in the allotted fifteen minutes. Back on the tank, I got a long drink at the sink, grabbed my hat from underneath my mattress, and went to the front to be closer to the tank door.

Someone over in Number 4 tank hollered, ''Heah they cum,'' referring to Cap'n Smooth and his entourage, Lieutenant Sundown and Buzzard. The front office could be seen from the Number 4 tank windows. Thirty seconds later Big Tom rang and the tank doors opened. This time, instead of Cap'n Smooth waiting at the end of the hall by the back door to count us as we went streaking by, he stood underneath the inside picket.

''Whenever you nigguhs git outta that back door, I want

177

ever squad to stop by in front uv 'at laundry, an ever nigguh gitta sack! First nigguh I ketch 'thout a sack when we git to 'at field is gon' git sump'n dun to his goat-smellin ass," and strutted down the hall to take his position at the back door. Aiming his voice back up the corridor, "Lemme have 'em, Boss!"

"Number 1!"

We hit the yard following Road Runner to the bundles of neatly stacked cotton sacks piled on the ground in front of the laundry. Road Runner grabbed a sack from the first pile and took off. The rest of us followed suit. Boss Deadeye was loping his horse to keep up as we sailed through the backgate, "Go Head!"

Ol' Sol was just showing its huge, orange face over the eastern horizon by the time we crossed the main turnrow. As far as the eye could see was row after row of blossoming cotton bolls. It looked like an endless plain of freshly popped popcorn. We turned off the main turnrow which led into the camp onto the Williamson turnrow. Each squad stayed about twenty-five yards behind the next. We trotted straight down the Williamson turnrow to catch our sets of rows. The rest of the field work force would string out to catch theirs after we did.

"Count off twenty-seven rows Ol' Chinaman," Boss Deadeye hollered to our tailrow man who worked the last row, and was responsible for spotting and counting off rows. Chinaman began to step them off calling out the number of each as he went. As soon as he hollered out the number, the con who had been assigned that number got on it and began picking. "You sonsabitches ketch 'em Gotdam rows an gitcha mawdickin asses offa this turnrow!"

I caught cotton row number fourteen. By the time I picked the cotton from two stalks, the rest of the squad was already twenty or thirty feet ahead of me. I raised my head up for a moment and couldn't even see the end of my row, it was so long. The squad was continuously moving ahead of and away from me.

My row was in the swing, middle of the squad, and the worst place to be. That's where the bosses ride while watching the squads work. Boss Deadeye was walking his horse right beside me. Out of the corner of my eye, I saw him leaning forward in his saddle eyeballing my every move as I carefully plucked each boll from the stalks. The faster I tried to pick it, the more I dropped. The more I dropped, the more time I wasted trying to get all the dirt, leaves, stems, and sticks out before putting it into my sack. Deadeye was so close I heard the crying of his saddle each time he shifted positions.

"Ol' Cap Rock," Deadeye hollered, "hit this sorry bastard's row a lick up thar an hep him git th' end uv his sack off 'is Gotdam turnrow."

Cap Rock was the push row man who worked the second row in the squad. He picked up his sack, walked across the twelve rows, and started picking cotton ahead of me on my row.

Then Deadeye started on me, "Nigguh, you betta go to feedin 'at bag, an movin them shit scratchers lak you aim to do sump'n! Aw, I know apickin cotton's neath yore style. I betcha a few weeks in 'at pisser jes might hep you tighten yore sorry ass up a notch."

It was open season on my row for Cap Rock, who picked a long strip and went back to his row. I finally picked my way up to the cottonless stalks he left. Just to be able to walk down the middle of the rows and straighten my back up for a minute was a blessed relief. When I leaned back down, I rested one elbow on my knee while I picked, to take some of the strain off my back. The skip Cap Rock picked in my row caught me up with the squad momentarily, but in no time I had fallen way behind again.

It wasn't long before some of the cons in my squad yelled for Water Boy Brown to bring them another sack. He brought an armload from the water wagon. Those pickers who needed them got out of their full sacks, tied knots in the strap part, and with green cotton bolls marked their prison names on them. Water Boy Brown draped the full ones over his water wagon and hauled them off to the scales. Most of the squad had filled up a sack and the other few, excluding me, would be getting one in a very short time.

About an hour later, "Awright, Ol' Road Runner, ya'll raisem up an head on to them scales."

We picked up our sacks, slung them across our shoulders, and ran behind Road Runner down several turnrows. We crossed over quite a few more before reaching the area where the scales had been set up. Huge sheets were spread out on the turnrow for us to dump our cotton onto after our sacks had been weighed.

By the time we reached the scales, I was out of breath from the long run. Road Runner hung his two sacks on the scales first. After the scale man hooked the rope around them, he hoisted the load so the sacks did not touch the ground.

Cap'n Smooth hollered out his weight, "He got 235 pounds uv cotton." He continued to call out the weights of the pickers as their sacks were hung on the scales. After emptying, they went to the water wagon, got a drink, and waited for the rest of us to weigh up.

"He's got 230, he's got 215, he's got 220, he's got 195." Cap'n Smooth stopped and commented when the weight dropped under 200 pounds, "Nigguh, you betta take yore Gotdam ass to wek an quit a draggin roun fore I do sump'n to you." Then to Boss Deadeye, "You gon' hafta put this rotten bastard to wek, cuz I bleeve th' sonuvabitch dun laid th' hammer down, jes flat dun quit." Everything stopped until he finished preaching his sermon about the low weights.

As I sat on my sack waiting my turn, I felt like jumping up and running right out across the field. To hell with the 30-30 and the bloodhounds. The weight keeper called my number. Cap'n Smooth looked at me when I stepped toward the scales dragging my sack. Beer Belly's words rang loud and clear as I hung it up.

Cap'n Smooth hollered, "Forty pounds! Kin you bleeve it? Forty fuckin pounds uv cotton! Boss, this ol' nigguh sho must be heavy wit you! Whatcha do Boss, let 'em ketch you fuckin a mule?"

The cons waiting to weigh up behind me started laughing. Boss Deadeye's face crimsoned and he had a wild-eyed look when he said, "Cap'n, I'm willin to forfit a whole month's wages if you jes look th' utha way fer five seconds so's I kin throw this wuthless sonuvabitch away." With trembling hands, he pointed his double-barrel shotgun at me and laid the hammers back. Those waiting to weigh up scampered out of the way in case he fired.

"Naw, Boss," Cap'n Smooth said jokingly, "I don' bleeve this bastard's even wuth the price uv a good load uv buckshot. Sides, you might splatter nigguh shit all over my boots an mess up my shine." Boss Deadeye lowered his shotgun.

"Where you frum, nigguh! I spose you onea them city nigguhs that ruther steal than wek. Where'd you say you cum frum?" Each time I attempted to answer, "Dry up that fuckin ol' mouth when I'm a talkin to you!" With his finger pointed close to my face, he shouted, "Do you heah me talkin to you NIG-GUH!?" bouncing his voice off my nose.

"Tell you whut, Boss, don'cha let this sorry bastard even slow down at that water wagon. He ain' picked enuff to pay fer a drank uv water." Back at me, "As fer you nigguh, you betta gitcha Gotdam goat-smellin ass back out yonder an go to wek! I'm gon' do sump'n to you if you cum draggin yore yaller ass back up to them scales wit anutha measly forty pounds. You heah me NIG-GUH!?"

He hollered down the turnrow to the officer watching the dump sheets for dirty cotton, "Lieutenant, you betta sho watch this nigguh, an don't let 'em dump ALL 'at cotton he's got on yore foot. Jes mite break it!" Walking toward the sheet to empty my sack, I heard him say, "Reason that sonuvabitch can't pick no cotton's cuz he wuz too busy hustlin up decent white men for his ol' mammy to screw 'stead uv learnin sump'n wuthwhile."

I emptied my sack and stood to the side waiting for the others to weigh up and empty. The lieutenant, whom the cons called "Sundown," said in a semi-audible tone, "You didn' have much that time, didja?"

"No sir."

"Well, they's plenny uv it out thar. You betta gitcha sef sum uv it."

When Chinaman emptied his sack and got a drink, we took off running back down the turnrow to where we'd left off. It seemed like we had been picking for an hour when Boss Deadeye hollered, "Ol' Road Runner, ya'll raisem up an go on over yonder whar they dun set up 'at johnny ground.''

Heading down the middles of the rows toward the turnrow, ''You dick-eatin bastards betta not be a knockin 'at man's cotton all over th' fuckin ground! Ever sonuvabitch stay walkin in his own middle. Furst nigguh I ketch acrossin over 'em rows aknockin cotton on th' ground's gon' git a load uv buckshot in his black ass. You nigguhs tighten up an git on up yonder wit that lead row nigguh 'fore I bust a ball down thru this canyon! Ol' Road Runner, go head! Take 'em on way from heah!''

Road Runner shifted gears and we struggled furiously for our other gears. We shot down the turnrow like a bunch of gazelles. Within minutes, we pulled up at the johnny ground. On one side of the turnrow the flunkies had set up folding tables and chairs for the bosses. By now, all the squads arrived and we were lined up to go through the chow line. The Number 1 squad first.

As we started through, Boss Deadeye shouted, ''Ol' Yaller Nigguh, don'cha git no pan. You jes stand yo rotten ass over yonder back outta th' way, so's 'em nigguhs thas been awekin kin git sump'n to eat.''

The other bosses joshed Boss Deadeye, ''Hey Boss, is this heah that nigguh whut broke 'em scales wit all 'at cotton this mornin?''

Another chimed in, ''Hell, Boss, that nigguh don' want no talk. You kin tell he's swole up. That nigguh's got his mind on sippin lemonade in that free world.''

Boss ''Eatem up,'' the undisputed master at harassing cons and bosses, added his bullshit, ''Since you ain' gon' feed that ol' nigguh, why don'cha lend 'em yo hat an let 'em fan suma these fuckin flies. As a gen'le rule, nigguhs whut claim they can' pick cotton gen'ly make damn good fly fanners,'' he said cramming food into his mouth. ''Boss, know whut? If I had that ol' nigguh in my squad, shit, I wouldn' even ASK 'em to wek. All he'd hafta do is jes fan th' flies an gatternippers offa me an my fuckin hoss.''

I stood off to the side waiting for them to finish eating. Some con said, ''Gotdam! Looka heah, heahs a big o' grass-hopper in my pan!''

The con next to him reached over pretending to grab it, "Lemme hav dat piece uv meat, man," he joked.

With the meal over Boss Deadeye hollered, "Awright, alla you Number 1 nigguhs, git out heah on 'is turnrow an line up in two's." We quickly paired off so he could take the head count. He rode his horse from end to end, "Go Head!"

I was back on my row again and nothing had changed. I kept falling behind, Cap Rock came over at Boss Deadeye's request to pick off my row, and Boss Deadeye stayed on my ass. My shirt stuck to my back and the sweat sloshed inside my brogans. My throat got drier and drier and the sharp pains in my back were excruciating.

Shortly, Boss Deadeye yelled, "Ol' Road Runner, that man's beckin fer us agin. Ya'll raisem up an head on to them scales."

The sun's hot rays had dried most of the early dew from the cotton. It was much lighter now, which was evident as Cap'n Smooth called out the weights.

"He's got 175!" That was Road Runner. Cap Rock weighed up next, "He's got 185!" He outweighed Road Runner because of all the cotton he had picked off my row. The weights ranged from 130 pounds to Cap Rock's 185. So far, Cap'n Smooth hadn't said a word to anybody who had weighed up ahead of me.

I hung my sack on the scales. Cap'n Smooth jumped back in a comical gesture and hollered out, "He's got fifty-five pounds! Boss, you musta whispered sump'n in this nigguh's ear! Nigguh, you betta go to gittin sum mo uv 'at cotton. That ain' near bouts enuff. You heah me?!"

"Yes sir," dragging my sack away.

Before I reached the sheet, he shouted, "Nigguh, don'cha be awearin 'at fuckin sack out draggin it up an down this Gotdam turnrow! Pick it up an tote it. You ain' got a double handful uv cotton, and you gonna jes drag it roun lak it's too heavy fer you to tote!"

I emptied up. Since nothing had been said to the contrary, I headed to the water wagon. Water Boy Brown poured up some more water from the two canvas-covered wooden barrels, refilling the four tin buckets. He could barely pour for squabbling with some cons who had already gotten their drinks. They were at the front of the wagon aggravating the two old mules, Ol' Coal Oil and Ol' Fannie. Ol' Fannie had been screwed so many times by convicts that when one of them patted her on the rump, she automatically raised her tail up. When a con touched either of the mules, it caused them to move the wagon a few feet.

Water Boy Brown finally said, "You ignant muthafuck-uhs, let dem mules lone fo I take onea dese axe hannles an ram it up onea ya'll's asses. Gotdam stupid muthafuckuhs!" he mumbled. "Dere's sum mo nigguhs back heah still tryin to gitta drank!"

Still they would not stop, no matter what he said. Like a bunch of mischievous little boys, they enjoyed teasing the mules and antagonizing Water Boy Brown.

The water was hot as piss and so salty it was almost slimy. But it was my first drink since we left the building and tasted good as Coca Cola. I noticed instead of wasting water by spitting it on the ground, it was spat into the empty cotton sacks. Whatever water was left in the cups went into the sacks too. Wetting it "makes th' cotton weigh mo."

When the tailrow emptied his sack and gulped down his last swallow of water, Boss Deadeye yelled, "Ya'll git on way frum heah, Go Head!"

Like bats out of hell, we speeded back to our rows and started picking again. It was late in the afternoon. A few courageous clouds dared to shield us from Ol' Sol," momentarily causing shade-giving shadows to dance across the fields. Barring an occasional abusive remark by a boss or the "go head" command and except for the rattlings of the cotton stalks being stripped of their precious white gold, it was quiet. All across the field black bodies dressed in white bobbed up and down like prairie dogs, bending, stooping, sweating, crawling, picking, and popping those sacks with an uncanny rhythm each time a handful was thrust inside.

I wasn't quite as far behind as I had been earlier in the day and Boss Deadeye was behind somebody else for a change. I hollered, "Pourin it down over heah, Boss!"

Finally, "Go head an po it down."

Turning my back to him, I directed every single drop into my sack.

We picked and picked. Cap'n Smooth had already gone to the building, leaving Lieutenant Sundown in charge of the field force. I understood why the cons called him that. The sun was sinking low and there was no indication that we would be knocking off any time soon. On the turnrow ahead, he leaned so precariously off the side of his horse the stirrup almost touched the ground. It looked like any minute his saddle was going to slip down under the horse's belly.

Sundown looked right sitting atop a horse. A real Gary Cooper-looking cowboy. He was tall and slim, and his tailored shirts fit like a glove. He sat unconcerned, smoking a cigarette and staring off into the sunset. They were motionless, except when the big, dark bay periodically swished her tail or he took a drag off his cigarette.

For once I was even with the squad because the work pace had slowed down considerably. Most of the squad was watching for Sundown to raise his hat. I passed several of them as I hustled for every boll of cotton I could get. I had more in my sack now than I'd had all day. The strap was cutting into my shoulder each time I pulled against it. The sun was gone, even the reddish-orange had disappeared over the horizon. We picked on. Sundown raised his hat at twilight.

Boss Deadeye yelled, "Awright, you Number 1 nigguhs, brang 'em sacks on back heah an put 'em on th' end uv yore row." After the head count, "Go head! Ol' Road Runner, take these ol' thangs on to that house." Hollering up ahead, "Boss, git them Gotdam drag-asses outta the way up thar an let this Number 1 squad cum by."

Some of the other squads had gotten to the turnrow before we did, but it was a law of the bottoms that no squad walked or worked in front of Number 1. They pulled over, "Ol' Road Runner, go head nigguh!"

While standing at the backgate waiting for Boss Deadeye to get his shotgun and pistol checked in, I noticed that neither the warden nor the captain was there with the Hog Law book. I didn't know what was going on, and didn't care so long as I could make it back to the tank and get on my bunk. That evening I found out it was a traditional policy of Big Devil's not to punish on the first day of picking season. "He gives us dat day to warm up an git broke back in."

Finished checking his weapons, "You nigguhs, go head!"

Inside the yard, midway between the backgate and the back door, we stripped so the line of waiting guards could shake us down. The ten of us who lived on Number 3 tank made a mad dash for the showers to get in and out before the rest of the squads got into the tank. As usual, Big George sat on the ledge above the commodes so he could eyegrind our naked, wet bodies. Thanks to Sundown, by the time we finished showering it was totally dark outside.

After supper I got on my bunk. To hell with the domino table and card games. I dozed off. Voices and the tank door opening and closing woke me. Toe Sucker had been put out of the tank again, for the umpteenth time. He had gotten a double lip-lock on somebody's toe during the night and must have nibbled a little too hard and woke his prey. Half-asleep, I raised up on my elbows.

Beer Belly in the bunk across from me said, "Ain' nobody but Toe Sucker hustlin sum mo toe jam."

Unable to go back to sleep, I heard whispering from the next row of bunks. Half opening my eyes, I saw a couple of cons pouring lighter fluid all over Iron Head's sheet-covered body.

The cons called him Iron Head because he could hit his head with his fist and it sounded like he was hitting an empty bucket. He was so good at his ventriloquist trick few realized he actually made the sound with his mouth.

While he loudly snored and snorted they finished dousing his bunk and returned to their own. One of them lit a cigarette and thumped it on Iron Head's sheet. A second or two later, WHOOSH!

Inflamed, he jumped up yelling and cussing, ran toward the front of the tank, then realized all the water was in the back. He ran down the alley hollering and slapping at the flames, trying to put his sheet out. He made it to the showers, jumped in, and turned on the wrong faucets, the hot water. He was dancing a jig and had the shower area looking like a steam bath.

The tank was in an uproar. The boisterous laughter caused Boss Wise-em-up to holler down, "They's sum wild-ass'd nigguhs in heah tonite. Suma you ol' wild-ass'd nigguhs gonna hafta talk ta that warden in the mornin. You betta git down on it.'' Then he asked Iron Head, ''Didja make sho you got all that far put out? Don' wanna set this whole fuckin buildin afar.''

''Yassuh, Boss, it's all put out,'' as he went back to what was left of his mattress. ''Wisht I knowed whut muthafucka it wuz dat dun dat. I betcha dat warden havta burn me offa his ass.''

Of course, everybody was pretending to be asleep now, but snickering under their covers. Iron Head mumbled on until Slope Diddy said, ''Say muthafucka, dry up dat fuckin mouff an go ta sleep fo you git dat ol' iron head melted sho nuff!''

Iron Head lay down on his bunk and quickly went back to snoring.

Tomorrow came and with it the inevitable. Hades couldn't possibly be any hotter. We had been entombed, packed inside a four-by-eight steel and concrete chamber. As we stood naked in our urine and sweat, the heavy stench was overpowering. The small supply of oxygen depleted with every panting breath the nine of us took.

No face basin, no water, and a fifty-cent-piece-sized hole in the center of the rough, unfinished concrete floor served as the lavatory. The nine of us writhed and twisted for space like maggots in a cesspool. All the darkness and sweltering heat vacuum-sealed inside when the solid steel door slammed shut. This was the pisser.

I was the second man to enter and hurried to one of the back corners. Each time someone squirmed for position everybody in the dark furnace was disturbed. A fight nearly broke out when a con tried to lie down. If one punch was thrown in the blackness, fists would fly like a bunch of blind men fighting.

My legs were cramping, I had to get out of that corner. ''Say,'' I said, ''I know a way we kin make it easy on our-selfs.''

A voice shot back, ''Ain' nuthin gon' make dis shit easy, man. Dey got us crammed in dis hot muthafucka lak sardines.''

Then another, "Whut kinda plan you got, man?"

"Look," I said, "if five of us line up from this corner I'm in to th' door, with our faces to the wall, then four of us can take turns sittin an squattin on the floor next to the other wall."

"Sounds awright to me," somebody said, "but, say man, how cum we gotta face the fuckin wall while them fo nigguhs is squattin down 'hind us?"

"Yeah, man, how cum?"

"Well, facin the wall would keep us from blowin our hot breaths on each other an we wouldn' be danglin our dicks in the faces of the ones on the floor."

"Yeah, but den yo ass would be."

"I know," I said, "but it won' stick out as far."

We agreed to try it, and rearranged ourselves in the cell. The nine of us stood, squatted, and sat in that hellish coffin until the next morning when it was time to go back to the cotton patch and try to satisfy the Hog Law book.

I thought I was going to starve to death that first cotton picking season. But as the season wore on and after at least a dozen more trips to the pisser and several more bouts with the cuffs, my picking skills got better and better. Just like Beer Belly said, those "miss-meal cramps" have a phenomenal effect on the development of cotton picking speed.

When the next cotton picking season rolled around I managed to average with the squad more often than not. By the end of the season in October, I was doing a lot better than Road Runner even. He'd gotten in bad health; his endurance and speed had waned. He lost that other gear and was struggling just to bring up the rear out on the turnrow. When the Hog Law book didn't get him cut out at the backgate, Boss Deadeye got him for "laziness." Finally, his laborious wheezing and coughing up blood got so bad, the medical team diagnosed he had symptoms of TB and had him transferred to the Walls hospital. After Road Runner got shipped, Boss Deadeye put Cap Rock on as the lead row.

I knew it was almost a cardinal sin if a convict talked back to a boss or refused to obey ANY order. He got an ass whipping, the handcuffs, solitary, or a combination of all three.

However, if someone got caught jacking off or fucking, Big Devil and the bosses made a joke of it, like with Fistfucker.

Fistfucker was heralded as the tank jack-off champion and played pants-pocket pool even while holding a conversation. Big Devil decided the best solution to the problem was to make him sleep in a pair of boxing gloves with his wrists tied to his bunk. Whenever he hollered "alley boss," Forty had to rush and untie him.

So when Flea Brain and Pork Chops got caught fucking, they had to stand side by side on the soda water boxes under the picket, the usual punishment when Big Devil deemed the offense an insignificant part of prison life. While standing on the boxes this time, they argued so much it led to a shoving match and both fell off. The picket boss hollered down orders for them to stop, but they kept right on quarreling.

Flea Brain had been aptly nicknamed because he acted like his brain was no bigger than a flea's. He spent every waking hour thinking and talking about the love of his life, Pork Chops. Flea Brain was the more aggressive and vocal of the pair. Pork Chops, on the other hand, was extremely humble, no spirit, like a broken-hearted dog in a pound. When he was a young man, the tear sack under his left eye was damaged by a blow from the barrel of a policeman's revolver, causing his eye to drip most of the time, and making him look even sadder.

Pork Chops helped keep himself and Flea Brain in smokes by washing the socks of cons in return for their cigarette butts. Nevertheless, Flea Brain would not allow the washing services to last very long. When Pork Chops went back to the same con twice to wash his socks, Flea Brain would cuss to the top of his tongue-tied voice, "Poke Chops, I gittin tied yo shit. You tink you smar mudderfucka, I be wachin yo ass, Poke Chops. Don'cha tink I ain'."

Pork Chops' left eye started dripping heavier when Flea Brain chastised him. He'd say, "Go on, man. Go on, man. Lemme 'lone, man," and try to get away from Flea Brain, who followed him all over the tank fussing. They "fought" in the tank all the time about any and everything.

After their lovers' spat in the hallway, the picket boss

made them sit in separate corners. Flea Brain began his amorous pitch as Pork Chops sat quietly in his assigned corner. "Baby, you knows I loves you."

Flea Brain babbled on and on. Finally, the picket boss yelled down for him to shut up, but he never quit professing his love. He harassed the picket boss and Pork Chops all night long with his tongue-tied, lovesick jabbering.

The next day, Sunday, Big Devil was in the guard's barber shop in the front of the building getting his weekly hair trim and shoe shine. Afterwards, he came through the short corridor that led past the commissary to underneath the inside picket. He looked like a Philadelphia lawyer in his blue gabardine suit, black shoes shining like glass, and light-gray, short-brimmed Stetson hat. Big Devil looked through his gold-rimmed glasses at them like they were two big piles of horseshit. Flea Brain immediately told the warden how he had caught Pork Chops traipsing around, "washin the same nigguh's socks twice."

By the time Flea Brain finished, Big Devil agreed, "Sumthin must be dun." To prevent future problems, Big Devil decided, "Sumtimes marryin has a way uv settlin crazy-assed nigguhs down."

Big Devil phoned the backgate picket boss and told him to send in Big Mama James, who was a trusty working in the welding shop. Since trusties work seven days a week, Sunday was just another work day. When Big Mama James came in the building, Big Devil told him to go back to the shop and make two wedding bands out of some nuts.

While Big Mama James was gone, Big Devil hollered upstairs to the Number 5 tank building tender, "Send that ol' preacher down heah!"

Rev came downstairs, "Good mornin, Warden. How are you?"

Ignoring his greeting, "Ol' Rev, I want you to perform me a weddin ceremony. You thank you got sense enuff to do that?"

"Oh yassuh, Warden," and ran back upstairs to get his Bible.

In twenty minutes, it was chow time. After the meal, all of us, excluding the white cons, were ordered to remain to witness the "weddin." Rev stood in the aisleway waiting with his Bible neatly tucked under his arm. Big Devil ordered Flea Brain and Pork Chops to strip and get up on one of our messhall tables. Then he told Rev to begin the ceremony. Big Mama James acted as best man and handed them the rings when Rev got to that part. They put the rings on each other's fingers and Rev pronounced them "man an wife." After which, Big Devil ordered them to embrace.

Most of the audience exploded in laughter. Since the wedding was at chow time and our pans were still on the tables, we showered the newlyweds with food scraps. The cons and bosses were really enjoying the warden's show. Especially us, because it afforded the opportunity, however short-lived, to go acceptably berserk without fear of punishment.

Finally, Big Devil half-heartedly ordered, "Awright, you nigguhs, knock that shit off!" Even after his command, somebody slung gravy which splattered his suit. He demanded quiet again and we settled down. He gestured for Flea Brain and Pork Chops to get off the table. Up to that point in the festivities, Flea Brain had been grinning and enjoying himself, while Pork Chops stood dejected with his hands folded over his privates.

"I'm gonna give you two nigguhs an early Christmas present."

Big Devil issued the order for Cap'n Foots to transfer Flea Brain to Number 1 tank, placing him on the other side of the building from Pork Chops. After they dressed, Flea Brain reached out to touch Pork Chops' hand for a last farewell as they filed out of the messhall. One going East; the other going West.

It was early December. The rain was freezing fast as it hit the ground. Icicles hung on the outside window ledges. The radiator pipes that hung along the inner ceiling popped sporadically. Already we had been laying-in the building for two days and were getting on each other's nerves. This was my second Christmas and almost my third year at Retrieve. I'd begun to feel like an ol' timer.

The saddest part about the Yuletide season was the way each of us tried to hide our loneliness. If we felt sad, however, it was by choice. Big Devil took great pains to make our Christmas merry. Cons were standing on bunks hanging decorations. Big Devil made the bosses chip in and buy them after Hollywood had this festive brainstorm and sold him on the idea.

The outstanding sissies on each tank were selected by Hollywood and the building tenders to do the decorating. Afterwards, Big Devil would inspect the five tanks to determine which was the prettiest. The chosen tank's members were allowed into the Saturday night picture show first. After the white cons, of course.

Very quickly, the tank activities slowed after the decorating spree. The sound of hard walking and jingling spurs broke the calm. We knew it was Cap'n Smooth even before he spoke. "Boss, open up all 'em tank doors so's them buildin tenders kin git out heah."

Boss Humpy hollered down, "You want one frum each tank or all uv 'em, Cap'n?"

Aggravated, "Ever damned one uv 'em!"

Levers were thrown and the noisy steel doors slowly opened. "That Cap'n wants all uv you buildin tenders ta cum on out heah under this picket!"

Three building tenders live on each lower tank and one on the trusty tank. In a matter of minutes all thirteen had gathered underneath the inside picket for a meeting with Cap'n Smooth.

"Tell you whut I want ya'll ta do," Cap'n Smooth began, "first, how many uv you nigguhs kin read an write?" Several shuffled their feet and looked down at the scrub-polished red brick floor, indicating they were the ones who could not. "Well, you nigguhs whut kin, I want ya'll to go back in them tanks an git th' names an numbers uv ever one uv 'em nigguhs who needs a set uv teeth."

Big George asked, "Cap'n, does you want da names an numbers uv jes dem nigguhs whut ain' got no teefs atall, or does you want dem nigguhs' names whut's got sum teefs lef?"

"Naw nigguh! I don' want ya'll gittin no nigguh's name whut's got sum teeth in his mouth. That warden wants to take care uv them nigguhs first whut ain' got no teeth atall.

192

Nigguh, whut made you ask a Gotdam crazy-assed question lak 'at in the first place? If a nigguh's got teeth uv his own, whut th' hell does he want sum mo fer?''

The question Big George asked must have had some validity or why did Cap'n Smooth climb up in the inside picket and phone the front office to get further clarification? Afterwards, he descended, ''Now, les go over this agin, so's I kin see if you nigguhs understand whut you spose to do. I want ya'll whut kin read an write to go back in them tanks, an git th' names an numbers uv ever nigguh whut ain't got *no* teeth atall. An git the names an numbers uv ever one uv them nigguhs in there whut's got one eye missin. Don't none uv you crazy bastards ask me if I mean 'em nigguhs that ain' got no eyes atall, cuz we ain' got no no-eyed nigguhs in heah,'' he said sarcastically.

When they turned and started to leave, ''Jes you nigguhs hold up! I ain' finished wit ya'll yet.''

One mumbled, ''Naw suh, Cap'n. We wuzn' leavin, suh. We jes thought you wuz thru wid us, Cap'n.''

''I'll tell you when I'm thru, nigguh. Now, where wuz I? Oh yeah, afta you dun got them nigguhs' names an numbers, an dun give 'em to the picket boss, I want ya'll to git a big-mouthed nigguh, a medium-mouthed nigguh, an one uv 'em little-mouthed nigguhs whut's got teeth from the eastside, westside an Number 5 tanks. Git 'em up to the front uv them tanks so's they kin bite them false teeth molds when Ol' Nolan brangs 'em down heah. Now, I'm thru wit you nigguhs. Take ya'll's rotten asses on back in 'em tanks an do whut I tol ya'll.''

''Yassuh, Cap'n.''

The cry went out on all five tanks to those who needed false teeth and artificial eyes. Big George presided over the eastside tanks' registration.

Yelling loudly so residents of both tanks could hear, ''Awright, you nigguhs lissen up! Dat Cap'n wonts alla ya'll's names an numbers whut needs a set uv dem false teefs an dem dat ain' got but one eye. Dat warden gon' give ya'll sum. So alla ya'll dat ain' got no eyes an teefs, cum on up heah an give yo name an number ta Ol' Slocum.'' Big

George had delegated the signing up responsibility, since his own writing skills were lacking.

Cons from Number 4 tank who needed an artificial eye or false teeth started marching through the now opened door, which separated the two tanks, to enter Number 3 tank, where the domino table had been cleared for sign-up use. Across the hall, the door separating the westside tanks had also been opened by Boss Humpy so their building tenders could sign up their less fortunates. I never realized there were so many with missing parts. A good third of the cons in the eastside tanks were crowded around the domino table trying to get their names and numbers listed first by Slocum.

Big George shouted, "Say, suma you nigguhs git back an give dat nigguh sum elbow room."

When the last con left the sign-up table, Nolan came down the stairs and stood at the 3 tank door, very neatly attired in his wraparound smock, white tennis shoes, and emergency room cap.

B.C., out of the Number 2 hoe squad and Bull's replacement on our tank, yelled out, "You nigguhs whut needs teefs, cum on up heah to da front so ya'll kin heah whut Doc Nolan's gon' say."

Marble Eye, who was in my squad, didn't hush quick enough for B.C. "Ol' Marble Eye, you gon' need more'n anutha Gotdam eye if you don' stop runnin yo ol' head! You gon' need a tractor ta pull my foot outta yo ass. You onea dem nigguhs whut don' lak ta be tole nuthin. You gits swole up when sumbody tells you a liddle sump'n," B.C. said while weaving his way through the crowded front of the tank toward the back where Marble Eye stood.

With one foot propped on his lower bunk, Marble Eye was holding a conversation with another con and completely ignored B.C. When he saw B.C. coming, he took his foot down and one-eyed his way to the center of the alley, "Dis gon' be twixt you an me, B.C. An pull-do muthafucka, you ain' gon' whup my ass!"

Marble Eye's bold response froze the other goons for a moment. Before they could establish position in alliance with B.C., we, the Number 1 hoe squad members from the two tanks, got between them and Marble Eye to ensure a fair fight. Boss Humpy had a front row seat as he looked down into the tank from his perch. Since it involved a building tender, he wasn't going to interfere.

Both were 200-plus pounders, with muscles like tree stumps from many years in the fields. Both were serving life sentences, mean as hell, and well matched—except for Marble Eye having just one eye. This was going to be a battle.

B.C. got within a few feet of Marble Eye and lunged. They met head-on in the alleyway and their bodies crashed together like two rhinos. Both hit the floor. Fists were flying as they fought side by side between the rows of bunks. They kicked and hit, each scuffling to get up first. The bunks reeled and rocked like they were being uprooted from their bolted-down positions in the concrete floor.

The cons and picket boss looked on. No one said a word as the fighters continued to pummel and kick each other. Blood was flowing freely from both. They fought on, blow for blow. Their knuckles were bloody, and thick red slobber hung from their noses and mouths. Neither gave an inch, but the power of their swings dwindled.

"Awright, thas enuff uv that shit!" Boss Humpy hollered. "You nigguhs break 'em up now!"

The building tenders moved through the crowd toward them and Big George said, "Say, B.C., ya'll break it up now. Da man's lookin at ya'll, break it up!"

Neither said much when the building tenders parted and shoved them away from one another. However, Marble Eye did mumble as he walked back up the alley, "You ain' gon' whup my muthafuckin ass an no utha nigguh."

And he meant it. If B.C. wanted to show off, he sure should've grabbed somebody from another squad and not Number 1. Everybody in Number 1 hoe would fight.

With this brief interruption over, it was back to the business at hand. Nolan was talking through the bars with Polly, a Number 4 tank building tender, to allow a few minutes for things to get back to "subnormal." Turning his attention toward the picket boss, "Boss, will you open Number 3? I need to git those imprints made."

Boss Humpy hated doing anything the cons asked, and he shot back, "Can't them nigguhs do it thru the bars? Ever one uv 'em got them long ol' mouths.'' But knowing Nolan was working under strict orders from the warden via the captain, the door's lever was belligerently thrown.

"Ya'll lissen up heah!" Polly hollered. "You nigguhs lissen up now!"

Nolan made the announcement, "The warden wants me to take imprints frum three uv yawl with all yawl's teeth. He wants a big-moufted nigguh, a medium-moufted nigguh, an a bird-moufted nigguh to make yo imprints in this mold. You nigguhs qualified, cum on up here."

Nobody moved forward, only feet shuffling and snickering. Nolan looked at Polly, and Polly looked at Nolan. They didn't have a plan for the arisen selection process crisis. Nolan spoke out, "An the warden said you buildin tenders is gon' hep do the pickin."

Polly hollered, "Awright, I ain' gon' do dis shit by mysef, the resta you muthafuckas git offa yo asses an git ta pickin."

Building tenders from both tanks began rounding up their choices.

Ape was urging Mama Better Drawers along, "Cum on now, baby. G'on up dere an bite dat shit so evuh nigguh dat gits a pair o' teef made frum yo mouf will hafta pay me for life. Cuz das lak evuh nigguh whut gits dem teef will be kissin my o' lady. An baby, you don' want no nigguh kissin you an not payin us. Now do you?" nudging him forward again.

Ape was cutting back two life sentences. He had gotten one added since he'd been down for choking a con to death with his bare hands. The victim had a knife in his hand, but Ape literally squeezed the air out of him before he ever got to raise it.

Mama Better Drawers was doing twenty for midnight burglary. Both were multiple offenders who had grown up at Gatesville School for Boys and graduated to hell. Ape and Mama Better Drawers seemed content with the life they had both grown so accustomed to.

By now, several of the star sissies had been shuffled to the front and were gathered around the middle domino table where Nolan and Polly sat. Except for Forty, all the building tenders were there in the interest of their specific punks. Each one trying to get his punk to calm down and "stop actin lak a damn fool."

"Say, Nolan," one hollered, "let our woman g'on an bite dat shit an git it over wid. You dun kissed her. You knows how sweet her lips is."

Trying to ignore the comment, Nolan gave out more directives, "Yawl look here, les git this over wit so I kin git on outta here. I got a lot uv shit to do to git these molds ready by tomorrow." The once-a-month real dentist would be down to pick them up. "Look, I know alla yawl wants yo, ahem, friend, to give the imprint. But I have to have three sizes—small, medium, an large. Jus by lookin, yawl know that suma these nigguhs is 'liminated." Nolan continued, "You nigguhs whut know yawl's 'liminated, move on back outta the fuckin way an let suma these utha nigguhs git up here."

A few of those standing around the perimeter of the crowd moved toward the back. Then a few more and a few more.

"Now, les git to pickin sumbody," Nolan urged. "Whut bout this nigguh?" he asked, pointing directly at Mama Better Drawers. This brought a howl and a chest beat from Ape. Nolan had played it on the safe side. Nobody offered any opposition to his first suggestion. A few cons whistled and hollered when Nolan said, "Okay, we got one. Mama Better Drawers'll bite the medium-size mold."

All the toothless cons bared their gums, grinning acceptance of Mama Better Drawers as the medium-mold imprintbiter.

Ape, in his thunderous voice, "Evuh onea you muthafuckas whut gits a pair o' my baby's teefs is gon' gimme a sack o' dust evuh week or I'm gon' do sump'n to his ass!"

Now, to choose the small and large. This was going to be difficult. Things were boiling down to B.C. and his punk Candy, and Air Hammer, former Number 1 squad member, and his punk Mama Good Drawers. B.C.'s life sentence was for murder and Candy was doing twelve for burglary. Air Hammer was doing fifty for robbery and Mama Good Drawers got thirty-five for poisoning somebody. All of them, except Candy, could hold their own in the muscle department.

Air Hammer looked at Nolan, "Doc, jes by lookin, you knows my ol' lady's mouf ain' big as Candy's." Nolan wasn't about to dispute Air Hammer's word.

B.C. made his pitch for Candy, "You right Air Hammer, yo nigguh's mouf might be liddler, but it sho ain' as priddy."

"Look, B.C., you knows muthafuckin well I ain' scaid o' yo ass, nigguh. An me an you kin settle dis shit in the back or rat now! Cuz it don' make a fuck ta me. I been kinda wantin suma yo ass anyway."

B.C. pondered his predicament. "Man, fuck it! Let Mama Good Drawers bite dat shit. I don' want my woman puttin his mouf on nuthin but my you knows whut. Cum on Candy, baby. Les me an you go in the back. I wont you ta pick my face."

One more to go, a big-mouthed mold biter. Everybody was moving away from the domino table and slowly drifted toward the back of the tank. For whatever reasons, nobody liked the idea of being selected to provide the large imprint. Except for a few cons sitting on the bench at the front of the tank, Polly and Nolan were without an audience.

"Cum on, Polly. Pick sumbody so I kin git outta here. It don't make a fuck who it is."

Polly wheeled away from Nolan and walked over to the five or six cons sitting on the front bench. If a big-mouthed con was what Polly was looking for, he certainly had found one. Sitting among those on the bench was Gatormouf.

Polly pointed straight at him, interrupting his conversation, "Hey you, you wid da big mouf!"

Gatormouf looked confused, even though Polly's finger was pointing straight at him. "You talkin ta me, Polly?" he asked in bewilderment.

"Yeah, you nigguh. You got da biggest muthafuckin mouf on da bench. Yeah, I'm talkin ta you. Git up offa yo ass an cum bite dis shit for the Doc."

Gatormouf didn't move, "Say man, how cum you fuckin wit me?!"

"Nigguh!" Polly yelled, "if you don' git yo ass off dat bench, you gon' need sum teefs yosef!"

He slowly made his way toward Nolan grumbling, "I

198

don' know whut ya'll fuckin wit me for, dey's a whole lotsa nigguhs in heah wit moufs bigger'n mine.''

Polly overheard, ''Who nigguh?! Name sumbody! You don' know nobody heah an nowheres else wid a mouf bigger'n yo's.''

''Well, if my mouf's so fuckin big, who in da hell gon' wear a pair o' teefs made frum my bite? Yeah, smart-assed muthafucka, tell me dat!''

Polly was tired of arguing, ''Man, fuck you! Bite dis Gotdam shit fo I put my foot in yo ass.'' Gatormouf reluctantly sank his teeth into the modeling material.

Christmas day arrived. The purple and red crepe paper hanging from the ceiling sagged from the heat of the radiator pipes. After today, it would be taken down, boxed up, and put away until next year.

The night before, we were issued a new shirt, britches, and pair of brogans, the year's ration. The clothes were made by the women prisoners at the Goree Unit. Getting our new clothes was like looking into fortune cookies. Inside the fly of our pants was written ''I wish'' or ''I love it,'' and other little messages. They even wrote their names, numbers, where they were from, how much time they were doing, and even poems under shirt collars and around the cuffs and tails—any place they felt would escape the eye of the clothes garment inspector. Even though the Christmas messages would come out after the first washing, they did add to the merriment of the Yuletide season as convict after convict discovered and showed what was written in his fly ''specially'' for him.

It was still early morning and not many cons were up and stirring about just yet. In another few minutes, the tank would be pulsing. Card and domino games would be starting soon, and Big Devil even allowed dice games today. This was the only day of the year that he pulled out all the stops. We could gamble openly in the games and not worry about getting busted. Wasn't much fear of a con being punished today, unless he smarted off at a boss.

Big Devil also gave orders to the picket boss to leave the door separating 3 and 4 tanks, and the one separating 1 and 2 tanks open so we could ''visit'' in the adjacent tank. Cons marched through the opened door like ants. Some just walked through, turned around quickly, and re-entered their own tank. Being able to get out of the tank had more to do with it than visiting.

After our Christmas dinner of turkey and all the trimmings was over, everybody was handed a small paper sack as we walked out the messhall door. In it were about ten pecans, a super-small winesap apple, an orange, and a small walking cane peppermint stick. Also as we walked out of the messhall, a cupful of salted peanuts was poured into our hats, which we had been told beforehand to bring to the messhall with us.

Most of the cons rushed back to the tanks and headed straight for the gambling tables. The small sack and hatful of Yuletide goodies was like giving them $500 worth of chips at the Las Vegas casinos. It was hilarious to listen and watch the betting in those games. "Shoot twenny goobers. Twenny goobers I shoot." At the rate they were counting out their peanuts, some of those games would last all night long. The peanuts were handled so much all the salt and skins had been rubbed off. The gamblers bet a few, ate a few, and squabbled all in between.

The Number 4 tank residents were the lookouts. They could see from their windows whenever somebody came from the front office. One of them sounded the alarm, "Heah cums Cap'n Smooth. He got two nigguhs with him totin sum boxes."

Beer Belly commented, "Maybe he be branging my prole papers."

Bad Eye answered, "Shit, you ain' gon' make no prole way frum dis hellhole. You kin forgit dat shit. Nobody knows where dis muthafucka is, specially dat prole board." Elaborating, "Hell, I been down heah goin on 'leven calendars an ain' never seen nairn down heah yet. Sides, dey needs a hellacopta an a pair o' spy glasses jus ta find th' road dat cums in heah. An dat's way too much trouble."

"Yeah," Chinaman chimed in, "thas de only reason I ain' dun run off. I don' know where in th' hell I am."

Cap'n Smooth came in the back door and up the hall. Two

house boys tagged behind him carrying a cardboard box apiece.

"Ya'll jes set 'em down heah under th' picket," Cap'n Smooth ordered.

After they sat the boxes down, "Anythang else, Cap'n Suh?"

"Naw, thas all. Let these two nigguhs back out, Boss," he hollered to Boss Humpy as the two trusties turned to leave.

"Merry Christmas ta you, Cap'n," they said in parting.

"Yeah."

The full name the cons had dubbed him was Cap'n Smooth Mouth, but spoke of him as Cap'n Smooth. He was transferred here from one of the northern units when Big Devil took over the camp. He had the notorious reputation for being the "hardest cap'n" in the system, even though he was in his sixties. He's best known for leaping off his horse onto the backs of field workers like Hoot Gipson of the old Wild West movies. He'd fight him man to man and wouldn't allow the bosses to intervene—win, lose, or draw. When he staged these cantankerous melees, he managed to draw a few, but never won "nairn."

Cap'n Smooth's idea of weekend fun was to come in the tanks and chase cons down with a pair of pliers to pull out their whiskers or the hairs on their heads if he felt it was too long. Sometimes, he put on convict whites he got from the laundry and eased his way into the tanks to catch unalerted crap shooters. He'd sit on a con's bunk unnoticed by the gamblers until he made his presence known, "It's my fuckin shot now." He took all the loot and threw it up in the air. Whoever caught it got to keep it.

The main thing Cap'n Smooth disliked was the "suckass" tactics the cons used on the officers. By now, the tanks' prime suckasses had gathered at their tank doors. With the curiosity of baboons, they were dying to find out what was happening, but didn't know how to approach him.

Finally it got the best of one, "Mornin, Suh, Cap'n." Cap'n Smooth didn't answer. Undaunted, "Cap'n, dem sho is sum priddy boots." Scratching his head, "Sho would lak ta shine 'em up fur you sumtime,'' he said in his best Stepin Fetchit voice.

"Nigguh," Cap'n Smooth said, looking at him like he was a twice-used condom, "git yore Gotdam ass on way frum 'em bars, 'fore I cum in thar an stick these purty boots in yore stankin black ass!" His temper riled, "You Gotdam, rotten-assed bastard! Cum up heah fuckin wit me on Christmas. I oughta throw yore mawdickin ass in that pisser. By God, if it wuzn' Christmas, thas whar you'd spend the next thirty or forty days!"

The harangued con dropped his head, stuffed his hands into his pants pockets, and began to shuffle away. Looking back over his shoulder like a whipped dog, he muttered, "Merry Christmas ta you, Cap'n Suh."

"You jes kiss my Merry Christmas ass," Cap'n Smooth snarled, "you low-down sonuvabitch!" Looking up at the picket, "Boss, now that that sonuvabitch dun quita fuckin wit me, I wantcha to call all them ol' nigguhs up heah to the front whut needs them false teeth, an git all 'em one-eyed fuckers up heah too."

"Ya'll hold it down in thar so I kin heah that Cap'n," Boss Humpy hollered down to the tanks. "That Cap'n wonts alla you nigguhs whut needs them false teeth an ol' eyes to cum on up heah to th' front. Rat now!" He added, "If ya'll wont this shit, you betta quit draggin them ol' asses roun an git on up heah!"

Cap'n Smooth propped his boot on top of one of the boxes as he talked to those gathered at the tank doors on both sides of the hall. "I'm gonna git that boss to open 'em doors an let you nigguhs cum out heah under this picket to git you a set uv these fuckin teeth thas in this box," indicating the one he had his foot atop. "An you ol' nigguhs whut needs eyes, they in that box rat thar. Ya'll understand that?"

Shouting to Boss Humpy, "Open them doors an let these nigguhs out."

The tank doors opened and the disadvantaged filed out in semi-orderly fashion. Bad Eye, One Gone, and Gotch Eye cautiously began opening the eye box, while Rat and Gila Monster gingerly opened the teeth box.

Impatient, Cap'n Smooth barked, "You nigguhs quit

apickin over them fuckin eyes an teeth! Just gitcha sump'n an git on way frum heah! You rotten bastards kin switch 'em roun when ya'll git back in them tanks.'' Rushing them, ''Gotdam sonsabitches, gon' fuck aroun all day pickin over 'em damn thangs. Jes grab 'em an git th' hell on back in them tanks!''

Pairs of hands ripped into each box grabbing what they could. Cons were putting their teeth and eyes in as they came through the doors. Most of the plates got mixed during the scavenging and the teeth recipients were busily swapping them to come up with a matching pair. After they did, some were holding theirs over cigarette lighters, heating them in order to bend them into ''proper shape.''

Rat, our famous baseball pitcher, and some of the others made a beeline straight to the gambling tables with their presents and pawned them as collateral to get into the games. I chose to get in one of the other games that played for cigarettes and tobacco. I didn't have any use for an extra eye or set of teeth—yet.

In a nearby game, an argument broke out between Blood Eye and Squat Low. When Squat Low won Blood Eye's eye, he put it in his pocket. Blood Eye didn't like it, ''Say man, take my eye outta yo pocket!''

''Fuck you, man! It ain' nonea yo eye no mo. Dis eye is mine til you pay me my stuff.''

''I don' give a fuck, take my eye outta yo pocket, Squat Low. You ain' gon' be totin my fuckin eye roun in yo pocket.''

''Whutcha wont me ta do wit it den?''

''Why don'cha put it in yo locker.''

''Put it in my locker? Nigguh I don' wont that thang lookin at me evah time I go in dere ta git sump'n.''

Blood Eye left, soon to return with an empty, all-purpose Bull Durham sack. He pitched it on the table, ''Squat Low, put my eye in dis 'bacco sack so you won' see it lookin. Ain' nuthin in yo locker my eye wonts to see no how. Less it's onea dem homemade fuck books you got.''

''Say, Blood Eye, you blockin da cards,'' Squat Low said as he scooped up the sack and put it in his pocket.

With his mind on the game, he really hadn't paid any attention to Blood Eye and the fight was on. It didn't last too long because some of the other players quickly broke them apart. But when it was over, Squat Low put Blood Eye's eye in the sack and back in his pocket. "I'll put yo eye in my locker when I git thru gamblin."

I asked Good Eye, who was in the game with me, "Say, how cum you pick that blue eye?"

"Shit on you, man!" he said offended. "Dat's da only color dey had. It don't make a fuck ta me whut color it is, I can't see outta it no how. Jes long as it keep da air outta my head an fills up dis Gotdam hole, dat's all I wonts it to do. So don't be fuckin wit me bout it, man."

After Cap'n "Santa" had come and gone, walking down the alleyway half-asleep got real spooky. The dim light of the twenty-watt bulbs cast eerie shadows on the proud eye-and-teeth recipients' faces. Even as they slept, those with the oversized teeth grinned, and those with a big, blue eye "watched" because their eyelids couldn't close shut over them. All the eyes were one size, extra large. Sending the jumbo, blue, artificial eyes down here must have been a good laugh for somebody at the Walls. Passing through the monster colony was worse than walking through a graveyard at midnight. I barely made it to the urinal in time.

The problems those eyes and teeth caused at the face basin every morning turned the area into a battleground. Two or three brawls broke out before we could make it to the chow hall. Some con's big eye fell into the sink as he washed his face, just as another was spitting out toothpaste.

"Say man, don' be spittin dat shit on my fuckin eye, less you wonts ta die!"

Back and forth, "Man, fuck you! You oughta keep dat big ol' humbolli marble where it b'longs, stuck up in yo ass! Dat's da only hole you got it'll cum close ta fittin."

The fists flew when someone's teeth fell out and got spit on; it was the bell for round one all over again.

11

The Number 1 hoe squad got a late Christmas present. The week after Christmas our guard and nemesis, Boss Deadeye, had a stroke and died. "Yea!" It was mid-January, and Number 1 had been laying-in since New Year's. We heard through the grapevine the warden was waiting on somebody "special" to replace Deadeye.

Korea, a trusty who worked as the warden's office porter, had come in for lunch and was at the 3 tank door talking with B.C. while waiting on the call for "short-line." The trusties ate thirty minutes ahead of the field force. "That Number 1 hoe won' be layin up on dey asses much longer."

B.C. commented, "I'm sho glad, I'm tired uv lookin at 'em."

"Whoever Big Devil been waitin on jes showed up, an he called him Boss Band."

The trusty chow bell sounded and Korea left.

I asked Black Rider, "Didja hear whut Korea jes said?"

"Yeah," he said dryly, "I heard. I sho hope it ain' who he say it is. I worked under him on that Number 3 Ramsey camp back in '45. They transferred him dere cuz he kilt a whole squad over on anutha camp. I sho hope it ain' him! Boss Deadeye wudn' shit 'pared ta him."

All ten of us began talking about the new boss. Finally, Tennessee spoke with authority. "It happen, it sho happen! Kilt evuh last one uv 'em." Clarifying, "Now I wuzn' in his squad when he dun it. Guess ya'll kin see dat. But I wuz on th' camp at th' time.''

Chinaman said, ''Say man, quit hem-hawin roun an tell us whut happen or shut the fuck up.''

Tennessee was taking his time with the story. Always out of smokes, he was enjoying the free cigarettes being passed around. After bumming a light to fire up the cigarette he had just bummed, ''Th' way I heard it frum suma th' trusties who weked roun dem bosses' houses when dat happen wuz dis.'' He left us hanging as he again stopped to expound. ''Now ya'll know how th' grapevine is. Sum you kin bleeve an sum you has ta wonder about.''

Anxiety got the best of Whitefolks and he could take no more, ''Say, lissen alla ya'll, lissen a minute.'' He took the floor, ''Tell ya'll whut, les don' give dis nigguh no mo lights, no mo cigaritts, no mo nuthin til he tells us whut he knows!''

We nodded our heads in agreement with his suggestion.

''Awright, awright, I'm gon' tell ya'll. Don' ya'll be in such a Gotdam hurry. Hell, we ain' got no where ta go.''

With a thick blanket of cigarette smoke filling the air, Tennessee began again. ''See, Boss Band had a house boy, least his wife did,'' he chuckled, ''whut cleant an cooked fer 'em. Th' way th' trusties tole it wuz th' house boy wuz bout ta root Boss Band outa house an home.

''Anyhow, th' house boy an Boss Band's wife got in a squabble bout cleanin up th' house. He spose to talk back to th' woman, sassed her out real good when she told 'em to do sump'n. Well, when Boss Band cum home dat evenin, she told 'em th' house boy had sassed her out. She tole Boss Band jes enuff to git 'em punished a lil' bit. Jes to show 'em she wuz still his boss, even if dey wuz gittin it on.

''Afta she tole Boss Band, he lef runnin fo th' buildin. He fount dat house boy in th' tank, an told 'em if he cum back to wek he'd kill 'em. Den he went to th' warden's house to demand sump'n be dun to his ass. It didn' matta ta Boss Band th' warden had jes sot down to eat his supper. Th' warden say it could wait til mornin, an he'd look into it.

''But th' warden knew how mean Boss Band wuz an had dat house nigguh hauled off in his car to anutha camp dat same night. Next mornin, Boss Band cum to th' buildin an fount out th' nigguh wuz gone. Th' warden wouldn' tell 'em where he sunt 'em.

"When th' turnout bell rung, Boss Band took his squad out an tole 'em to wek on way frum th' uthas. Dey sped up an weked on way frum th' utha squads. Whilst dey had dey backs turnt ta 'em choppin, he opened up wit dat pump scatter-barrel. He mowed 'em down, two an three atta time. Dem whut he didn' git wit dat scatter gun, he finished off wid his .45. Dey say he blowed suma dem nigguhs half in two. Holes in 'em big nuff to put yo two fists in, all foteen uv 'em!

"Das why dey calls 'em Kill-A-Band. Cuz when we useta set roun talkin bout it afta it dun happen, we useta say, 'Man, dat boss kilt a whole band uv nigguhs!' His reason wuz dem nigguhs tried to 'git in th' saddle' wit 'em. Eben afta he dun kilt dat many folks, he nevah missed a day's wek er nuthin. All dey dun wuz transfer 'em over to th' Ramsey camp.

"We heard thru th' grapevine dat he sho straightened out dat Number 1 hoe over dere in a hurry. Hell, he wudn' at Ramsey a month an kilt two mo." Laughing a little, "Dat's when his wife lef him. Dat muthafucka's got a graveyard alla his own. I sho hope it ain' him. Ef it is, dis nigguh sho gon' put on his travelin shoes!"

Our afternoon leisure was interrupted by a command from the inside picket boss, "Alla you Number 1 nigguhs, cum on outta them tanks an git out on that yard!"

We filed out of our tanks and down the hallway, walking for a change. January's wintry breath strip-searched us at the back door. The sun, just by appearing, showed its bravery. Walking through his shadow to line up against the wall, I glanced at the face half-hidden beneath the wide-brimmed hat. With the sun at his back, he stood motionless. It took a minute or so for the twenty-six of us to stagger ourselves against the wall so each of our faces could be seen by him.

After we were in formation, in a gravelly voice he asked maliciously, "DO YA'LL KNOW WHO I AM?" Nobody said a word. He broke the momentary silence, "Well, I know who ya'll is, an ya'll gonna find out who I am damn quick!''

He was about six feet tall, maybe weighing 160 pounds, and looked to be on the older side of sixty. Thumbs tucked into the pockets of his jeans, with his weight shifted to one side, he looked intently at each of us.

Kid gloves were neatly stuffed into the empty holster hanging from the extra belt he was wearing. Each bullet compartment contained a round of .45 ammunition. With that many bullets around his waist, he certainly didn't plan on running out. He wore a gabardine khaki shirt, black keen-toed boots, and spurs minus the rowels. There was no crimp in the crown of his black hat, the brim was flat all the way around, exposing the silvery, long sideburns.

When he raised his head enough so the brim no longer hid his sinister-looking face, I quickly squinted a peek at his eyes. Their icy-blue color contrasted with his heavily tanned, weathered skin. He seldom blinked, roving his eyes over us.

"I'm gonna tell ya'll one time, an one time alone how I'm gonna deal. First off, if airy one uv you tries to run off, I'm gon' kill ya. If airy one uv you 'sputes my word, I'm gon' kill ya. If airy one uv you don' do lak I tell ya, I'm gon' kill ya. If you lay th' hammer down under me, I'm gon' kill ya. And if I jes take a notion to, I'm gon' kill ya.''

Never blinking an eye, he continued his commandments in the same monotone. I was holding my breath between each blunt statement. *Was there nothing he wouldn't kill us for?*

"I don' wont no conversation wit nonea ya'll. Jes ya'll do lak I tell ya. I don' know whut ya'll dun heard bout me, an I don' give a damn. But I heard you nigguhs jes been drag-assin.'' Louder, "I'ma tellin you now, if ya'll drag 'em ol' asses roun under me, I'm gon' kill ya. That last boss ya'll had didn' git a Gotdam thang outta ya'll 'pared to whut I'm gon' git. I bet not see airy nigguh comin thru 'at backgate wit his shirt not astickin to his ass. Ain' gon' be no dry nigguhs in my squad.'' Shouting, "DO YOU HEAH ME NIGGUHS!?''

A few said, "Yassuh'' or "We heahs you, Boss.''

"When I'ma talkin ta alla ya'll at the same time, an I axe

ya'll do you heah me, ever nigguh betta stop whut he's adoin an answer me back 'Oh Lawd'! If I'ma talkin to onea ya'll, 'fore you say ANYTHANG to me, you betta say aforehand 'Oh Lawd.' Is that clear? I'm gonna say it agin, an you nigguhs betta answer me right! DO YOU HEAH ME NIGGUHS!?''

In unison, "OH LAWD!"

"If you nigguhs don' answer me back lak that when I'ma talkin ta ya, then I'm gon' bleeve ya'll tryin to big-ass me. An if I EVUH ketch any uv that ol' punkin goin on in this squad, I'm gon' kill ya!"

We had been out on the yard about twenty minutes listening to his death sermon. He reached into his shirt pocket and pulled out a spiral note pad and pencil, slowly sizing us up with his cold eyes. Back and forth, looking up and down the line, then settled them on me. "Ol' Red!"

Brain-locked, I fumbled out a partial "Yes . . .," then remembered the magic words, "Oh Lawd!"

"Cum heah! Kin you read an write?"

"Oh Lawd! Yessuh."

Handing me the pencil and pad, "Go to the fur end an start writin 'em nigguhs' names down, jes lak they's lined up 'ginst 'at wall."

I turned to leave, "And put yore name down first!"

"Oh Lawd! Speakin ta you, Boss. Do you want me to write these nigguhs' real names down or their utha names?"

"Jes the real uns. I'll learn the uthers as we go."

It wasn't an easy task. Several of the cons couldn't spell their names, and neither could I. So we just guessed at it and I hoped he wouldn't notice. After writing all the names I handed his pencil and pad back, and returned to my place at the end of the front line.

He looked over the names for a moment, and closed the pad. "Awright, thas the way I wont ya'll to ketch 'em rows, jes lak yore name is writ in this book. You nigguhs gon' wek 'zackly lak ya'll lined up 'ginst 'at wall. If I ketch airy nigguh wekin on a row outta his place in 'is book, I'm gon' kill 'em. Now, carry ya'll's asses on back in the buildin an be ready to meet that bell cum mornin. DO YOU HEAH ME NIGGUHS!?''

"OH LAWD!"

Walking away, he said over his shoulder, "Boss Band! Thas who I am."

Back inside the tank, I went straight to my bunk and flopped on it, still in shock. I couldn't believe he picked me to carry the first row. Me?! Whew, shit!! Gazing at the bottom of the bunk overhead, I thought of running away and even suicide. Fuck! I don't want to be no lead row man, but his haunting words "if airy one uv you don' do lak I tell ya, I'm gon' kill ya" burned in my ears.

My gloom was interrupted when I noticed Black Rider standing next to my bunk giving me the "last look" like I was already dead. That evening I caught the chow line. Once I sat down at the table, I couldn't eat; my appetite was gone. My belly had more knots in it than a Navy rope and was growling like an old Philco radio dialed between stations. I tossed and turned all night and bolted upright awakening myself near daybreak, wringing wet with sweat. I knew it was useless to try to go back to sleep, "Alley, Boss!"

"Lemme have 'em, Boss!"

My knees were shaking as I waited for the next call.

"Number 1!"

Like a lightning bolt, I charged down the hall with the Number 1 hoe squad right behind me. When the last man cleared the back steps, "You got twenty-six uv 'em, Boss," Cap'n Smooth hollered.

"Thas right."

Clearing the backgate, we got our first work command from him, "Evuh nigguh gitta hoe!"

Leading the pack, I veered for the hoe racks. In nothing flat, we had our aggies and took off like rats fleeing from a burning barn. My walking gait was good. Leaning into the wind, I balanced the hoe handle against the crook of my arm with the blade hoisted high in the air.

"Ol' Red!"

"Oh Lawd!"

"Head 'em on over to that highline turnrow an ketch in."

"Oh Lawd!"

Glancing over my shoulder, I saw the other squads coming behind in the distance. We were a good forty yards ahead of the closest one, Number 2. He galloped his horse to stay up with us as we burned rubber going down the turnrow. Three or four miles later we were there.

"Tail row nigguh! Count off twenty-six rows. Ya'll ketch 'em, an git on way frum heah!"

After Bad Eye stepped off the first row, I caught it—just like it was "writ in the book." I couldn't remember the exact order I listed all the names, but I knew Cap Rock's was the first after me. He got his push row position back. Because Bad Eye's name was the last one on the list, he fell heir to Chinaman's job.

Thousands and thousands of empty rows stared us in the face. The work force had to "air" the rows out by hacking and pulverizing the soil. It was close to planting time again and this helped dry the land out faster. We hacked down one side of a row to the end and came back hacking down the other side. The weather had been clear the last several days and the winter sun dried the top layer of soil.

I was middle ways into the field on my row before I looked back and saw the last squad, Number 8, catching their rows. I sank my hoe blade deep as I could each time I dug it into the soft, black gumbo. We had to do more than just break the crust, the rows had to be flattened. On the way back down our rows, we passed Number 2 hoe. They were still about twenty yards from reaching the end for the first time.

Even though a cool, crisp breeze blew across the fields, my shirt was sticking to my back. Just like the lawgiver said, "Ain' gon' be no dry nigguhs in my squad." I gutted the inside of my row each time I sank my aggie blade into the earth. It was still hard to believe I was the lead row man, the pacesetter.

Lunch was short on the johnny ground. We were rushed through our meal by Cap'n Smooth, "Ya'll betta hurry up an eat that ol' hog an bread, an git on back out yonder an finish up them rows."

We made a pit stop at the water wagon and headed back to work. *It wasn't as bad as I thought,* I said to myself, with each savage hack. Number 1 hoe had been sailing all day.

None of the other squads even got near us. I was holding my own and keeping my row out front. We hacked up and down row after row after row. The sun was going down. Cap'n Smooth had left; Sundown was in charge. He would keep us out until the sun's last glimmer. He didn't hassle the cons but he sure hated to knock off.

The other squads had slowed down just a hair as quitting time neared, but Number 1 hoe was still driving hard when somebody hollered, "Dere it is, it's in th' air!"

We made a dash for the turnrow. After he counted, "Ol' Red!"

"Oh Lawd!"

"Take 'em on to that house. Go Head. Hey Boss! Pull them Gotdam heifers over out the way, an let these Number 1 bulls cum on by," Boss Band shouted up ahead.

With the right of way cleared, "Ol' Red! Bear down!"

"Oh Lawd!" speeding up the walking cadence four more notches.

At the backgate we waited for Boss Band to check in his weapons and give the "go head" signal, "Ol' Red!"

"Oh Lawd!"

"Git over yonder! Resta ya'll nigguhs, go head!"

For what? I dared not ask.

I stood at the backgate until the last man in Number 8 hoe went through the gate. Out of all the 200-plus field workers, I was the only man cut out.

After shakedown, Cap'n Smooth marched me through the gate. As we walked toward the building, "Speakin ta you, Cap'n."

"Whut?"

"Cap'n, whut'd I git cut out for?"

He spat tobacco juice, "Dry up that ol' mouth. I don' want no talk, nigguh."

Once inside, "Boss, hand me down a pair fer this nigguh." After cuffing me tightly to the bars, "These cuffs'll git a nigguh's heart right."

Hanging about four hours, the pain made me forget my anger. The cuffs were one thing all the cons agreed on, "They can make the blind see, the lame walk, and the deaf hear."

212

The hours snailed by until finally the bright lights were on and the turnkey unlocked me. I made it to the latrine quick as I could, splashed water on my face, and got ready for breakfast. Even though the last time I ate was at the johnny ground, I wasn't all that hungry. Just tired as hell and aching. My rib cage felt like somebody had taken a crowbar and pried them six inches apart.

"Number 1!"

At the end of the day when we got out on the turnrow and headed for the building, I didn't let up. The squad was strung out behind me like a string of beads, running to keep up. Occasionally, I heard complaints behind me to "slow dis muthafucka down, man."

We were panting when we arrived at the backgate. I was so exhausted I was about to drop, but wasn't about to show it. I had run them raggedy all day.

"Go Head!"

I could hardly wait to get on my bunk after supper. I was half-asleep when several Number 1 hoe workers came over to my bunk. "Say man," Cap Rock said. I opened my eyes. "Whut th' fuck wuz dat shit all bout? Rippin an runnin up an down dem fuckin rows lak you wuz crazy or sump'n, an dat man wuz on our asses lak stank on shit. We wuz lucky he didn' cut us all out at th' backgate."

Jack Hammer added, "Yeah, man. You wuz messin wit our hog an bread doin dat!"

"Well," I said, "seems thas the way ya'll wanna do it. None uv ya'll don' thank I kin carry the lead row nohow. Hell, I didn' ask for it! What wuz I spose ta do? Not take it?"

Their blank stares told me that no matter what I said, I was still unwanted.

Cap Rock spoke up again, "If dat's th' way you feel bout it, you know you gon' hafta burn ever onea us out. Cuz afta dis shit you pulled, we gon' CARRY yo lil' ass awhile! An I don' thank you kin hold 'em."

"We'll see," I said as they walked away. I closed my eyes again, trying to drift off to sleep. Cons having nightmares, screaming out, crying and moaning all through the night made sound sleep hard to come by. Plus in the wee hours the lecherous building tenders went on the prowl. And the creatures of the night, Ol' Toe Sucker & Company, came out.

Like Toe Sucker, these vampires lived in the tank's ghetto, the back bunks closest to the commodes. When the tank lights are dimmed, that end is the darkest. Along with Toe Sucker, these phantoms waited until others went to sleep to attack.

A couple of them were just bold pests and fairly harmless. If they saw a con's leg hanging off his bunk, they'd tip-toe up to him, feel and rub on it, and jack off. The sneakier ones really didn't go for blood and were content just to pass by an exposed leg or thigh, touch it quickly, go on to the back and jack off while sitting on the commode gazing back up the alley at it. The few who actually climbed in the bunks with sleeping cons and started hunching them got their asses beat so much they finally kicked the habit.

Lying awake, I thought about the Raw Hide and Bloody Bones bedtime story Emma told me when she had "company" and wanted me to go to sleep in a hurry. I carried that damn salt box to bed with me many a night, just in case I couldn't go to sleep fast enough. It only took a little salt to get rid of him, but for these wee-hour roamers I kept a bar of prison soap in a sock so I could put a knot on one of their heads if they crept up to my bunk.

The endless cycle of seasons brought us back to corn harvesting. When we first started pulling it, four huge John Deere combines were sent to the camp to help us out. Every row the combines harvested was a row we wouldn't have to pull by hand. Those fourteen-foot sacks full of corn got mighty heavy to drag down them long, city-block rows.

Number 1 hoe was moving through the wind-tangled stalks like a swarm of hungry locust. When we got to the end of our rows we emptied the heavy, gut-busting sackfuls into the trailers parked on the turnrow.

We were "high rollin" and close enough to take a better look at those rumbling green giants. The machines were doing the whole operation at one time: pulling, shucking, and spitting the kernels into a tractor-drawn cart running alongside.

I looked up from my row to see Big Devil's Chevrolet speeding down the turnrow, leaving a swirl of dust behind. His presence in the field automatically caused everybody to speed up. He stopped directly in front of our squad and got out.

While sitting on the hood talking with Cap'n Smooth and Sundown, Big Devil pointed toward the combines. I was dumping my sackful into the trailer ten or fifteen feet from them when Big Devil beckoned for Boss Band. He walked his horse over to the car.

"When yore nigguhs finish emptyin up, take 'em over yonder an ya'll ketch in next to them combines. Brang them rows back thisa way," motioning across the field.

"Whut if we ketch up wit 'em?"

"Go roun 'em," Big Devil quipped devilishly.

"Awright, you Number 1 nigguhs, git them Gotdam sacks emptied up an git on way frum 'at trailer. Suma you nigguhs gon' git a loada buckshot in yore ass if you don' tighten up!"

"Ol' Red!" Whenever he called out my "name," it sounded like he was calling a horse.

"Oh Lawd!"

"Head 'em ovah yonder an ketch in next ta them combines. Take 'em on!"

As we flew to the rows to catch in, Big Devil sent the other squads in the opposite direction. This left only the Number 1 hoe squad pulling corn on the same side of the turnrow as the combines.

We covered the couple hundred yards, fanned out, and caught in headed the same way as the four combines. Cap Rock and I were out front, speeding down our rows. The rest of the Number 1 workers were angled off, in hand shaking distance of each other. We pulled within twenty yards and were catching up.

Big Devil borrowed Cap'n Smooth's horse. He looked like he was riding a pogo stick bouncing up and down in the saddle as the horse galloped toward the combine supervisor. The cons operating the equipment, along with their supervisor, were transferred from unit to unit to help with the corn and maize harvests.

When he reached the supervisor's pickup, the supervisor jumped out and pulled off his hat. After their brief conversation, the supervisor walked out across the field, and waved his hands until he got the operators' attention. He gave them a hand signal to rev up their engines, pull out the throttle, and run the machines wide open. The combines began pulling away from us until . . .

Boss Band shouted, "Ol' Red!"

"Oh Lawd!"

He fired a shot into the ground behind me. It was close enough to kick the dirt up on my back. "You bet not let them fuckin combines gitta way frum you! The resta you thangs betta lay wit 'em!"

He rode his horse back and forth behind the squad, using his reins as a whip to drive and prod. "Git them Gotdam rows on up yonder wit that lead row nigguh!"

He shot again—somewhere. I pulled corn so fast it was like I put it on automatic. All the squad could see was the tail end of my sack. The scent of that gunpowder was all the additional motivation I needed. My sack was getting heavier and heavier to drag, slowing me down.

Boss Band spotted my cumbersome handicap, "Ol' Red!"

"Oh Lawd!" I thought he was going to shoot again.

"Whenever you git a sackful, jes git out uv it, an leave it lay. Resta you nigguhs pull up even wit that lead row nigguh's sack an git out uv 'em."

He hollered across the turnrow for Water Boy Brown to bring some empties. He dropped the large bundle in the middle of the squad. We grabbed two empties apiece and tore out again. The combines finished their rows and were heading back on others with a fifty-yard lead on us.

Boss Band galloped to catch up, yelling final instructions to the water boy, "Have sum mo sacks waitin at the utha end when we git thar."

We spread out across our twenty-six rows and caught in behind the combines. Big Devil watched through his binoculars. I glanced over at Cap Rock, "I'm goin after 'em. Pass

the word an tell 'em to cum on. Let's show them muthafuckas we kin do it!''

When the word reached Bad Eye, we double-clutched it
after those combines like a pack of whippets. My sack was
full middle ways down the row. I dropped it, unfolded the
empty hanging from my free shoulder, and lit out again.
When they evened with my full sack, they did the same. The
machines had the edge, they never stopped.

I was gaining. I filled up another sack and got an empty.
This time when I bent down and straightened up again I
reached the end of my row the same time the combines did.
They were catching more rows, and going the other way.

The squad finished their rows and got fresh sacks. We
took off down the turnrow to catch in, this time right beside
them. Boss Band fired again. That last shot evened EVERY-
BODY with the machines. The combines were running wide
open—but so were we.

The noisy engines drowned out Boss Band. He must have
said something, but we didn't hear. He rode his horse to the
front of the squad and I saw his mouth shout out, ''Go
Head!'' as he leveled his scatter-barrel at us.

We passed the combines and beat them to the end by at
least thirty feet. The operators shook their heads in disbelief
when we went by. There would be no catching us now. We
were reaching the ends of our rows a good twenty yards
ahead of them every time. We kept it up all day. Big Devil
was so pleased with our performance he radioed the agricultural director at the Central Unit to send the heavy equipment trucks to come pick up the combines, and ''take 'um
sumwhere they need 'em.''

After supper, Cap Rock walked up beside me at the face
basin, ''Lil' ol' nigguh, we gon' run yo ass so damn fas you
ain' gon' know if you comin or goin!''

''Say man, fuck alla ya'll rat dead in the ass! What th' hell
am I spose to do when he shoots an tells me to tighten it up? I
don' plan on gittin shot for goin too slow! If you can' keep
up, tough shit! Didn' none uv ya'll wait for me when I useta
be way behind. If you don' lak the way I'm carryin the lead
row, why don'cha tell it to th' man!''

''Look, man, you know you can' hold me if I really want

to pass yo ass. An you sho can' beat me pickin cotton! Only reason I been lettin you stay aheada me is I don' wanna job you to th' man.''

"Bullshit! You ain' been 'lettin' me do shit! Cap Rock, I kin outwork you any day of the week!''

"I'm damn sho gon' see when cotton pickin time cums roun agin! Thas how I got my name,'' he said, referring to an area in West Texas known as ''the Cap Rock,'' noted for growing cotton. "I wuz born an raised in a cotton patch,'' he boasted.

"An that's where they gon' bury yo ass if you keep on fuckin wit me! Cap Rock, we don' havta wait til cotton pickin time. Me an you kin git it on anytime!''

Later that evening Slocum, who had just returned from the Walls hospital from a hernia operation, told us Road Runner had died about three months ago.

It was so bad now that the months ahead would outweigh a motherfucker by ninety pounds. The workers in the squad tried to run me down one by one. On a daily basis, somebody challenged me to a ''burnout'' by working ahead or walking in front of me on the turnrow. And nobody is supposed to be in front of the lead row man.

Most of the cons were just mouth and if they could hog you they would. From experience I knew the first blow generally won the fight, so the very moment anyone threatened, I struck. Boss Band never cut me out for fighting. So rather than race with them one by one, I began hitting them with my hoe, fist, or whatever, to make them stay in line behind me. I chopped Kool Ade in the head with my hoe and damned near took off one of his ears for walking ahead of me on the turnrow. When he fell, Boss Band made me and some of the squad drag him off to one side for the water wagon to pick up when it came by.

It was cotton chopping time again, and we must have been working fast enough to please Boss Band. At least he hadn't shot yet. I looked out of the corner of my eye and saw that Railhead Shorty had pulled up beside me. "Say man, gitcha ass back in line where you blong!'' I growled. He kept chopping his row even with mine, grinning and gunning his motor by chopping a little ahead of me. I hollered, "Oh Lawd! Gittin 'em over heah, Boss!"

"Go Head!"

We took off. Nearing the end of our rows for the first time, we chopped side by side. Hurrying to beat him out on the turnrow and to the next set of rows, I tripped over the raggedy legs of my pants, got up quickly, and tore after him. I saw no signs of his letting up as he swooshed his aggie blade between the young cotton stalks plucking out the weeds, leaving the standard four stalks to the hill.

I shifted into "double-nuther" gear and went by him so fast it threw his timing off. In an effort to catch up, he stopped chopping and walked up even with me, leaving a long skip of grass behind him.

Boss Band rode over to check our rows, saw the grass Railhead Shorty left, and made him go back to re-chop it.

He stayed right at his heels, cursing him with every breath, driving him to catch up. Railhead Shorty made it to the turnrow and dropped down on all fours. Boss Band tried to trample him with his big black horse, Ol' Satan, who had a cold-blooded disposition and would attack when we got too close.

Railhead Shorty barely rolled out of Satan's path. Boss Band tried again. He got to his feet, staggered and stumbled toward the squad, but fell again. Boss Band hit him with the barrel of his shotgun as he tried to get up. Blood splattered, Railhead Shorty was sprawled out in the middles.

"Ol' Chinaman, Ol' Mae Widder! Cum back heah an drag this rotten bastard out yonder on 'at turnrow. Tell 'at water nigguh to po sum water on 'em when ya'll git up thar."

They grabbed an arm apiece and began dragging him. "Onea you nigguhs cum back heah an git that sorry sonuvabitch's hoe an take it wit 'em."

Both dropped Railhead Shorty's arms at the same time, and started back for the hoe. "I jes need onea you nigguhs!" They put on the brakes. Boss Band shouted angrily, "Ol' Chinaman! Git this Gotdam aggie 'fore I shoot both uv you ignant bastards! Tell that water nigguh when he gits this nigguh revived tell 'em he betta ketch up wit us, cuz if I havta go to that house 'thout 'em I'm gon' kill 'em. Resta you nigguhs git on way from heah! Go Head!''

We finished chopping a couple more sets of rows. Railhead Shorty was on his way back and soon as he got to us he caught in and started chopping.

Boss Band slowly walked Satan over and stopped him about ten feet from me. I felt his eyes burning in my back, ''Ol' Red!''

''Oh Lawd!''

''Whar you frum, nigguh?''

Here we go with that ''whut color wuz yore mama'' shit again. ''Longview, Boss.''

''Well, they ain' got no cotton to mount ta nuthin in Longview,'' he commented.

''Nawsuh, they sho don't.''

''Whar you learn how to chop cotton lak 'at?''

''Right heah, Boss.''

''How long you been heah?''

''Goin on five years, Boss.''

''I wuz watchin yore row when ya'll wuz goin up thru thar to see if you wuz gon' be leavin a buncha them weeds. Gotdam me, I never seed a nigguh racehossin up an down a row lak 'at, an clean it thatta way.''

He paused a moment. ''Thank thas whut I'm gon' name you. OL' RACEHOSS!! Thas whut I'ma namin you. You heah me nigguh!?''

''OH LAWD!''

''When I calls you that, you betta answer!'' Then shouting to the squad, ''Did the resta ya'll nigguhs heah that?!''

''OH LAWD!''

''Ol' Racehoss, ya'll take 'em rows on away frum heah! Go Head!''

From then on, ''Ol' Racehoss'' was my name. The bosses called me that, and the cons called me just plain Race, for short.

When we got to the field the next morning and caught our rows, Cap Rock took off down his and got ahead of everybody in the squad. I kept a steady cotton chopping beat, allowing him to get no more than three or four feet ahead of me. He had a good drag, and held the lead all the way to the end. Even out on the turnrow when we headed to catch some more rows, he walked slightly out in front of me, jobbing me. The squad knew what was going on, and by now, so did Boss Band. Cap Rock was "askin" for my job.

Back on the turnrow after lunch he walked out ahead again. Boss Band hollered, "Ol' Racehoss!"

"Oh Lawd!"

"You betta quit yo drag-assin, an git ta carryin 'at lead row!"

I stepped on out and regained the lead position, "Gitcha jive-ass back in line, Cap Rock!"

He slacked back just a hair. Looking over my shoulder as we sped down the turnrow, I hollered, "Oh Lawd! Speakin ta you, Boss!"

"Whut?"

"Takin Ol' Cap Rock a roun or two when we ketch in!"

"Go Head!" We'd been cleared to duel.

He pitched Bad Eye the fourteen-inch file he kept hanging from the horn of his saddle, "Put a good edge on both uv them nigguhs' hoes."

This took a few minutes. When Bad Eye finished he re-turned the file and re-took his place on the tailrow. Cap Rock and I waited for Boss Band to give the signal.

"Go Head!"

Neck and neck we left the blocks. We quickly pulled away from the squad. Boss Band hollered at us, "Ya'll, carry them rows on away frum heah!"

The pace was brutal, and my race with Railhead Shorty the day before had made my body sore. We covered at least four feet each time we dragged our hoes down either side of our rows. One of the first things I learned, "When you choppin cotton, jes git the grass an don' move no mo dirt than you hafta."

I barely skimmed the ground's crust with my hoe. On the next set of rows, I took a slight lead, pulled away, and kept lengthening the distance. After about two hours into the race I lost count of the rows we'd chopped, but I was far ahead of him.

Boss Band called me back, "Ol' Racehoss! Cum on back ovah heah in the squad. This goat-smellin' sonuvabitch dun laid the hammer down!'' He herded Cap Rock back into the squad, trying his best to ride him down with Satan. "If I ketch anutha onea you bastards in fronta Ol' Racehoss on 'em rows, I'm gon' kill you!'' Adding, "An you nigguhs stop acrowdin him when ya'll out on 'at turnrow. Next nigguh I see acrowdin him, I'm gon' blow th' top uv his Gotdam head off! DO YOU HEAH ME NIGGUHS!!?'' he bellowed.

"OH LAWD!!''

Cap Rock and the others wouldn't dare push me any more. They would work and walk where they were supposed to and let me set the pace, Boss Band would see to that.

The hungry years under the Band forged me a body "'thout a ounce uv fat on it.'' My legs were lean and muscular like a distance runner's; like a racehorse's. My chest looked like I'd been pumping iron. I'd been slow baked in the sun's oven like the men of the desert. Hands rough as sandpaper with layers of hard calluses lining the palms. No more blisters from the brogans without socks.

Boss Band pushed me beyond any limits I dreamed I had. He forced the word *can't* out of my vocabulary. He gave no alternatives, it was do or die. At times I felt like throwing up both my hands and screaming "Kill me! Kill meeee!!''

He compelled me to recognize, to look, to become aware of where I was and what was going on all about me. I had become confident and I had opened my eyes to nature. I'll never forget the day I fell in love with the *rain*.

That day, it had been so hot I saw little heat devils jumping on the glistening turnrow. The only dry spot on my body was my throat. That day, the heat made me dizzy and I began to imagine things. I thought I saw a hawk light upon a cloud in that endless blue sky which held the glaring sun diamond in its navel. Two or three cons had already collapsed in the heat.

We started hollering for rain like a bunch of croaking frogs. In less than two hours a light shower came from the Gulf and cooled us off. The rain cloud wept her tears and left. We moved to a dryer cut across the turnrow and worked on. Ol' Hannah must have laughed while drying and suck-

222

ing the sap from my bones. At least a dozen men had fallen and were dazed, and lying under the water wagon. I was near collapse, I just hadn't dropped. The rain blew her cool, soothing breath across my face just before she came again.

I glad-watered but nobody noticed, I was wet all over, thanks to her. Her persistence forced Cap'n Smooth to wave his hat.

Another day Hannah hung high and bore down, asking for it every step we took. All day we'd kept up a hellish pace. As if possessed, the Band drove us with unrelenting fury, and we'd made three revolutions around the other squads. Drag-stepping in our heelless brogans, we glided down the turnrow, enveloped in our own cloud of dust, a shivering mirage.

Suddenly, Satan let out a loud, eerie neigh, and fell over dead, pinning Boss Band underneath. We finally drove the big, black bastard down and jobbed him to the man. He wouldn't be biting us in the ass any more when we got too far behind.

Jack Hammer, Thirty Five, and Mule rushed back and grabbed Satan by the legs, hoisting him off Boss Band. Like the Pony Express, the livestock supervisor delivered a fresh steed. Looking more evil than ever, he unsaddled the carcass and quickly saddled his replacement. And the Band played on, "Go Head!"

That evening at the backgate Boss Band cut the three rescuers out to be punished. The next day in the squad he called them back, "I'm tellin ya'll heah an now, ain' nairy one uv you nigguhs heavy wit me. I oughta kilt ya'll fer doin sump'n I didn' tell ya do. Gitcha Gotdam asses back to wek!" He fired in the ground behind them as they ran back to catch their rows.

At night in the tank we sat around and joked about who jumped the highest and how long he stayed in mid-air after Boss Band shot behind us. Tonight, it was Jack Hammer, Mule, and Thirty Five on the butt end. When Boss Band shot behind them, Mule remained running in flight a good eighteen seconds, according to our "stop watches." He was declared the top "air walker" in the Number 1 hoe squad.

It was July; the cotton was growing well. Soon, we would

start picking. After we chopped it for the last time, we headed to the woods. Acres of bottom land could be cleared before the cotton blossomed. The only good part about working in the woods around the snakes, scorpions, and leeches was that it provided us with a source of meat. Since it was seldom served in the messhall, we were allowed to take any varmit we could catch to the building to get it cooked. All we had to do was holler "gittin it over heah, Boss!" and take out after it.

Boss Band loaned out his pocketknife to clean the catch. One of the feet was left unskinned so the cooks could tell what it was and how it should be cooked. Possums, coons, rabbits, squirrels, armadillos, and any other edibles were run down and caught. Nothing was safe near Number 1 hoe. When somebody in the squad hollered "dere it go," "it" was dead meat.

Some cons were so fast they could catch a running rabbit in a matter of seconds. Each man in the chase got a share of the kill. It was taken in that evening after work and served at supper the next night. Terrible fights broke out when the cook got the meat mixed up and gave it to the wrong cons.

I wasn't allowed to run varmits, I had to keep the lick going. Because of this, I got cut in on whatever was caught. Runnin Time caught an owl once and had it prepared in the kitchen. I was going through the chow line right behind him to ensure my piece of the fowl.

The cook came from behind the steam table and handed him a pan containing the cooked bird with the shortest drum sticks I'd ever seen. Runnin Time now had a pan in each hand, but wasn't passing up a thing on the steam table. Owl or no owl. When we got to the chocolate pudding, Runnin Time held the pan of owl forward.

The flunky looked confused as he waved the ladle over the pan for a place to pour it. They were holding up the line. "Say man, where you wont me ta po dis shit?"

"Dumb-ass nigguh, if dis wuzza turkey an dem wuz cranberries, you'd know where to put it. Po it over dis fuckin owl!"

That night I ate my first and last piece of chocolate covered owl.

Due to the density of vast underbrush, the woods afforded the best possibilities for escape. With such limited visibility, there was no way the bosses could see all of us all the time. In the woods, we were the closest to the "Big Brazie" river, which was the main escape route. Boss Band counted constantly.

Tarzan was in his finest element in the woods. He loved it, and if anything, the woods weren't wild enough for him. He was a husky, barrel-chested, gorilla-looking con, with long hair growing on his muscular arms. He didn't have any top or bottom front teeth, which made him look like he had fangs. When he opened his mouth, it looked like a huge python's.

Whenever Tarzan caught a varmit, he didn't waste time waiting for the cooks. He used his fangs to snap its neck. Then he'd bite the head off and spit it on the ground. He didn't want to eat "no brains," but ate everything else, blood, guts, hair, and all! Usually, whatever he ate was still kicking as he chewed.

Always, after he finished a meal, Tarzan let out a loud, jungle-like holler that caused Boss Band's horse to rear in fright. All the birds in the trees would fly away and the small animals scurried to safety. I would have loved for Tarzan to walk up on Bloody Bones out in the woods. That oozie bastard wouldn't have lasted five minutes around him and would have been gobbled up, without the salt.

With all that blood on his face and around his mouth, Tarzan reminded me of a little playmate I grew up with, Marie. But us kids called her "Meat Reetie." She was Floyd's sister, even uglier than he, with two-inch Buckwheat plats all over her head.

Miss Bertha took Floyd, Marie, and me to the creek to catch crawdads. For some reason she always handed the raw liver she bought for bait to Meat Reetie to tote. We'd be walking in front of her toting the poles and buckets and look back to see her mouth and face covered with blood. She'd look at us so innocently, with the most blank-looking expression, while smearing it all over her face trying to hide the evidence. Miss Bertha ended up spitting snuff juice on small pine cones, and we'd catch plenty of crawdads anyway. Meat Reetie looked funny; Tarzan did not.

Nobody liked to sit next to him in the messhall. We always tried to leave an empty seat between him and us. He slobbered and spat food all over the table as he chewed ravenously. When he said, "Pass de salt," we all leaned back to let his foul breath pass on by. We certainly didn't want to get breath-poisoned by the "funky breathed muthafucka," as he was referred to under our breaths.

Going to the woods was like going to the Big Top, a circus without the tent. It wasn't unusual to see cons pulling brush or axing trees with live baby snakes dangling from their ear lobes. They applied pressure on the snakes just below the head, forcing them to open their mouths, then clamped them on. Looking at those Medusa-earred jokers, I knew the classification committee had really blown it . . . again. Tarzan wasn't the only crazy one out there and the woods seemed to bring out our wilder sides.

Because the thick brush and foliage obscured Boss Band's view, it provided cover for Cowfucker. He was always on the prowl for any loose cow who strayed into our work area. That sentence he got for "cattle theft" hadn't curbed his lust one bit. I don't know how he could catch one of those half-wild cows without a horse and a real rope, but he kept right on trying.

The story told on the camp about him is that he was a student at an East Texas college and was sneaking off campus fucking a cow. The relationship developed to such proportions that "she" started coming on campus "lookin" for him. She would stand outside his classroom window, and moo for him to come out.

It's claimed he would actually leave campus with the cow in tow under the pretext of taking her back to her rightful owner. This happened so often that the college officials put him under surveillance and finally caught him in the act. Cowfucker was standing on a five-gallon bucket laying it to her. Since his "woman" belonged to one of the wealthy ranchers, the sheriff gave him a "genjuine old-fashion ass-whuppin" right there in front of her, hauled him off to jail, and he wound up down here. It's hard to imagine preferring cows over a campus full of coeds but he boasted many times that "If a cow could cook I'd marry one."

It had been raining recently and the forest was steaming. Boss Band split us into three work groups; the cutters, the trimmers, and the brush pullers. We all loaded the heavy logs except Whitefolks. Boss Band didn't know he had a bad back, but we did. Nobody wanted to lift logs with him as a partner so when we split up into our regular three-man loading teams, Whitefolks kept pulling brush. Boss Band had a policy about loading logs, "Thar ain' no fo nigguh-sized logs out heah. Three's high as they go."

The cutting teams felled quite a few of the tall timbers. It was time for us to pull back to help the trimmers catch up. Then we'd load. Enormous piles of trimmings and underbrush hissed and crackled in the flames no more than fifty feet from our backs. What little wind there was blew all the fiery heat in our direction.

After we helped the trimmers and loaded, my four-man cutting team went back to axing. We worked at a furious speed to get further into the woods away from the fires. Two men cut at the same time on opposite sides of the tree. Each pair struck our blows in time with our grunts to avoid hitting the other pair's swinging axes.

When I heard Boss Band holler "Ol' Glodine!" I glanced back at the brush pullers. I saw that Glodine's ass was really dragging. Boss Band had been driving him all day. "Don'tcha be adraggin no mo uv them damn lil' ol' twigs up heah ta this far. Go back yonder an grab sum mo uv them limbs. You Gotdam rotten-assed ol' whore! I oughta blow a Gotdam hole thru you! Go ta wek!!"

Glodine had a strange look on his face when he hurried over to my tree to gather limbs. He walked up so close that Bad Eye had to stop cutting.

"Whut's the matter wit you man?!" I asked.

"Will onea ya'll chop off my han if I lay it on dis tree?"

"Man, you crazy? Hell naw! I ain' gon' chop off yore fuckin hand," I said.

Bad Eye, a mean bastard doing life, said, "Put it up dere, I'll chop th' muthafucka off."

I stood stunned as Glodine laid his right hand against the

227

tree mumbling, "I can't take it no mo, I got ta git way frum Boss Band an dis place."

Big Louzanna and Cryin Shame, the other pair, stopped cutting when Bad Eye asked, "You sho you wonts yo han chopped off? Ain' gon' be no uh-oh. When I hits, it's gone."

Gritting his teeth, Glodine muttered, "Do it, man."

Bad Eye WHACKED it off, right across the knuckles. Glodine never made a sound, cradled what was left of his hand, and dropped to his knees.

I hollered out, "Oh Lawd! Got one wit his hand hurt over heah, Boss!"

Boss Band rode over, "Whut happen ta that nigguh's hand?"

Bad Eye blurted out, "Oh Lawd! Boss, it wuzza accident. Th' nigguh walked up heah rat in th' way."

Boss Band stared at each of us a moment, then rode away. He radioed back to the building with his walkie-talkie for a pick-up truck to "Cum take one in."

We were still standing around after the excitement until Boss Band shouted, "You nigguhs git ya'll's asses back to wek! That ain' th' first time ya'll seen nigguh blood. Git back to wek! Go Head!"

The next day we were three men short. Replacements for the Number 1 hoe were slow to come by. Elefin Head and Cryin Shame got a rare lay-in. They caught poison ivy and "swole" up so bad they couldn't go to work. I saw them before we left the building and they were hardly recognizable. The last thing Elefin Head needed was for anything to swell up his head; it was already two sizes too big.

Cryin Shame actually looked better. With his face swollen out of proportion, he wasn't his regular old neanderthal-looking self. He was so named because it was said, "He so ugly it's a cryin shame." Somebody in the tank was always jazzing him about his looks and said things to him awfully hard to take.

"Ugly muthafucka, ain' no tellin whut yo daddy musta 'cused yo mama uv doin when he seed yo ugly ass."

"Nigguh, if yo daddy's ugly is you, he got to be sumwhere in a zoo. Who you take afta?" Before he could answer, "Naw, don' tell me! I don' wanna know dere's anutha muthafucka on earth ugly is you."

The cons cracked up at their facetious remarks, and Cryin Shame laughed right along with them.

Their affliction gave me an idea. When we got back to the woods, I was going to get into some poison ivy so I could lay-in and rest up too. Soon as we reached our destination in the woods and started axing, I caught Boss Band not looking and made a beeline for the first patch of poison ivy I saw. I opened my shirt, scratched my chest and arms with some briars until I bled, then rubbed the poison ivy all over my scratched skin. I sneaked back to the crew and took up my position and resumed cutting.

I was in misery the rest of the day. The salt in my sweat was burning the scratches and I was itching like crazy. *That must be a sign it's working,* I thought as I showered that evening. I could hardly wait until morning to wake up and be all swollen and get to lie back down. Next morning I immediately began inspecting myself. Nothing had happened. When Big Tom rang, it was back to the big top for me.

Whether Boss Band knew it or not, we had grown accustomed to his style. He had a way of tipping his hand when he started fidgeting with his shotgun. This was one of those days. The activity in the woods was going full blast as we hacked our way deeper and deeper into the bottoms. The falling trees and noisy axes failed to quell the sound of the gunshot. We paid little attention to it because some boss was always target practicing or shooting at "somethin" in the woods. Our foursome continued cutting.

Whitefolks kept his voice low as he picked up the brush near my crew, "Boss Band jes shot Rapehead! I thank he's dead."

"Why'd he do that?" I asked in disbelief.

"Shhh! Not so loud man, I don' want 'em thankin I'm meddlin in his bizness."

We tapped the tree lightly with our axes trying not to drown out his half whispers. "I wuz throwin sum brush on th' pile back dere, an jes turnt to leave when I heard th' shot. I looked aroun an seen Rapehead fallin to th' ground wit a hole in his bosom big as a black diamond watermelon! Boss

Band wuz talkin to hissef lak he always do, an I heard him say sump'n bout Rapehead wuz tryin ta hide frum him 'hind th' pile.''

Whitefolks left our area and went back to pulling brush. We passed the word along to the others. Two or three of the bosses working close by walked their horses over to "see." Shortly, a pick-up truck came and we loaded Rapehead's body. Boss Band slow-walked his horse over near my crew and stopped about fifteen feet away. We were working and watching him at the same time as he sat gazing off into the woods.

"Rotten bastard, didn' b'long in this squad, didn' b'long on earth, neitha.''

That evening when we got to the building, Rapehead's body was lying at the back steps. All the squads had to step over him to get inside, a grisly reminder of what would happen if we "tried to 'scape." I knew now what Tennessee told us had some truth to it. Boss Band was a travelling executioner.

I leaned off my bunk and whispered up to Black Rider, "Say man, wonder what really made Boss Band so cold?''

"Thas th' way th' muthafucka cum outta his mama's belly.''

I lay back down feeling he was right.

On Sunday morning, as usual, the inmate preachers were circulating in the tank encouraging different ones to attend the afternoon service held in the auditorium. We were one of the last units to get a chaplain. The job was given to a feeble old fart who looked like he already had one foot in the hereafter. He pastored over a small church on the outskirts of Brazoria. When he drove up in the parking lot, it took him five minutes just to get out of his car. With the use of his cane, he slow-stepped his way straight to the warden's office. Big Devil made a point to be in his office on the Sundays "Ol' Preacher" was scheduled to preach. Their little chats usually lasted until chow time.

The inmate preachers would be watching and waiting for the moment he emerged from the warden's office. When he did, they got the "Heah Ol' Preacher cums" signal from the

4 tank lookouts. Excitedly, they started yelling to the picket boss, "Comin out, Boss! We gotta go hep da chaplain."

With standing orders from the warden, the picket boss unlocked the tank doors, "Alla you ol' preachers thas gonna hep that ol' parson cum on outta thar!"

They met him at the front gate, almost mobbing him as the eight or ten of them jockeyed for positions. One snatched his walking cane, almost making him fall down, and two grabbed him under each arm and were almost carrying him. Another toted his huge Bible, and somebody else had his hat. The rest danced and frolicked in front of him all the way to the building.

Once inside, they let him walk. He headed straight for the messhall with his followers dogging his heels. He wasn't allowed to eat in the guard's dining room, so he ate in the messhall with us. He was Uncle Tom, Uncle Moses, and Uncle Everybody Else, all wrapped into one. And they treated him that way from the warden on down. To keep him from feeling too bad, the inmate preachers were allowed to sit at the table with him and keep him company. To further illustrate it was "nuthin personal," they put a tablecloth on his table. After his belly was full of food and suckass adulation, the inmate preachers assisted him up the stairs to the auditorium.

Upon arrival, another assisting crew took over. These less privileged inmate "preacher-aides" weren't allowed to eat with him, but helped him suit up in his pastoral attire. Robed, with a huge cross hanging around his neck, Preacher took his seat behind the portable pulpit among the six main deacons. They waited for Molly, the choir leader, and the Retrieve a capella choir to complete their rendition of "Nearō My God To Thee."

The choir finished and the deacons helped prop the old man up against the pulpit. Preacher raised his outstretched arms skyward, and called out, "Ya'll know ya'll got th' best WARDEN in th' system?" Looking back at the deacons, "Do I heah a amen on THAT!?"

"A---men!! AaaaMen! Amen!"

"I'm gon' talk ta ya'll today bout truf, amen. Truf, amen, thas whut we gon' talk bout. Facts is one thang, but unfacts is sumthin else. We ain' talkin bout unfacts, naw! We gon' talk bout th' TRUF!! If you know whut th' TRUF is, then you know whut I'm talkin bout, amen? Suma ya'll dun furgot whut th' TRUF is, and you been livin in a day-dream!!''

Several "amens" came from the audience. Preacher was getting revved up. "How long will it be?! HOW LONG?!'' he shouted at the ceiling. "How long is it gon' take fo you cum into th' light, an know th' TRUF, the FACTS?!!'' He had the main deacons stomping on the floor, shouting "amen" after "amen," and nodding their heads in agreement with every statement.

"Th' TRUF!! Thas whut we heah to talk bout today.'' Leaning forward over the pulpit, looking us straight in the eyes, "Ya'll already know that most uv you b'long in heah. An ya'll jes hafta 'cept dat. I don' hafta stand up heah an tell ya'll dat. Ya'll already knows it!! AMEN!!?''

This "truth" was "amened" the loudest of all.

"Talkin bout FACTS! If you didn' b'long in heah, you wouldn' be in heah. Suma ya'll be dead if you wudn' in heah. Dis place give ya'll a new leash on life. The Lawd's been good ta ya'll.''

He was bombarded with "amens.''

"Talkin bout FACTS! I don' hafta tell ya'll there's only two ways outta heah. Ya'll already know th' mo trouble you make, th' mo trouble you gits. Ya'll oughta strive to please yo keepers, amen? Cuz if you STRIVEEEE,'' covering his ear to keep from deafening himself, "to please yo keeper, th' WARDEN will surely set you free. AMEN? AMEN!! Thas th' *right* way out. Or, you kin git buried heah, an hope yo spirit will leave. Amen?

"Sumbody gotta speak fer you. Sumbody thas got a word that means sumthin. Th' WARDEN kin speak them words, amen?''

"Amen, amen.''

"It's up to you whut you want him to say. Do YO PART! An you kin rest ashuured th' WARDEN'S gon' do his'n. It says rat heah in my Bible, talkin bout TRUF, amen? It says rat heah,'' shouting louder while pointing to a page, "if you make one step towards me, I will make ten towards you. DO

232

YO PART!! Lean on th' LAWD an DO YO PART! GAWD! and th' WARDEN will do the rest! Les pray.''

Some had to be awakened to rise for prayer. We had all heard the ''Warden Sermon'' before, it was the only one he ever preached besides ''The Eagle Stirred His Nest.'' But, I thought he would have at least mentioned something about Rapehead.

Preacher's other pastoral duty was to be our counselor. But somehow, every problem any con went to him with was quickly solved by Big Devil. It didn't take long for us to figure out it was best not to confide in him. And for God's sake, don't ask him to do something like mail a letter. Instead of just saying ''I can't'' and not do it, he went straight to the warden and snitched.

The counseled ones kept getting their asses whupped by the bosses and building tenders after talking with Preacher and got wise to him. So, after church was dismissed the congregation fled. Only the deacons, inmate preachers, and preacher-aides remained behind to help him take the holy harness off and hold a special prayer service. After ministering unto the flock, it was time for him to leave, and they escorted Preacher back to the front gate until next time.

It was no secret that Number 1 hoe was working under a whimsical maniac who drove us mercilessly from sun up to sun down. After Boss Band killed Rapehead, we developed a million-and-one new ways to watch him while we worked. When he scratched his head, we flinched. We watched him much closer than he watched us. In his heyday, Road Runner's fastest gait would have been too slow for the torturous pace we maintained for this man. Even though we worked the hardest and fastest, we knew death sat on a horse just a few feet behind us. Boss Band had wiped out Baby Raper too, for ''tryin ta 'scape.''

One day he called me back in the squad, ''Ol' Racehoss, is you evuh wondered how cum I ain' dun kilt yo yaller ass?''

''Oh Lawd! Nawsuh, Boss!''

''Well, I'll tell you why. I don' let nobody pick the nigguhs I kill. I'll do that mysef.''

After four years under the Band, the Number 1 hoe members had become the devil's advocates. Hardly a week passed without one of us getting into trouble on our tanks. We didn't take any of the building tenders' bulldogging shit and stopped them from ganging up on anybody on 3 tank. They knew we had nothing to lose. For us, going to solitary was merely a few days rest from dodging bullets.

Big Tom sounded, and when we cleared the back steps, Cap'n Smooth motioned for us to stand to the side. After the other squads cleared the yard, Big Devil came out of the building. When he wanted special work done, he pulled us out of the field to do it.

"Boss Band, take these Number 1 nigguhs up there by the entrance, an clean up that ol' graveyard. I'm 'spectin sum folks down heah an I want that thang cleaned up real good." In an irritated tone, "I don't know why'n hell they put a Gotdam graveyard rat next to the entrance to begin wit. It ain' nuthin but a eyesore!"

With the warden's instructions over, "Ol' Racehoss!"

"Oh Lawd!"

"Head on over to that hoe rack. Evuh nigguh gitta hoe! Go Head!"

The graveyard was a half mile from the yard. In a few minutes we were opening the fence gate. Boss Band rode through behind us and walked his horse over to one of the fence corners. Facing us, he backed up until the horse's tail was touching the barbed wire. He knew not to get too close when we worked away from the main work force. Some of us were just as trigger happy and eager to sink our hoes into his skull as he was to put a bullet in ours.

The Johnson grass was so tall it completely hid the graves. We started chopping, but he stopped us, "Ol' Racehoss!"

"Oh Lawd!"

"Ya'll lay them aggies down. Pull all that grass up by the roots an throw it outta thar. I don' aim fer us to havta cum back up heah day afta 'morrow."

Quickly, we uncovered the mounds. The markers bore no names, just dates. Some of them went back to the 1930s. I heard conflicting stories about who was buried in this old graveyard. Some said they were black, but others called it "peckerwood hill." At first, I wondered how could they be white, but then remembered this used to be an all-white camp at one time.

After we pulled all the grass out, the sixteen mounds had to be reshaped and smoothed over. We picked up our hoes, but Boss Band stopped us again. "Ya'll jes leave them hoes 'lone an start pattin that dirt back on them mounds by hand. I wont this thang to be real priddy fer that warden," he said sarcastically. "Plus, it'll give ya'll a chance ta whisperrr . . ."

Suddenly, Band leaned to one side, fell off his horse, and lay on the ground clawing at his chest and gasping for air. We looked at each other for a second in disbelief.

Elefin Head whispered, "I bleeve Boss Band's dyin."

We walked closer, and stood watching. Cowfucker started calling his name, "Boss Band! Boss Band! Can you hear me?"

"Shit!" Bad Eye said. "You jest wastin yo breath. Dis bad muthafucka's dead!" he said while poking him with his hoe. "Les take his shotgun an pistol an split! Hell, ain' nobody up heah but us. We kin git a good head start if we leave now. C'mon ya'll, whut th' fuck we standin roun fer? Dis muthafucka can't stop us."

Thirty Five said, "If we leave heah wit this muthafucka dead, they gon' swear up and down we had sump'n ta do wit it."

"Well," Bad Eye said, "whut we spose ta do? Jes stand heah an watch th' flies blow his dead ass?"

I said, "Naw, we ain' gotta stand here an watch 'em, but I agree wit Thirty Five, we sho oughtta stay. I'm goin over there in the corner an sit down on my ass til somebody shows up."

The others agreed, and we finally convinced Bad Eye to go along. We sat down together in the farthest corner away from Boss Band. Glancing occasionally in his direction his shotgun and pistol looked very tempting, but Thirty Five was right. Chinaman pulled out a fresh bag of "dust" (Bull Durham) and passed it around.

Lieutenant Sundown, usually the officer who checked on us when we worked away from the other squads, rode up and saw the riderless horse standing inside the fence. Half joking, he asked, "Whut ya'll dun did wit Boss Band?"

I answered, "We ain' dun nuthin wit him, Lieutenant. There he is layin over yonder."

Thirty Five added, "We wuz wekin, an he jes up an fell off his hoss. We didn' know whut wuz th' matta wit 'em."

Sundown trotted around the outside of the fence to get a better look. "Cum on outta thar an line up out heah on this road so I kin count ya'll. Ol' Chinaman, git Boss Band's hoss."

After he counted, we sat down beside the road. Sundown radioed the warden on his walkie-talkie. Then he asked, "How long has he been layin thar?" He got several different time spans hurled at him all at once.

Big Devil drove up quickly, got out of his car, and walked around the fence to look. "An ambulance is on the way, but that ain' gonna hep him none. Didja talk to these nigguhs bout whut happen ta 'em?"

"They all say that he wuz talkin to 'em, an rat in the middle uv it, he jes fell off his hoss. Sounds ta me lak he had a heart attack."

"Yeah, guess so. Ol' Racehoss, cum heah."

When he asked me what happened, I told him the same thing we told Sundown.

The ambulance arrived. While the attendants were loading him, Mae Widder mumbled, "That muthafucka sho died hard. He ain' gon' hav no hoss in th' hell he goin to. Dey gon' han dat muthafucka a hoe an put 'em on the lead row wit all dem nigguhs he dun kilt 'hind 'em, drivin his ass. Thas where I wanna go when I die, so I kin hep 'em."

After the ambulance drove away, Big Devil got back in his car. As he was turning it around to head back to the building, he hollered out the window, "You stay heah wit these nigguhs. When I git to the buildin, I'll send Boss Robles out heah to take over the squad."

Sundown waved an acknowledgment as the warden sped away. "I know ya'll sho gon' miss Boss Band. Ain'tcha?"

Sundown's question got only silence. And more silence. Nobody faded him on that shot.

12 ▌▌▌▌▌▌▌▌▌▌▌▌▌▌▌▌▌▌▌▌▌▌ ☐

The next day in the fields he called the squad together. "My name's Robles. Ya'll kin call me Mr. Robles or Boss Robles. I'm gonna call ya'll by yore names afta I learn 'em all. So don' gitchạ dandruff up if I say 'hey you' til I git a handle on 'em. Okay? Anutha thang, I ain' gonna be cussin ya'll out. I don' feel lak thas gonna be necessary. Do ya'll?"

A few heads shook in agreement.

"If any uv you would ruther I call you by somethin other than yore name, thas fine by me. When we work off by ourselves, we kin let 'em down."

He continued to speak in a manner we were very unaccustomed to hearing—no cursing, no threats. He was talking to us like men who were capable of understanding what he said. "Ya'll do what yore supposed to do and act lak men; I'll deal with the warden or anybody else I have to. Ain't nobody gonna be tellin me who to cut out at that backgate. Somethin else too, nonea ya'll don' have to git permission befo' you talk to me. But since Racehoss is our lead row man, I'd 'preciate him doin most uv the talkin when it concerns this work. He knows more about it than I do."

Boss Robles looked to be in his mid-thirties. He wasn't a big man, standing about 5'7", kinda chubby, and had a pleasant, friendly voice. There was no scowl of disdain on his face—yet. He carried no shotgun, just a six-shooter. He didn't call us "nigguh" and encouraged us not to call each other that. I heard he was a recent hire and working with the fencing squad as a utility boss before Big Devil called on him to work us.

We were just as surprising to him as he was to us and we stupefied him with the way we worked. He soon learned that he had inherited a squad of "stone down gorillas," the highest compliment one con gives another. All he had to do was sit on his horse and keep up with us.

It didn't take long to find out if he was for real or not. We were picking cotton with the Number 4 hoe squad picking next to us. Their boss, Eatem Up, walked his horse over to shoot the breeze with Boss Robles.

"Howdy do, Boss."

Boss Robles said "howdy," very uninterested.

But Boss Eatem Up wasn't the type one could ignore when he wanted to talk. Walking their horses side by side, Eatem Up kicked off again, "Gotdam, it's hot! Ain't it?" he said as he took his hat off to wipe his forehead.

"Yep."

"Say how'd you manage to git that Number 1 hoe squad? Damn, you mus know sumbody. I been carryin this Number 4 fer six years. I ask'd that man to give them nigguhs to me afta Boss Band died. I bleeve they worried that po Boss to death. I'd lak to carry them bastards fer jes one month.

"Tell you one thang, you sho hafta watch them ol' nigguhs, Boss. If you don't watch yore bizness, suma them nigguhs'll drap yore britches n' fuck you rat out heah in this field!"

This got a quick, angry glance from Boss Robles, but he held his peace.

After cramming his jaw full of Redman Chewing Tobacco, "Alla them ol' nigguhs you got kin pick hell outta that cotton, but if you don't prod an drive th' shit out uv 'em, they'll jes tell you ta kiss they black asses an lay down on them sacks."

Boss Robles continued looking straight ahead.

"You gonna hafta fuck wit 'em an have eight or ten uv 'em put in that pisser or hung up on them fuckin bars. Jes ta hep keep th' lead outta them ol' asses n' let 'em know you mean bizness. Nigguhs is jes lak mules, you hafta make 'em

238

do whut you wont 'em to. A little shower uv leather," patting the eight-plait bull-whip he used on his squad, "'cross th' fat part uv they ol' stankin asses evah now añ then is th' best thang you kin do fer 'em. Hell, they love it. You ain' gonna bleeve this, but I had a nigguh come up an thank me fer puttin this whup ta his ass."

Chinaman interrupted his conversation when he hollered out, "Gittin on th' job ovah heah, Boss!"

"See Boss, thas whut I mean. I betcha a quarter that nigguh don't bit mo need ta shit then I do. Thas they way uv fuckin roun. Evah time onea mine do's it, I make 'em brang sum back on a stick." Shouting back at his squad, "You nigguhs betta git down on that ol' head runnin an git sum Gotdam cotton in them sacks!"

Only able to elicit an occasional "yep" out of Boss Robles, Boss Eatem Up talked about everything from their low salaries to the weather, but hadn't come up with a topic yet that interested Boss Robles. "Whar you frum, Boss?"

"West Texas."

"Well, I'm frum Conroe mysef. Got me a big ol' fat half-Injun woman ta cook biscuits an hep keep me warm in th' winter time," spitting tobacco juice on the ground. "I go home on th' weekends I ain' on duty. Wit a job lak this, a man's sho gotta regulate his fuckin, ain't he?"

Boss Robles never cracked a smile.

"Say, didja evah heah th' one bout th' nigguh an white man that wuz on death row? Well, I'll tell it to you jes in case you ain't. See, they had this nigguh an this white man on death row. They wuz in cells side by side. An they wuz gon' hang 'em th' next mornin. Well, that nite that fuckin ol' white thang wuz up most uv th' night pacin back an forth jus a bawlin. It got on that nigguh's nerves an he hollered an tole 'em, 'Shet up all 'at cryin an go to sleep.' That ol' white thang hollered back, 'How kin I sleep? Don'tcha realize they gon' hang me in th' mornin!?' That nigguh tole 'em, 'Well, I ain' cryin an they gon' hang me too.' That ol' white thang said, 'Yeah, I know, but ya'll's use to it!' ''

Boss Eatem Up doubled over with laughter. Seeing no response from Boss Robles, he said, "Say Boss, you sho don' talk much, do ya? You know I been a tryin ta git sumbody to lissen to me fer th' last six years," looking real serious. "I got a invention that'd cut th' cost uv pickin this damn cotton ta nuthin. Won' nobody lissen. Best part is, it won' hardly cost nuthin to git it goin. It'd save on manpower an everthang."

Finally, he got a response. "How're you gonna do that?"

"Ah ha, gotcha 'tention did it?! I betcha wanna git in on sum uv th' profits, don'tcha?"

"What kind uv invention is it?"

"Well, it ain' zackly whut you might call a invention cuz it's been roun furever. People jes ain' smart nuff to use it. I garn-dam-teeya, it weks ever time. I'll tell you whut it is, but you gotta promise to keep it to yoresef."

He had Boss Robles's attention.

"Tell you whut we kin do," looking all around like he was about to divulge some deep, dark secret. "We kin git us a boat an go out in th' ocean an git us suma them octopussies, brang 'em back, an crossbreed 'em with these nigguhs. We'll have us sum eight-row-at-a-time cotton pickers that'll run on plain ol' watermelon juice!"

He cracked up at the way he had pulled Boss Robles's leg. Boss Robles waited until Eatem Up had stopped laughing, "Boss, I wantcha to git away frum me an my squad. And I don' wantcha comin roun no more wit that kind uv talk. You stay away frum us. Do I make myself clear?"

The seriousness in his voice was enough to convince Eatem Up to leave. He turned his horse and headed back to his own squad. Before he left, "If thas the way you feel bout it, hell, I wuz jesta funnin you."

We were going through the cotton like a cyclone for the third time, picking the "tags," scrap cotton left in the bolls. This would be used to make clothes and bedding for the prison population. I was into my seventh cotton picking season and all doubts were settled who was the fuckin' best.

At the beginning of the season, Cap Rock and I squared off in a cotton picking shootout with six decks of squares bet. I beat that chump by 90 pounds. It was sweet revenge for the days he picked off my row under Boss Deadeye. He finally knew his place in the squad—behind me. Now my cotton weights topped the field. I didn't need to piss in my sack no more.

It was early September, and we were more than three-quarters finished with our cotton crop. We finished first every year. Big Devil was nominated each year for the "Warden of the Year" award. He was the only one in the system to win it four years in succession. Naturally, he was going for five.

His strategy was to pull us out of the field along with the other top three squads and send us over to one of the other farms to "hep 'em out." This left the remaining four squads to keep on picking what was left of our crop until we returned. We had been assembled in the auditorium for Big Devil's preparatory speech.

"I'm gonna send ya'll over to th' Clemens farm to give 'em a hand. We fur nuff long wit ours to be outta danger fo bad weather hits. Clemens dun fell way behind this year. Ain' no way they gon' git dun by rodeo time, less we go hep 'em. Suma you nigguhs been over there befo. I'm gonna warn you now if ya'll fuck up over there, you gon' git punished over there.

"I'm gonna send the lieutenant 'long wit ya'll's bosses, an he'll be in charge. I want ya'll to go over there an behave ya'll's selves an don' be afuckin wit them nigguhs. Ya'll will be leavin furst thang in th' mornin."

Clemens, another all-black unit, housed mostly first offenders. Many of us "graduated" from there. It had nearly twice as many cons as "hell" with their 750-plus count. They could field an army of workers compared to us. True, we had grown to 447, but half were dog boys, cooks and messhall flunkies, house boys, garden squad, tractor squad, lot squad, shop squad, maintenance squad, dairy squad, turnkeys, building tenders, commissary clerks, and so on. This left eight hoe squads in the fields, with twenty to thirty men each to maintain over 16,000 acres under cultivation.

The next morning we were loaded onto two cattle trucks fitted with metal cages specifically designed for transporting convicts. With about fifty cons to a truck, the Number 1 and 2 hoe squads were inside the cage on the first truck, and Number 3 and 4 were in the other one. The trucks had seats welded to the floor outside the cages for two bosses to sit on. Boss Robles and "Cochise," the Number 2 hoe squad boss, sat at the rear while Sundown rode in the cab with the driver. Pick-ups pulling trailers with the horses and dogs brought up the rear.

We ate thirty minutes early, and the sun was barely rising when we got on the highway. The fifteen-mile trip took about half an hour and the driver drove us straight to the field. Heading down the turnrow to unload, we passed the Clemens squads in the field working. Some stopped picking long enough to wave and cheer as we sped by. They knew help was on the way. I counted fourteen squads as we went by.

When the trucks stopped, we were about a mile from the Clemens workers. After our four squads unloaded, we had to wait: no cotton sacks. Sundown was mad as hell. Clemens was supposed to furnish everything.

While waiting for the sacks to be delivered I couldn't help but notice the condition of the cotton. It was tall, and full of morning glory vines and Johnson grass, like it had never been hoed.

About five minutes later, the water wagon arrived with some sacks. All regulation eleven footers. I couldn't remember the last time we used eleven-foot sacks. We quickly gobbled up the pile, grabbing two sacks apiece.

As the water boy turned his wagon around to leave, Sundown asked, "Is this all th' sacks ya'll got? I kin tell you now, this ain't enuff to hold 'is bunch. You betta git us sum mo. By th' time you git back, suma these ol' bullies'll be waitin.''

"Yassuh, I be rat back.''

"Boss Robles, go rat down yonder whar that turnrow makes a L an ya'll ketch in an brang 'em rows on back thisa way.''

When Sundown finished, "Racehoss, les git 'em started,'' Boss Robles said.

The stalks were loaded and by the time I picked to the end, I had a full sack. I tied a knot in the end of it, got a green boll, marked "Racehoss" on it, and left it lying on the turnrow. Several others had filled their first sacks too, and were changing harnesses.

My second sack was over half full when the water boy came back. When I reached the end this time, I dropped another, marked it, and grabbed two more. The others who needed them did the same. We finished picking about three sets of rows before Sundown decided it was time for us to weigh up.

"Boss Robles, brang yores on outta thar an les go weigh up."

When we reached the area where they had set up the scales, Big Devil and the Clemens warden, whom the cons had dubbed "Silly Willy," sat on the hoods of their cars waiting to hear our weights. I slung my two- and-three-quarter sacks of damp cotton across the scales, and their weight checker did a double take before hollering out, "He's got 265!" Silly Willy didn't believe it and made me hang them back on the scales again. It was right the first time. Cap Rock's wasn't much different, 240.

To empty up I had to pass them, and Silly Willy asked, "Whut'd ya'll call that nigguh?"

"Ol' Racehoss."

"I kin damn sho see why," and he offered to swap Big Devil three trusties for me.

Big Devil just looked at him and grinned, then hollered at me, "Ol' Racehoss, you betta quit layin back on that sack an go ta gittin me sum mo cotton!"

"Yessuh!"

We got a quick drink and headed back. Word travelled about how much cotton we weighed up compared to the Clemens squads. On that first weigh up, our four squads picked "almost forty bales" Sundown said. He told us we wouldn't weigh up again until after lunch.

At lunch time, we loaded onto their tractor-drawn trailers and *rode* to the building. We didn't have to "run" that long distance to and from the building. "Yea!" We got there and were quickly ushered up to the auditorium.

The inside picket boss told us, "When I call ya'll, I wont ya'll to go in the messhall in yore own squad so's I kin git

243

anutha count. An that warden wonts ya'll to stay together, an not be amixin up wit our nigguhs.''

We lined up by squads at the top of the stairs and waited. The mess steward beckoned when he was ready, ''Okay, ya'll kin go on in.''

The Clemens cons were already eating before we were allowed to enter. A special section had been reserved with a row of empty tables purposely left to keep us separated. A complete hush fell over the messhall when the infamous Number 1 hoe squad walked in. They stopped eating and gazed as we passed their tables. Boss Band had made my ''name'' and the Number 1 hoe a legend in the bottoms.

Their stares told how we must have looked, and made me realize how different we were. Because of Boss Band we'd been nicknamed the ''death squad.'' We did look like the walking dead compared to the Clemens cons.

They had a fresh-from-the-crate appearance, still wrapped in baby fat. We looked tough and driven. Our heads were noticeably balder and our eyes were hidden hollows that used our faces for backgrounds. Sunken cheeks revealed jowls protruding against hard, weathered faces.

We were raggedy as a nickel mop. Our sleeveless shirts exposed arms like coils of steel. Our britches were held up with shoelaces and pieces of rope; they wore belts. They watched and whispered as we ate in sullen silence.

After lunch we picked our way closer and closer to the Clemens work force. Suddenly, Tarzan let go with his famous jungle scream. Boss Robles' horse reared and bucked. It must have scared Boss Robles half to death. This was his first Tarzan yell experience since he'd been working us. After he got his horse quieted down, he managed a weak smile, ''Whut on earth wuz that all about?''

''Ain' nuthin, Boss. Ol' Tarzan jes made a ketch,'' Thirty Five rendered.

Boss Robles was still confused until he saw Tarzan bite the head off that lizard and start chomping. He almost fell over backwards. He rode off a ways and started puking. After regaining some composure, ''Damn!''

It was after two o'clock and we hadn't weighed up since we got back from lunch. With all the cotton in our sacks that

244

we didn't weigh up before, our next weights would really be heavy. I had filled up my third when Sundown signalled for us. No one in the squad had less than two. When we got out of the cotton patch onto the turnrow Sundown immediately noticed that we were just "totin a lil' dab" to the scales.

He stopped us, "Whars th' resta ya'll's cotton?"

I spoke up, "It's on the utha turnrow. We had more'n we could tote."

Boss Robles quickly added, "Lieutenant, they filled up so many sacks I tole 'em to leave 'em."

"Awright Boss, ya'll take whutcha got on to th' scales an wait."

Sundown radioed Big Devil, "This is walkie-talkie three to walkie-talkie one."

"Yeah, go head, Lieutenant."

"Whut's yore twenny, Warden?"

"I'm over heah by Dow Chemical. Whut's th' trouble?"

"We got a problem, Warden. These nigguhs dun picked mo cotton than they kin tote. Les we piss ant it, we ain' got no way to git it to th' scales."

"Ya'll jes stay where you at. I'll be there in ten minutes. Ten fo?"

"Ten fo."

Over Sundown's walkie-talkie, we heard Big Devil transmitting with Silly Willy. "Walkie-talkie one Retrieve to walkie-talkie one Clemens."

"Yeah, I heard," Silly Willy responded, "whutta you wont me to do?"

"Well you kin git them trailers out ta th' field an haul our cotton to the scales. Thas whut them trailers is fer anyhow."

"Jes hold yore hosses, I'll gitcha sum trailers headed thatta way. Ten fo?"

"Ten fo."

By the time the tractor drivers brought our sacks and we sorted them out, Silly Willy and the entire Clemens field hierarchy had gathered. Even "Bear Tracks," the Ramsey warden, was there. He must have been in the vicinity and heard the message too.

"He's got 315." I quickly unhitched my sacks and emptied.

While waiting for the others, Big Devil called me, "Ol' Racehoss, cum over heah."

"Yessuh."

"How much you have?"

"315, Warden."

"How much you have this mornin?"

"265."

He was having a field day showing off before the other two wardens. "Thank you gon' git me a thousand today?"

"I will if we stay late enuff."

Bear Tracks asked, "This lil' ol' nigguh evah picked a thousand pounds befo?"

"I don' know, have ya Ol' Racehoss?"

"Nawsuh, not yet."

Bear Tracks continued, "I got a nigguh over on my farm we call Thousand Poun Blue I'd lak to see tie down wit yore nigguh."

"Thank you kin beat 'em, Ol' Racehoss?"

"Yessuh, I kin beat 'em."

While the wardens detained me, Boss Robles took the squad back to the field. When I got back, I told them about the contest they were setting up.

At the day's end our four squads beat the Clemens work force so bad, Silly Willy punished all fourteen squads. That evening when we got to the building, the Clemens pickers almost overflowed the yard standing on barrels and soda water boxes. They were hanging in the halls and the pissers were full. We really jobbed them, but it wasn't done maliciously, just naturally.

Early the next morning the three wardens converged on the turnrow for the "cottonathon." After leaving the conference site, Sundown came and got me. It had been decided the contestants would pick in a separate cut, and Sundown would oversee the race.

Out on the turnrow, with Sundown walking his horse close behind me, "Ol' Racehoss, I heard that ol' nigguh frum Ramsey kin pick pretty good. I tell you one thang, that man sho been a braggin on you. Thar's a lot ridin on this contest, if you know whut I mean."

"Yessuh."

The two other contestants had been assembled by the time we got there. Soon as I walked up, "Ol' Racehoss, lay yore sack over yonder 'side th' turnrow. We gonna give ya'll sum fresh 'uns. First, lemme go over the rules wit you, I dun tole these two. We don' want no buncha leaves, stalks an stems put in them sacks. If ya'll git caught wit any mudballs in them sacks, I can't speak fer these uther wardens, but I'm gon' do sump'n to yore ass. Is 'at clear?"

"Yessuh."

"We agreed to give th' winner two cartons uv cigarettes. Second place'll git one carton, an third gits five packs."

While Big Devil talked to me, the two cons had stood off to one side. When he finished he motioned for them. "Ol' Racehoss, do you know these uther two nigguhs?"

"Nawsuh."

"Well, the next thang we oughtta do is innerduce ya'll," he said smiling at the wardens. "This nigguh heah is Ol' Totem Pole, and this'ns Ol' Thousand Poun Blue."

Silly Willy entered Totem Pole, the lead row in Clemens's Number 1 hoe squad. He didn't look a day over twenty-one and was a tall, gangling con whose profile did resemble a totem pole. Just by looking at him, I knew he didn't have a chance. He didn't look hard enough yet.

Thousand Poun Blue, on the other hand, looked more like us. He was stockily built, about thirty or so. His clothes were the same dingy gray, and just as raggedy. His alleged cotton picking prowess, coupled with his blue-black complexion, had earned him the monicker. He was the lead row in the Number 1 hoe squad at Ramsey, which was a repeat offender unit, housing white and black cons—segregated of course.

All the time Big Devil talked to me, Thousand Poun Blue was giving me the once over. Now, face to face, we stared at each other like two warriors about to do battle. Both of us completely ignored the youngster from Clemens.

We got fourteen footers this time. Big Devil told Sundown to get us started. As we walked away, Thousand Poun Blue turned to Bear Tracks, "Warden, Suh, kin we hav any kind uv cigarritts we wonts?"

"Any kind you wont, Ol' Blue."

Heading to where we were going to pick, Sundown gave us final instructions, "When ya'll gitta sackfulla 'at stuff, git out uv it, and leave it lay. Sumbody'll be by to pick 'em up. Ya'll betta be sho an mark ya'll's sacks good so's you kin tell 'em apart. Anutha thang, how many rows ya'll ketch is up ta ya'll. You kin pick one at a time or a dozen at a time. Don' make a shit ta me."

The cut selected for us was some of Clemens's best. It was low, about three feet tall, and loaded. The soil was semi-soft from the morning dew, just right for fast crawling.

Totem Pole asked, "Lieutenant, Suh, how you wont us to ketch in? I mean who you wont to carry th' furst row?"

"Don' make a shit ta me."

It wasn't hard working that out among ourselves after Thousand Poun Blue caught the first two rows and lit out. Totem Pole was next and I ended up in third position. We caught two rows apiece. Totem Pole had good hand speed, but he was fighting it. Middle ways into the field, he fell back into the low part of the V. Blue and I were picking side by side.

I began to pull away from him, slightly. I knew that once I got ahead, that was it. I reached the turnrow first and caught the first set of rows coming back, "my" rows. Sundown told us when we got to the end, "Jus wheel aroun an head back th' uther way." I beat Blue to the end by about four cotton stalks.

I straightened up to rest my back a second and saw the wardens watching us with binoculars. Now Blue was picking in the middle and Totem Pole was third on the outside. Since I had no idea how long we were going to pick before we weighed up, I let it all hang out while the cotton was still damp.

When I got to the end of my second set of rows, I had another full sack. Empties were at the ends of each set if we needed them. Looking up at the cloudless sky, the sun said it was around ten o'clock. Sundown had us pick on. It was close to lunch time when he finally gave the signal. The water boy picked up our full sacks and had them lying on the side of the turnrow when we got to the scales.

Totem Pole weighed up first. "He's got 220," the weight

caller hollered. Blue hung his two and a quarter sacks on the scales, "He's got 240." I hung mine, "He's got 275."

Bear Tracks looked at Sundown and asked, "Where in th' hell did that nigguh git all that cotton frum?"

In his customary nonchalant manner, Sundown took a puff from his cigarette and looked off in the horizon. "You ain' seen nuthin. Hell, I ain' even hollered at 'em yet."

We barely got back to picking before Sundown knocked us off for lunch. This was the first time I had been with my squad since the contest started. Soon as I got on the trailer they started firing questions. "How much you have?"

"275."

"How much they have?!"

"That Clemens nigguh had 220; the nigguh frum Ramsey had 240."

The Clemens messhall was buzzing when we entered. "That nigguh from Retrieve beat both uv them nigguhs th' furst weighin."

"Fuck, I don' know why dey even put Totem Pole in it. Shit, I kin beat dat nigguh."

"I heard that nigguh Racehoss is a walkin gin."

When we got back to picking after lunch, I could tell that a lot of the wind had gone out of my two opponents' sails. I picked on away from them, stopping only to mark the full sacks I left strewn up and down my middles. The hot, broiling sun dried all the early September dew from the cotton. I knew my weight would be lighter the next weigh up, but so would theirs.

Sundown gave the signal to knock off. This time when we headed for the scales, I walked the lead point of our arrowhead formation.

I hung my three on the scales first and had 260, Blue weighed up 225, and Totem Pole had 215. We got a drink and headed back. One more to go.

All the squads had been knocked off for the last weigh up. The Clemens cons were amassed on one side of the turnrow and the Retrieve bunch on the other. Silly Willy ordered quiet so *our* last weights could be heard. I hung my two sacks on the scales and the Clemens captain hollered, "Ol' Racehoss got 185."

The convict weight keeper quickly tallied my total and handed the figures to the captain. "Thas a total uv 720 pounds fer Ol' Racehoss." Blue hung his up next, "He's got 195, fer a total uv 660." Then Totem Pole, "He's got 170, fer a total uv 605. Ol' Racehoss is th' winner!"

Bear Tracks jumped off the hood of his car, rushed over to Thousand Poun Blue, and hit him in the face, knocking him down. He stomped him repeatedly. I was glad this was our last day here. I was ready to go back "home." I know the Clemens bunch was glad to see us leave.

Big Devil must have radioed ahead because we had fried pork steaks and mashed potatoes with gravy waiting. It reminded me of the time the grand jury convened in Brazoria County and came out to the unit for lunch. It was in July, but turkey and dressing with all the trimmings was served on the line.

Big Devil came to the messhall. "I'm gonna let ya'll lay-in this weekend. Ya'll git them crops finished up this comin week an we'll have ice cream next Sadday."

A weekend lay-in during cotton picking season was as scarce as the hair on our heads. Working seven days a week with a short half on Sunday was a grinding three-month pace. The next morning about ten o'clock the commissary clerk called me to the commissary and told me I had three cartons of cigarettes to "spend."

"Boss Robles cum by an paid fer one uv 'em."

When I finished swap-shopping I had a carton left. I bought a new razor and blades, three cans of toothpowder, several bars of sweet soap, lighter fluid for my old Zippo, two bags of oatmeal cookies, and a couple of cans of sardines. Enough supplies to last me awhile. *Not a bad day's work,* I thought as I re-entered the tank carrying my goodies. I loaned out five packs for the two packs interest they would bring, and saved the others to gamble with and smoke.

With two days to rest, what was left of our cotton crop didn't last as long as a snowball in hell, and we got our ice cream.

I had never been to a prison rodeo. We were more than 100 miles from the Walls (Huntsville Unit) and I didn't like

250

the idea of freezing my balls off in those open-air trucks. It starts the first Sunday in October, and is held every Sunday during the month. Retrieve was scheduled to go the fourth Sunday this year along with the other two Brazos Bottoms units, Ramsey and Clemens.

The rodeo list had been posted with all those eligible to go. Going to the rodeo was a "privilege, not a right." All the trusties' names headed the list, then the tractor drivers, and others who had "jobs," then the field work force. Big Devil used the Hog Law book to determine who could go from the field work force.

After I reviewed the list I had to write the warden a note like I'd done in the past, asking that my name be taken off. To some, going to the rodeo was the big event of the year.

Chinaman, my regular domino partner, came to the table where I was playing.

"Say Racehoss, is you goin to th' rodeo?"

It was my play, "I don' know if I'm goin or not."

He waited until I made my play, "Well, when you gon' know, man?"

"Why?"

"Cuz I wanna know, thas why."

There was no use trying to ignore him, he wasn't about to go away. I had known him long enough to know that sometimes he was a pain in the ass.

Trying to concentrate on the game and listen to Chinaman at the same time, "Look man, I'll letcha know!"

He left, only to take a seat on one of the nearby benches. When the game ended, "Say Racehoss, man, is you made up yo mind yet?"

Then he poured it on, "Look Racehoss, man, you don' know whut you missin. Sum uv dem ol' gals goin by in cars sho be settin high. Shit they knows who we is n' do it jes so we kin see. And dem broads at the rodeo have on britches so tight man, if you stuck a pin in 'em dey'd bust."

Enthusiastically, "Shit man! I don' go up dere to watch dem nigguhs git bucked off no hosses n' tryin to ride sum big o' musty-assed bulls. I go to hussle me sum jack stuff.

"Man, I 'member last year when we went up dere. I seed a broad wit a ass so big an fine it give me night fits. Dem

251

britches she had on wuz so tight I could see the jaws! Had lips fat as Sugar Ray Robinson's boxin gloves. When we got back I nelly jacked mysef to death.''

I pondered for a minute all he'd been telling me and thought *what the hell. I could sure use some jack-material. I've just about used up all my memories.* ''Okay, man, I'm goin,'' I said, ''an you quit followin me fuckin wit me!''

Saturday night before the fourth Sunday in October, Big Devil walked underneath the picket, ''Boss, open up all uv them tank doors an send them nigguhs in the messhall thas goin to that rodeo!''

''Alla you nigguhs thas goin to that ol' rodeo, the warden wonts ya'll in the messhall!''

He walked through the messhall barking commands, ''Cap'n, I want you to have them laundry nigguhs brang a set uv clothes in heah for alla these nigguhs. I want ever nigguh to have a new paira brogans an a belt. Brang 'em a paira drawers.''

''Yessir, Warden. I'll take care uv it.''

''Take care my ass! I want it dun now!''

Cap'n Foots left the messhall running. Later, we went back to our tanks with an armload of Christmas in October garments.

At four A.M. the call went out, ''Alla you nigguhs whut's agoin to that ol' rodeo, les go eat!''

We were rushed through our meal and remained seated. A few minutes later, Big Devil came in, all decked out. He was going too.

The cage-fitted cattle trucks backed inside the yard close to the back door. ''Awright, ya'll lissen up heah,'' Cap'n Foots commanded. ''When I call ya'll's name gimme yore number n' go on down th' hall n' git on th' truck!''

Big Devil waited near the back door to inspect us and see that we loaded sixty to a truck. Within the hour, our three trucks cleared the farm with Big Devil leading the way.

As soon as we got to the highway, sheriff and highway patrol cars were waiting to escort us. Another group was waiting when we entered the next county. It was daybreak before we reached the Ramsey and Clemens trucks waiting to join the convoy at a highway intersection.

252

Unfortunately, we had Boss Eatem Up riding at the back of our cage. "I'm gonna tell ya'll sump'n, I ain' gon' have ya'll ahollerin out th' sides a' this truck at them ol' nappy headed gals. Furst nigguh I ketch awavin n' agawkin gon' git sump'n dun ta his goat-smellin ass. I wont you nigguhs to be quiet! Nuther thang, ya'll ain' gon' be a runnin all over this Gotdam truck."

I wondered how in the hell we were going to be "runnin all over" when we were almost sitting on top of each other. Before we got fifty miles down the highway, several cons had already pissed on themselves. Somebody forgot the piss cans. But, with so much wind blowing through the cage, they'd be dry by the time we got to the Walls. Somehow, I got on the wrong side of the truck when boarding and couldn't see off into the cars that went by. Nobody was about to switch for less than two decks.

It was almost noon when we got there and we quickly unloaded and were herded into the latrine area. Afterwards, we sat on those hard seats for almost an hour before show time. In the meanwhile the Goree girls kept us entertained by showing us their "stuff" when the guards weren't looking. We looked and wished.

The whole show lasted about three hours and then we were heading back to the hell.

I sat in wind-chilled silence thinking about the day's events, remembering some of the hundreds of pretty girls I'd seen. My head was so damn cold I couldn't help but remember we were the only cons there with bald heads. It started raining before we got halfway back. It was after eight that evening when we stepped off the truck. Cap'n Foots was at the back door, "Ya'll go on in the messhall, take off them clothes an tie them shoes together."

Indian givers. We stripped, and filed back to our tanks where our clothes were ready and waiting. I finally thawed out and went looking for Chinaman. "Look man, a million years frum now, don' never ask me to go to anutha onea them muthafuckas! It ain' worth it." He just stood grinning at me like Fu Manchu.

13 ||||||||||||||||||||||| ⬜

A herd of wild elephants foraging in the African jungle wouldn't make as much noise as we did stripping sorghum cane. The task was threefold and Boss Robles left it to me to get us organized. I chose the fastest workers to do the cutting and the slower ones to handle the loading. Everybody in the squad helped strip the razor-sharp leaves off the cane going down the rows. Coming back, we split up into sections. The cutters hewed the stalks while the loaders came behind gathering and loading it onto the trailers. When the loaders fell behind, we cutters helped load to keep them caught up.

When we stripped in the afternoon, it wasn't too bad, but not so in the early morning when the cane was still wet with dew. The leaves let go reluctantly. My hands were semi-soft from the moisture, and almost every time I reached up to the top of a stalk to strip it down, I cut my hands. My bloody palms looked like they had been sliced repeatedly with a razor blade. I ripped off a piece of my pants leg and wrapped it around my palms. When we knocked off for lunch and got out on the turnrow headed for the building, I noticed I wasn't the only one. Once we reached the building and got to the tank I headed straight for the face basin. After washing my hands, I saw what a real mess they were.

The turnout bell rang. Back to the cane field. After lunch we quickly finished up where we had left off and caught another set. My hands were bleeding again from more fresh cuts.

About midway I stopped, "Boss Robles, my hands is in bad shape," turning my palms up for him to see, "an some uv the others is too."

After looking at my hands he shook his head. "I see 'em, Racehoss, but I flat don' know whut to tell you, 'cept ya'll take yore time an try to be careful strippin them leaves."

The last part was okay, but there was no way we could take our time. Not us. I worked on a little farther, thought about the pisser, and dropped my cane knife. Fuck it! I quit! And sat down on my row.

The rest of the squad quit. Soon, squad after squad sat down in the middle of their rows and placed their hands over their heads like we had done. The call went out, "Them nigguhs dun bucked!"

Meanwhile, Cap'n Smooth told the bosses, "Roun 'em all up in one bret an gather up them can knives."

Cap'n Smooth ordered security phase two: "Ya'll drive 'em tractors an trailers up heah alongside these nigguhs an park 'em," talking to the tractor drivers who were hauling the cane to the syrup mill. They quickly obeyed his orders and, soon as they completed the operation, he ordered them to sit with us.

"Suma you bosses wit them shotguns, tie yore hosses an git up on 'em trailers." Like commandos, they responded and took their posts. Boss Robles was excluded, he only carried a revolver. The "commandos" took it a step farther and laid the hammers back.

With all secured, Cap'n Smooth directed his attention to us. "If you nigguhs don' git up offa ya'll's asses an git back to wek, you gonna wish you hadda."

He walked Ol' Cherry, his big strawberry roan, right into the crowd. We shifted and slid left and right to keep from being stepped on. He stopped in the center of the circle, "You Gotdam impudent bastards betta git up offa ya'll's asses an git back to wek! Ya'll heah me?!"

We didn't budge. He walked Cherry throughout the crowd. We squirmed, twisted, and reshuffled to stay out of her path. He shot a glance at some of the other bosses who were still on horseback. They got the message and began walking their horses in and out of the crowd, hitting us with the reins, "Git up offa ya'll's asses an git to wek!"

They quickly got back in their positions by the trailers when they saw Big Devil's car coming.

Dust was still flying when Big Devil and three pickups loaded with officers and bosses halted on the turnrow in front of us. Some were carrying baseball bats and axe handles.

When he got to us, "Who started this shit?!" After no reply, "Cap'n, you know who started it?"

"Well, Warden, that Number 1 hoe wuz the one to quit first, if thas whutcha mean."

He tried to get Boss Robles to single one of us out, but he wouldn't. He told the warden we all quit at the same time. Determined to find out "who," he used another tactic. "Alla you Number 1 nigguhs that wanna go back to wek, stand up."

Nobody moved.

"Any the resta you nigguhs that wanna go back to wek, stand up," surveying us.

We all remained still. He motioned back to the waiting bosses to move in closer with their bats and axe handles. Every available man had been brought along, even the mess steward. Big Devil called to Cap'n Foots, "Brang 'em cattle prods outta the back seat uv my car."

Cap'n Foots delivered the half dozen or so "stingers," and Big Devil handed one to whatever bosses happened to be standing nearest him, and ordered "use 'em." Armed with a bat in one hand and a battery operated cattle prod in the other, this bunch started kicking and jabbing those on the outer perimeter.

Then they moved into the inner circle and poked us indiscriminately, trying to elicit a response of some kind they could really attack. After this failed, Big Devil ordered them to stop.

He pulled back most of his key officers for a conference and decided it was best for us to stay in the field until things were resolved. "Don't wont them nigguhs a tearin up 'at buildin.'' A good two hours had passed since the sit-down began.

I suppose it was prison policy to report a mass rebellion such as this to the bigwigs at the Walls, because before long we heard a plane buzzing overhead. It was the Texas Prison System's own. The horses stirred nervously as the small aircraft circled the field at low altitude and landed on one of the turnrows about a mile away.

Big Devil was there waiting. A man got out, hurriedly entered the awaiting vehicle and they drove away from us.

The unit's entire security force had assembled in the field, forming a huge ring around us. The bosses pulled some trailers together on the turnrow and formed a platform. Car doors opened, the visitor and Big Devil slowly walked toward the platform and mounted.

"My name is Jack Heard, I'm the Assistant Director. I'm here to find out why ya'll refuse to work. I talked to the warden, now I wanna hear what you men gotta say. I want somebody to tell me why you quit.''

Silence. He must be crazy asking someone to stand up and talk in front of all these guards and Big Devil to boot. What's going to happen to the one that does it? He sure as hell won't fly back to the Walls with him.

He repeatedly asked that somebody stand up and speak, but nobody would. Finally, "If somebody wants to speak up, I give you my word nothing's gonna happen to you for it. Is anybody gonna come forward and speak up or am I gonna have to issue orders to put ya'll back to work?''

Most of the cons in my squad cast their glances at me. I took a moment to weigh the promise he had made and stood up. When I did, he beckoned me to come forward.

"What's your name?''

"They call me Racehoss, Sir.''

Big Devil added, "This is the lead row nigguh in the Number 1 hoe squad.''

"You wanna tell me why you refuse to work?''

"Yessir.''

"Well, tell me then.''

"Sir, I ain' sittin down cause I don' wanna work. It's cause my hands is all cut up,'' showing them to him. To my surprise, Cap Rock walked up and showed his. Then all the rest raised theirs to show.

"How'd this happen? Why don't ya'll use gloves?"

"What caused it is the sharp edges on the cane leaves, Sir. When they wet, it's hard to strip 'em off without cuttin our hands and fingers nearly to the bone. We don' have no gloves, Sir. They don' sell 'em in our commissary, an even if they did, mosta us couldn' buy a pair."

He looked at Big Devil, "How come you don't have gloves for this type of work?"

Big Devil squirmed, "We got 'em on order Mr. Heard, we ain' received 'em yet."

His decision was quick, "Take these men to the building. I don't want 'em back out here til you get gloves. Is that clear?"

"Yessir, Mr. Heard."

After the head count we started walking down the turnrow. Mr. Heard stopped us, "Hey! Ya'll come on back here and git on these trailers."

For supper that evening we got two pork chops apiece, mashed potatoes, gravy, biscuits, and apple pie for dessert. All we could eat!

This strike ended quite unlike the buck the time in the spinach patch when it was freezing. Everybody quit then, except Hollywood. Big Devil took him back to the building in his car, gave him a job, and punished the rest of us. The 100 percent seemed to make a difference.

The next morning about nine thirty a truck arrived from the Walls. The turnkey unloaded a dozen cardboard boxes full of cloth gloves, made by the Goree girls. We were each issued a pair, and we waited for the turnout bell while reading our love notes written inside the fingers.

Once out the backgate, Boss Robles had me head for the trailers. We were going to ride to the field! Big Devil purposely had the trailers parked a good three or four city blocks from the backgate, just to show he was still on the throne. As we rode to the field, I thought about Boss Band. He had probably turned over in his grave!

The work situation in the fields changed dramatically. Boss Robles always had treated us like men, but now he

258

acted proud to be our boss. The other squads looked up to and admired us. We became the big brothers in the field. I was able to slow the work pace down so all the squads could keep up. Something totally unacceptable in the past.

Boss Robles lifted the silent system that we had worked under for so long. There was no longer the threat of death if one of us stopped working long enough to roll a cigarette. He streamlined the row hacking operation too. He stopped us from hacking down one side of our row all the way to the end and hacking down the other side coming back. Since we walked right down the top of the row anyway, he convinced Cap'n Smooth we could cover more ground if allowed to slow down a little and hack both sides of our rows while going down them. He was more concerned with the quality of our work than how fast we did it. Of course, picking cotton was still every man for himself and we still had to face the Hog Law.

Boss Robles struck up a mild friendship with the old boss over the Number 5 hoe squad. Boss Skeals was too funny to pass up and I liked to listen to him when we worked beside his squad.

He never stayed close to them like the other bosses did. He'd be at least twenty-five yards behind. His dialogue was filled with threats. By two o'clock he'd cut all his cons out for the day. But rarely did he ever do it at the backgate.

Totally unconcerned, "You nigguhs betta blacken dem rows, blacken 'em, I tell you. You nigguhs go ta sinkin dem hoes up to th' eye. Go to movin dat dirt roun lak you aim ta do sump'n. Now I know ya'll is all bad an I'm makin suma ya'll mad. But I don' give a damn. Ya'll ain' the baddest nigguhs I dun ever seed. I seed a whole lotsa nigguhs badder'n ya'll is.

"I'll bet evuh onea you ol' thangs is down heah fer murder ta let ya'll tell it. Shit, th' only thang ya'll evuh dun kilt is biscuits in dat man's messhall. Git ta wek an git dem rows on way frum heah!! I bet ya'll thank I'm gon' follow ya'll's black asses all over dis man's plantation an not do sump'n ta you. I kin tell you rat now, thas a damn lie! Jes wait til we git ta dat backgate."

Boss Skeals had been carrying the Number 5 hoe squad

259

for many years, but he couldn't name four cons who worked under him. Well beyond the sixty-year mark, he had a grubby old prospector look about him. He always needed a shave and his clothes were always dirty, stained with missed tobacco spits. He had a terrible odor and a running sore on the right cheek of his ass. A big wet spot showed through the seat of his pants whenever he wasn't in the saddle.

He had worked around black cons for so long he developed the mannerisms and even talked like them. He had more experience guarding convicts than any of the field bosses. Prior to coming to Retrieve, he served twenty years as a guard at the Angola Prison in Louisiana. He loved to talk about Louisiana. The cons in his squad who had served time in Angola or happened to be from Louisiana had it made. All they had to do was let him talk and throw in an occasional "thas right Boss," and go through the motions of working.

That is, until he saw Big Devil's car in the fields. When that happened, he immediately switched his conversation to chewing the con out for "laggin back," threatening to cut him out at the backgate if he didn't tighten up.

I overheard him doing that one day with Braggs, one of the few he knew by name. He was carrying on a two to five year Louisiana conversation with him. Somehow, Big Devil's car got by him and he didn't see it in time to straighten his act. He pulled his car right behind our two squads and parked.

"Boss Skeals!" the warden shouted. He didn't hear and kept right on talking. "Boss Skeals!" a little louder this time. Somebody in his squad finally said, "Boss Skeals! Boss Skeals!"

"Whut th' hell you wont, nigguh?! Can't you see I'm talkin? Thas whut's wrong wit you nigguhs now, always buttin in sumbody's bizness!"

The con finally got a word in, "Boss, I wuz jes tryin ta tell you th' warden is back dere callin you."

"Ol' Braggs, you bout th' sorriest nigguh I evuh seed," leaning forward in his saddle to really let him have it. "Don't you thank I gits tired uv watchin you drag yo ass aroun? Whut'd you say?! Nigguh, you bet not open yo mouf!

"How cum you won' go ta wek? How cum you make me beg you ta wek, nigguh? Why you so bitterly 'ginst it? Is wek evah kilt anybody in yo family? Is you evah heard tell uv anybody dyin frum it? I tell you whut nigguh, I'm damn sho gon see if I can' BEG dat man into doin sump'n ta yo rotten ass when we gits back ta dat house!"

Big Devil sat on the hood of his car trying to keep a straight face. After thoroughly chewing out Braggs, "Did I heah suma ya'll say sump'n bout dat warden 'while ago?"

"Yessuh, Boss, we been tryin ta tell you th' warden's been callin you."

"Well, why in th' hell didn' ya'll say so!? You damned ol' thangs be runnin them ol' moufs so Gotdam much, a man can't heah hissef fart. Git ta wek!"

Removing his hat quickly was the fastest move he'd made all day. He slowly turned his horse around and began walking it toward the car.

"How you feelin, Warden, Suh? You doin awright today, Suh? Sorry I tuk so long in acomin, I didn' know you wuz back heah. But as you knows, these ol' nigguhs be runnin them ol' moufs worse'n a bell clappin in a goose's ass. I jes got thru tellin one uv 'em he betta quit runnin his ol' head. I'm sho glad you showed up. He'll take his ass ta wek now."

"What nigguh is it thas givin you trouble?"

"Warden, Suh, you know whut I cum ta learn?"

"Whut's that Cliff?"

"Alla dem ol' wide mouf apes look so much alak I can' hardly tell 'em apart." Scratching his chin, "I can' thank uv dat nigguh's name to save my life. But I know whut I'm gon' do, I'm gon' cut th' whole damn batch out, dat way I'll git dat rotten bastard. Whut wuz it you wonted to see me bout, Warden?"

Big Devil had as much fun as anybody listening to his thigh-slapping humor, but wasn't about to let him off the hook for not adequately guarding his squad. "Skeals, you betta go to watchin 'em nigguhs an make 'em go to cleanin them rows. Yore nigguhs is goin down thru there leavin halfa that wek.''

''I'm sho glad you seed that, Warden! I been callin dem rotten bastards back all day. I'm so tired uv it I jes don' know whut ta do. Dey won' lissen ta me, Warden. Warden, now dat you is heah, kin I axe you a favor, Suh?''

''Yeah, whut is it Cliff?''

''Warden, would you take my hoss an ride out in dat field an tell dem rotten bastards o' mine how BAD you wont sump'n dun to dey black asses?''

Nobody was about to sit in the saddle after him. ''Cliff, whut I called you fer is to tell you I kin see ya'll's rows a mile away. Them nigguhs o' yourn is jes flat out big-assin you.''

''You right, Warden, you sho right! Only thang keepin me frum killin sum uv dem rotten bastards is I don' wanna give yo farm no bad name.''

''Whutta you mean?''

''Whut I means is th' way you runs th' damn thang. You th' bes warden I ever been under. Ain' no mounts o' money dat could git me ta take on yo worries. Thas why I do's evah thang I kin ta try not ta worry you no more'n I hafta. Is sump'n worryin you, Warden?''

''Yeah! Sump'n's worryin me. It's worryin hell outta me the way you let them ol' nigguhs o' yourn jes drag 'long, lak they waitin for the damn flies to blow 'em.''

''Warden, I'm sooooooo glad you said dat I don' know whut to do!! Jes soon as you leave I'm goin over yonder an put dem rotten sonsabitches ta wek, one way or anutha. I dun had enuff.''

''How cum you can' do it while I'm heah, Cliff?''

''Well, Warden,'' looking at him point blank, ''I respects you too much, I don' wont you no where round when I gits back ta dat squad. I couldn' stand fer you ta see whut all I'm gon' do. Sides, I couldn' sleep tonite knowin I dun messed up yo suppa.''

Big Devil didn't have a come back for that much tarnished humility. Shaking his head, he got in the car and drove away.

All the squads got to the end in good succession and we

quickly lined up and headed back. I slowed it down a notch to allow Number 8 to work their way up even with the rest of us. We were still snickering at Boss Skeals's conversation with Big Devil.

When all the squads got lined up and were working side by side again, I looked over at Cap Rock, "Les rock 'em." Cap Rock picked up the lick, and the con next to him, and the next, and so on down the line until our 200 hoes were hitting together thunderously, causing the earth to tremble beneath our feet. I cut loose with one of our work songs:

"We got forty-fo hammers rangin in one line."

"Forty-fo hammers rangin in one line."

"Ain' no hammer heah that rangs lak mine."

"Rangs lak mine."

"It rangs lak silver, an it shines lak golddddd."

"Rangs lak silver, an it shines lak gold."

"The price for my hammer rangin ain' never been told."

"Ain' never been told."

"So les raise 'em up higher, and then drop 'em on down."

"Drop 'em on down."

"They can' tell the difference, when the sun goes down."

"When the sun goes down."

We must have sung Boss Skeals and his horse to sleep. While we were singing, his old horse had wandered behind another squad. Both had their heads hanging down. Boss Cochise detected Boss Skeals had fallen asleep and alerted the others not to awaken him. The horse and Boss Skeals came right out on the turnrow still following the wrong squad. We watched him go down the turnrow, dead asleep.

Once all the squads were out on the turnrow the bosses felt they'd let the joke go on long enough. Cochise hollered, "Hey, Boss Skeals! Hey, Boss!"

Boss Skeals flinched and sat up erectly. Eyes blurry, he looked around and didn't see the three or four cons he knew. "Yeah, whut is it, Boss?"

"Boss Skeals, I hate ta 'sturb you, but you been followin the wrong squad." The other bosses cracked up.

Boss Skeals waited until they finished laughing, "Dey all nigguhs, ain't dey?"

Besides Boss Skeals's antics, the tractor squad was another main attraction. They put on a show for us when they plowed nearby. They plowed the rows straight as arrows with the front wheel of their tractors reared up like a motorcycle daredevil.

Thirty Five plowed while steering with his feet and rolling a smoke. Crazy Folks filed on a "piece a' sump'n" he hustled at the shop making rings, tie clasps, and other sellable "jewelry" as he tilled the soil.

The "toast ridin" feat was the grand finale. They all lined up and leaped off their moving tractors, ran along beside them, undid their water jugs, took a drink, "salud," crossed over in front, and remounted on the other side. It was no secret that those jugs were usually filled with "chock," a home brew made from Irish potatoes, sugar, yeast, dried fruit, and water. At any given time any of them could have been busted for PWI (plowing while intoxicated). It was no secret either, that the tractor squad was "the warden's niggers."

To keep the roads smooth, on Sundays the warden would have Pug and Brady drop the cultivators on Brady's hot rod tractor and hook on the cable-drawn two-by-twelve planks to drag-sweep the main turnrow. When we were up in the auditorium, we could see them through the windows as they performed their no-holding-onto-nothing-allowed "plank skiing" stunt. We bet on each ride.

They took turns riding the planks while the other zigzagged the tractor across the road, trying to throw the plank rider off. Going full speed, the driver would lock one of the wheels and turn sharply to create a wide, sweeping "pop the whip" effect. When this didn't get it, the driver was the loser and they'd switch places. According to our score, the match was 3-1 in Pug's favor.

Something was really going on; I thought maybe the Feds had taken over. Never had so many big shots from the Walls Administration visited our unit back to back. The week before it had been a group from the Education Department down to teach us a word association memory technique, and

264

then it was the prison system's clinical psychologist, Dr. Gates.

"Any man can change for the better, but he's gotta want to. He's got to have that itchin, achin, burnin desire for self-betterment." When I first saw Dr. Gates I thought he might have been the Governor. He told us, "I'm going to start a pilot program of group counseling sessions where we can talk out our problems through discussions and interacting with one another.

"The program'll begin next Thursday afternoon and will be held each Thursday thereafter for sixteen weeks. Those who are selected to attend will only work a half day on Thursdays. Selection of the twelve participants will be left to the warden's discretion."

"He sho didn't hafta say dat," somebody mumbled.

The only logical reasons I could come up with as to why Big Devil selected the twelve of us was either he'd gone crazy, or didn't give a damn if it worked or not and was just appeasing the administration. We were all field hands, except Hollywood and Rev.

After Big Devil finished laying down "the law" about classroom behavior, "Ya'll got any questions?"

Nobody had any. That is, except Flea Brain. "Yassuh, Warden. How cum ya'll don' put Poke Chops in heah wit us?"

Big Devil didn't dignify Flea Brain's question with an answer, instead he shot him a scornful look and dismissed us. Thursday rolled around. "Funny school day," the cons had labeled it. The count was clear and Boss Humpy let us out.

When we entered the auditorium, Hollywood and Rev were already seated, chatting with Dr. Gates. They got a head start because their trusty tank door was kept unlocked and they could wander about at will. We sat nervously waiting to be included.

"Good afternoon," Dr. Gates greeted. "I already met these two fellas. Why don't we get acquainted, I'm Dr. Gates. Now let's start with this fella right here, what's your name?"

Flea Brain didn't give anybody a chance to speak and

blurted out, "How cum ya'll ain' got Poke Chops in dis class?"

"I didn' know ya'll were allowed to eat up here." Joking, "Next time I'll try to remember to bring something."

The class erupted, and so did Dr. Gates, which I'm sure made Boss Humpy wonder what in the hell was going on. Finally we laughed ourselves down and Proud Walker explained between laughs, "Dr. Gates, he ain' talkin bout poke chops you eat."

"Well, if we're not talking about the kind you eat, somebody wanna tell me what we ARE talking about here?"

Proud Walker, in his finest hour, was quick to decipher the Pork Chops intrigue. "Dr. Gates, he talkin bout anutha nigguh NAMED Poke Chops."

"Nowww I got it. Thanks for helping me out."

The class had gotten back to semi-calm, and Dr. Gates directed his attention to Flea Brain, "What's your name, fella?"

"Flea Brain."

"How come they call you that? Do you know?"

"Yassuh, it's cuz my brains ain' no bigger'n a flea."

"How do you know that?"

With foolish pride, "Das whut th' Warden say an th' Warden don' lie."

"And you believe that your brain 'ain't no bigger'n a flea' just because the warden said it?"

You better watch out Doc, you're treading on thin ice. If you don't, Wise-em-up's nightly heralds of "you gonna hafta talk ta that warden in the mornin" will ring true for you.

"Well, now that I know Pork Chops is a who, why do you want him in the class?"

Flea Brain was not the bashful type when the subject was Pork Chops. "Jes cuz I luvs him an he need to be where I is an I need to be where he is. See, me and Poke Chops be together a long time."

"In other words, you feel that your friend Pork Chops should be in the class because you're in it."

"Dr. Gates, he be mo'n a 'frien,' Poke Chops be my woman," and sheepishly added, "an sumtimes I his'n."

Silence.

"Oh. I see."

Overwhelmed by his frankness, Dr. Gates jumped at the opportunity to do a full flea brain analysis. "Do you feel it's wrong to have sex with a man?"

"Dat's all dat's in heah. I gits punished when I gits caught jackin off. Most uv us can' git to dem cows, mules, an horses lak dem lot nigguhs. Whut we spose ta do?"

Flea Brain had stymied the good doctor. "If you don't want to be in the class because Pork Chops ain't in it, then the best thing for us to do is get you out of it. You go on downstairs and have a seat underneath the picket. I'll talk to the warden on my way out."

After Flea Brain left we spent the rest of the afternoon listening to the good Doc describe his escapades as a "RAF pilot in WW II." Even with Flea Brain gone, he had his work cut out for him. There was the silent bunch, Earthworm, Crazy Folks, Bad Eye, Cowfucker and me. Nelly Nuthin, Proud Walker, Bow Wow, and Fistfucker were the vocal dunces who tied up the class with their illogical questions and arguments.

Rev and Hollywood were the ad-libbing duo. They tied up the class expounding on Dr. Gates's statements. Their suckassism was the most boring part of the class, but Proud Walker would come to the rescue with his cockeyed questions that caught the good doctor off guard.

Dr. Gates was going hot and heavy, "A man is judged by his behavior. A man is no better or worse than his behavior makes him. You are no more or no less than what you've become up to this very moment. We're the sum total of our behavior."

He should have finished before he stopped to ask if we were "with him." Proud Walker apparently wasn't. "Dr. Gates, sump'n bout dis I don' unnastan . . ."

As the weeks wore on, the good doctor repeatedly talked about pride, fair play, humbleness, and respect for others, whenever Proud Walker hushed long enough to let him finish a thought. He was doing his level best to convince us we could "change." But he didn't know this was no place for fainthearted gentlemen.

At the end of the sixteen weeks we held our graduation exercise in the auditorium and received our certificates of completion. My first . . . for anything.

The next morning, Friday, it was business as usual. After Big Tom sounded, Cap'n Smooth hollered up the hall, "When you Number 1 and Number 2 nigguhs come out, pull over to one side an wait. Awright, lemme have 'em, Boss!"

"Number 1!"

Soon as I cleared the steps, I veered the squad over by the laundry. Number 2 did the same. It took about fifteen minutes to get the count clear; then Big Devil came out onto the yard.

"Boss Robles, Boss Wilhite (Cochise), ya'll go git sum shovels an picks. Take ya'll's squads roun in front uv my office an I'll meet ya'll."

"Yessir. Okay, Racehoss, let's go git us some tools."

We got them and met him on the shell road in front of the office. "Boss Robles, Boss Wilhite, I want ya'll to go rat out there," pointing to the open field of Johnson grass, "on the utha side uv 'at parkin rail and commence diggin."

We stood poised and ready to dig up the world. "Tell ya'll whut, I best walk over there wit ya'll an show you 'zackly whut I want." Walking across the road, "Brang ya'll's squads an follow me."

He walked to the center of the field and pointed down, "This is where I want ya'll to start."

"Whut're we diggin, Warden?" Cochise asked.

"A fishin pond."

"How big's it gonna be?"

"Well, it'll be plenny big enuff when I git dun wit it."

Looking at the area I thought, *he ain' bullshittin*. And with two squads digging it with picks and shovels, I'd discharge the rest of my sentence on it. Big Devil "walked it off." According to his calculations, the pond would end up being 100′ by 100′. "And we're goin down bout six to eight feet."

"Warden, you ain' plannin on goin fishin in it no time soon, is you?" Cochise asked.

Big Devil smiled mischievously, "Jes soons ya'll git it dug."

"Warden, you gonna stock it?"

"Gotdam, Wilhite! It wouldn' be no damn fishin pond if it wudn' no fuckin fish in it."

Boss Robles, waiting for an opening, asked, "Warden, you got any more orders 'fore we git started?"

"Yeah, take yore Number 1 nigguhs an spread 'em out in a circle heah in the middle. You nigguhs spread out in a circle roun me. Spread out wide 'nuff apart so ya'll got room to wek."

Then he had Number 2 encircle us. "Now thas th' way I want ya'll to start. You Number 1 nigguhs start diggin in the center heah, an pitch 'at dirt back to these Number 2 nigguhs. They'll throw it back outta the way, we'll build up the levee as we go. Awright, ya'll git at it."

The area was near the officers' housing, namely Cap'n Smooth's house. Most of the cons and bosses hate working close to the houses, and especially that close to the warden's office.

After the second week of digging, we had the "pond" all to ourselves. We didn't do it on purpose, but we jobbed the shit out of Number 2 hoe. We'd been digging out so much dirt and pitching it back, they couldn't shovel it back fast enough and we had a hole that looked like a double ring doughnut. This pissed Cochise off and he started cursing them for not keeping up. Cap'n Smooth's wife overheard his "foul language" and ran him in to the warden. Big Devil came out to the pond and sent them back to the fields. Fuck!

But Big Devil compensated for the loss of manpower. We worked in the hole as our "regular" job five days a week and all the screwups in the building, as well as in the field, carried on the project nights and weekends as punishment.

After about ten weeks the hole was taking on the shape of a huge pond. The more we dug, the more I despised the sight of a shovel and a pick.

Tuesday evening when we came in, Boss Humpy hollered down in the tank, "Ol' Racehoss, lay-in in th' mornin to ketch 'at chain!"

"Yahoooo!!" I couldn't help it. It had been so long since I talked to the parole man I'd just about given up. After almost eight years, I made it.

14 ▐▌▐▌▐▌▐▌▐▌▐▌▐▌▐▌▐▌▐▌▐▌▐▌▐▌▐▌▐▌▐▌▐▌ ▭

. . . and violated parole for aggravated assault with a deadly weapon.

Deja—fuckin—vu! Stepping back into hell again. I felt like kicking my own ass as I walked through the backgate. I had been out just long enough to get my belly full of pussy, and my nose cut off in an auto accident and sewed back on. With no credit for the time I was out, I picked right up where I left off, going yonder way on the rest of that funky thirty-year sentence, which amounted to about ten more years. With commutation time, eighteen calendar years discharges a thirty-year sentence.

Soon as I got my things put away in the same old Number 3 tank, the picket boss sent me to the front office. "Welllllll, Ol' Racehoss! Couldn' stay out, couldja? Jes can't make it in that free world, kin you? Nigguh, you wudn' gone long nuff fer 'em to give away yore bunk, wuz you?"

Not so, I got another bunk and locker, but I didn't interrupt just to dispute that. I'd rather have been shot down and shit on at sunrise than to have to face him, let alone listen to his shit.

Then he noticed the scar that hadn't completely healed, "Whut happen to yore face? Whut'd you do, git to fuckin wit sumbody's gal?"

271

"Nawsuh, Warden. I wuz in a car wreck."

He thought for a minute, "Go upstairs to the E and R Department (Education/Recreation Department) in the mornin, an tell Meabs I said to put you on Ol' Sonny Wells' job. I'm sendin him to the Walls to cook fer the director. Thank you kin handle 'at?"

"Yessuh."

"You do whut he tells you an you bet not let them nigguhs be a usin 'at place fer no whorehouse neitha."

"Yessuh."

As I was about to leave, "I'll call in there an tell the inside picket boss to let you out wit the rest uv them buildin nigguhs in th' mornin."

The next morning I ate breakfast on the shortline, and afterwards I went upstairs to my new work station. I went in the little office, sat down and began looking over the paper work piled on each of the two desks. Hanging on the wall behind the larger desk was Mr. Meabs' master's degree in physical education from Southern Mississippi.

The floors were already shining from last night's clean up so I got the feather duster and started dusting off the library books. It was getting pretty close to eight o'clock.

When he topped the stairs and entered the auditorium, I stopped dusting and spoke. He kept right on strutting like a blind rooster, as if he didn't hear me. I followed him, stood in his doorway, and waited for him to get settled at his desk before giving him the warden's message.

Without looking up at me, "Who're you?"

"Racehoss, Mr. Meabs. Yesterday the warden told me to tell you to put me on Ol' Sonny's job."

"You got a GED or high school education?"

"No sir."

"Kin you type?" still avoiding eye contact.

"No sir."

"Kin you run a picture show projector?"

"No sir, but I can learn."

He started grumbling about all the paper work and typing that had to be done. With a noticeable lisp he said, "What in the heck I gon' do wit shumbody who ain' got no education, can' type, and can' run no projector? I sure wis th' warden would lemme be in on choosin people to work in here.''

I spent practically the entire day in the auditorium, and he hadn't said another word to me. Since I didn't know what routine he expected I went to him and asked.

''Well, Racehoss, th' main tang is keep th' auditorie spic an span, cause we can' nebber tell when th' warden migh' cum up here an look aroun.''

''By the way, do you mind if I use the typewriter to practice on after we close up the auditorium?''

''It's awrigh' wit me. You knee git permission frum th' warden to stay up here atta count time.''

After Mr. Meabs left, I unlocked the projector room, examined the equipment, and by the time our Friday night show time rolled around, I ran the projector with ease.

Each night after all activities were over I cleaned up the place and lugged the old Royal typewriter downstairs to sit under the picket to practice so I wouldn't disturb the white cons. It was coming slow. Occasionally, Mr. Meabs let me ''hep'' in the office stapling papers, removing paper clips, and sometimes filing. Bit by bit I became familiar with the office routine, started studying, and eventually got my GED.

My typing was good enough now for me to type all the reports as well as manage the office in his absence. Mr. Meabs started showing up at nine o'clock instead of eight. Then ten, eleven, two, etc.

In the meanwhile Hollywood had suckassed Big Devil into believing he could help make us better. And got permission to formulate the Brotherhood: a self improvement program held every Saturday night. We ''changed'' so much it became Big Devil's favorite rehab program.

First hour—Fellowship

The star sissies served unsweetened poly-pop in paper cups Hollywood had panhandled from Foots. While the band played (''UUGH!'') Okinawa sang ''Cum Back Baby'' and ''Blind Man Standin On the Corner'' (''UUUUGH! ARRRG! BOOOOO!!'').

Second hour—Role-playing situations between the cons and bosses. Tonight, I played the role of Mr. Meabs. I had

273

worked around him long enough to mimic his fast-paced lisp to perfection. The audience was rolling in the aisles with laughter. After my performance, the night lieutenant, who sometimes sat in on the meetings, came up to me and said he never laughed so hard before and was still laughing as he walked downstairs to his station in the messhall.

The next morning before he left, he ran into Mr. Meabs and told him in jest he didn't know he had a convict twin, "Ol' Racehoss kin sound jes lak you. Last night at Brotherhood I laughed so hard I cried when he imitated you."

Mr. Meabs came straight to the office. "Whut's this I hear bout you mockin me las nigh?"

"I wudn' mockin you, Mr. Meabs. We role-play at the meetings all the time. That's the main part of the program. I just showed how you won' speak to nonea the convicts. And how I—"

He cut me off and told me "Nebber" use him as a subject again and stormed out. Working in the office with him after that was hard. He sulked and pouted like a little boy, and hardly spoke to me. He started monitoring my work to the point of harassment, searched for dust along the window sills and examined every piece of paper work. When he found a mistake he wouldn't let me correct it. Instead, I had to do the whole thing over.

The PIP (Point Incentive Program) Quarterly Report time had rolled around. We were graded quarterly for work, conduct, attitude, and "other" program participation. I stayed late several nights in the auditorium typing the 470 individual forms getting them ready for mailing. It took almost a week, but I had them ready by the first day of the month ending the quarter.

During that week, Mr. Meabs spent little time in the office. All the cons on the camp had been PIP rated, except me. All the forms were ready for his signature. The third day after our reports were due, the warden got a call from the Walls Education Department inquiring about them. He called me to his office and chewed my ass out.

"Warden, they ready, except for my sheet. They won't accept partial reports, all I'm waitin on is Mr. Meabs to grade me."

274

"I don' give a damn whut the holdup is, ya'll betta git them damn reports off to them Walls!"

"Yessuh, Warden."

Mr. Meabs didn't come to work until late that afternoon. As soon as I saw him, I reminded him about my rate sheet. He hardly slowed down long enough for me to talk to him.

"I be back in th' mornin an grade you."

The next morning I placed my form on his desk, on top of the stack. He couldn't possibly miss it. He didn't show. Later that morning Big Devil sent for me.

"Fuck it!" I went back to the office, looked in the files and pulled the last quarter's report. I had 110 points out of a possible 300. I circled the same ratings he gave me before, signed his name, and got the package off in the truck mail.

The next morning he came to work on time for a change. Soon as he walked into the office, "Where you PIP forms?"

"Mr. Meabs, . . . the reports are gone. I mailed them off yestiddy."

"Who grade you?"

"Mr. Meabs, the warden was on my ass. He called me out to his office again about them reports."

"Who grade you?"

"I did. I copied my last quarter grades."

"Who shined 'em?"

I swallowed down some air, "I signed 'em."

"You mean you forge my name?"

"Yessuh, if that's what you wanna call it."

He had me, and we both knew it. Everybody knew the warden's policy, "If you git run in, you git punished." It didn't matter if the con was in the right or not. In less than fifteen minutes, I was standing in front of the warden's desk. Mr. Meabs said I was impudent, forged his name, used my own judgment, and didn't consult him.

"Ol' Racehoss, I thought you wuz doin a pretty good job up there. But, guess I wuz wrong." He phoned the inside picket boss and told him to send the day duty officer out to his office. "Boss Tetus, take Ol' Racehoss roun there an put his ass in 'at pisser."

I lasted eighteen months on the job.

On the way, "Whut th' hell ja do, Ol' Racehoss?"

"Nuthin."

As we approached the compact building just outside the backgate, "How you doin, Boss? Got any empties back thar?"

"Sho Boss. Hell, ain' been nobody back thar in a week." Interrupting himself for a second, "Take off yore clothes an git up on them scales."

I stepped on the scales and he ran the weight balance back and forth a few times before, "a hunnert an forty-two pouns," and recorded it on a door card.

"Well, Boss, I best be gittin on back, he's all yourn."

"Yeah, well, cum back an see me when you got sum mo bizness. Okay, les go Ol' Racehoss."

After passing a couple of cells, "You got the whole hotel all to yosef. Which room you wont?" He opened and closed a few of the doors, took a brief look inside, "Whew!" while holding his nose. "They all th' same, which 'un you want?"

"Okay, if thas the way you feel bout it, I'll jes put you way back heah in the last 'un. That way if we git sum mo customers, you be outta everbody's way," he wise-cracked.

When we reached the last cell he unlocked the solid steel door, stepped inside, and unlocked the inner door. I stepped up inside and my eyeballs jumped to grab the last flicker of light before he sealed the 4×8 tomb. The concrete slab jutting out from the wall for a bed, a four-bit-sized hole in the center of the floor served as a commode. No electrical outlets for lighting, total darkness. A cup of water and a biscuit a day and every sixth day a full meal. I knew the routine. Solitary and I were no strangers.

But, I had grown soft from being out a year and then working inside for the last year and a half. I didn't expect to be put back in here, especially on some bullshit. When I worked in the fields, it was a refuge, a place to get away for a few days to rest.

If the boss could have seen through my back, he would have seen the tears streaming down my face. The slamming of the two steel doors still rang in my ears. Sitting naked on the slab in pitch-black silence, I hung my head as the tears bounced off the floor onto my feet. Other times, I took a seat and sang all the songs I knew over in my mind. But this time I felt like I was smothering, buried alive.

Sweat poured. Gritting my teeth, I hugged and rocked myself, trying to squeeze back the consuming fear. What if something happened? A fire, flood, war—would they remember to come let me out so I could run too? Tears flowed. I panted for the thin air and squeezed myself tighter and tighter.

I pounded my knuckles and banged my head against the unyielding concrete. Then the sudden sound of rushing water demanded my immediate attention. Frantically I felt along every crevice and seam, hoping not to find water seeping in. Louder and louder. I got on my knees and held my ear over the floor's hole. I started scratching the hole. Nothing. Covering my ears with my hands, I discovered the source and listened to the blood rumbling up and down my fingers.

With the agility of a panther, I sprang up and ran around the walls. Then rolled on the floor like a ball. With outstretched arms, I clung onto the low ceiling by my nails. I mauled myself, scratching and tearing my body. Slumped, exhausted on the slab, I covered my face with both hands and cried out, "Help me, God!! Help meeee!! . . ."

A ray of light between my fingers. Slowly uncovering my face, the whole cell was illuminated like a 40-watt bulb was turned on. The soft light soothed and I no longer was afraid. Engulfed by a presence, I felt it reassuring me. It comforted me and made my tears flow back into my eyes. No pressure any more, I breathed freely. I had never felt such well being, so good, in all my life. Safe. Loved.

I stood against one wall, viewing my wretched self sitting on the slab and screamed out, "No! No! No!"

And the voice within talked through the pit of my belly, "Don'cha worry about a thing. But you must tell them about me."

I lay back on the slab. A change had taken place. Never before had I felt so totally loved. That's really all I ever wanted. The biggest need in my life fulfilled in an instant. And I loved that Presence back. My capacity to love was restored and it proved I wasn't without feelings; I wasn't dead.

It unlocked the shadowed prisms of my mind. Through feelings, every thought was crystal clear. My life winded down before my eyes like the film in a projector set on reverse. The Presence made me glad to feel love again in my heart for Emma. This was the first time I ever looked at the situation and took into consideration that she had her problems too. I just happened to have been there, and glad I was.

I realized I was just as guilty for blaming her as she was for blaming me. It took that yoke off and sent all my regrets into exile; they became painless memories.

The Presence stayed during the entire twenty-eight days. When the boss opened the door, I hesitated. I didn't want to leave my cell. "Betta brang yore ass on frum thar fo I keep you in heah!"

When we reached the front, I stepped up on the scales to be weighed again. He was stunned, "147 pounds!" He rechecked the door card. According to the scales, I had gained five pounds. He said somebody had been slipping me food, but did not pursue it and let me go on to my tank.

After that, God was real. He found me in the abyss of the burning hell, uplifted and fed my hungry soul, and breathed new life into my nostrils.

As soon as I walked back through my tank door, I felt guilty for not blurting out what happened in solitary. But I knew if I told it, they would think I was crazy. I felt better when I figured out that maybe it meant *when I could*.

I took a shower, wasn't quite finished lacing up my brogans, getting ready when Boss Humpy hollered down, "Ol' Racehoss, that warden wonts you in his office."

In a few seconds, "Comin out, Boss."

On the way to the front gate, my mind was running a hundred miles a minute. *What the fuck could he want this time*, I thought as I stepped through the gate.

"Yessuh, Warden," as I entered his office doorway.

He finished signing some papers on his desk, looked up and handed them to me. "Take ease in there an give 'em to Boss Jack."

I quickly walked back into the outer office, handed them

to him and returned. He reared back in his chair and looked me over. "Ol' Racehoss, do you thank you got sense nuff to iron my shirts 'thout burnin a hole in 'em? Thank you kin fry eggs 'thout the lace on 'em?"

"Warden, I don't know much bout cookin and I ain' never ironed nobody's shirts befo." If he was offering me a house boy job, no way. I'd rather go back to the fields than work around the houses. Even back to the pisser. Working around the women meant nothing but trouble and I had enough trouble without any help from them.

"Well, I kin see you don't wanna wek at my house."

"Nawsuh, Warden. It ain't that I don't wanna work at yo house, it's jus I never dun that kinda work befo. I'm mo uv a field hand."

As he cleaned under his nails with a small pocketknife, "How much typin didja do fur Meabs up in the auditorium?"

"Most uv it. I did all the monthly an quarterly reports."

"Didja type letters?"

"Yessuh."

"You thank you kin keep yore mouth shet an not bea tellin 'em nigguhs in the buildin my bizness if I put you to wek out heah in my office?"

"Yessuh."

"Boss Jack! Cum in heah. This is Ol' Racehoss," he said after Boss Jack entered. "He's gonna be wekin heah in the office wit you an kin hep out wit sum uv the typin, or whutever you need 'em fer." Looking at me, "You'll be wekin under Boss Jack, but I still run the farm."

Boss Jack's expression changed; he didn't like the bragging remarks. He went back to his desk in the outer office. The devilish look on Big Devil's face as he picked up the phone told me he enjoyed needling him. He dialed the inside picket, "Boss, I'm sendin Ol' Racehoss back in an I want you to move 'em up to th' trusty tank. Yeah, an leave word fer 'em to let 'em out in the mornin wit the trusties. Right, he'll be wekin out heah in my office. Yeah, thas right, jes add 'em to yore trusty count. Ol' Racehoss, when you go back inside the gate, stop by the laundry and tell 'em I said give you sum new whites to wek out heah in."

Everything had happened so fast. I changed in the laundry room from my old dingy gray clothes into the new starched and pressed whites. Just like that! I had been given "the job," the warden's bookkeeper! I expected the worst, to be back on a row with a hoe by now. As a rule when we got busted off a job and put in the pisser, it was back to the fields. And I remembered, "Don'cha worry about a thing."

As soon as I was inside the building, "Ol' Racehoss, git alla yore stuff, I'm movin you up in Number 5 tank."

I quickly emptied my locker, put everything in my pillow case, and went upstairs. I walked over to the barber area and started chatting with Hip Cat, the barber. He said there was no special night for shaves and haircuts, and he gave them whenever the cons asked. He was a pleasant contrast to Crip, wore fireman-type suspenders, and looked like he was past fifty.

I already knew the trusty tank door was kept unlocked, "jes let th' picket boss know where you goin." We had a pretty long talk before the trusties started coming in for lunch.

On my first night in the trusty tank I found out that when it came to gambling and watching *Gunsmoke,* they were no different from the bunch in 3 tank. The TV benches were full of loyal fans. In the opening scene when Sheriff Matt Dillon walked out in the streets to draw his guns with the crook, stopped and relaxed his left leg, the cons went wild. The moment the sheriff moved into his drawing stance was the part that got it! They all were on Matt's side. After watching their enthusiastic reaction to *Gunsmoke* I knew it was just another tank full of cons, only called something else.

After eating breakfast on the short-line, the call for "trusties" went out. We cleared the backgate, each one went to the peg board outside of the pisser building and punched OUT. When I got to the board, my name wasn't on it.

"Stand to one side an let the rest uv these nigguhs cum on by." After they checked out, "Where in the hell do you thank you goin Ol' Racehoss?" half joking. "Ain' no peg up thar fer you."

"I'm goin round to the warden's office, Boss."

"Whut you gon' be doin in th' warden's office?"

"Workin, Boss."

"Well, you jes stand heah til I call th' inside picket. Ain't nobody tole me nuthin bout it."

After he slammed down the phone, I had to listen to the rules governing trusties coming in and out of the backgate. "I ain' gon' letcha back in the yard unless you been shook down. Jus cuz you trusty don' mean nuthin ta me. You don' hafta strip, but you'll be searched. Is that clear?" I started walking away and he said, "I'll hafta make you a peg."

"Yessuh."

After the warden arrived he called me into his office and handed me a set of keys.

"This is a extra set uv keys to the front door, desks, an file cabinets. I don' know which is which, you have to figure that out. Boss Jack usually gits heah round eight, an he'll tell you whut he wants you to do. One uv them keys fits my desk too. You might need to git sumthin out uv my drawers sumtimes."

"Yessuh," returning to the outer office area.

Talking from his office, "I tell you sumthin you oughta do quick is you kin, learn whut's in 'em fuckin file cabinets. Boss Jack's the only one who kin find a damn thang in 'em and most uv the time he's gone when I need 'em. I cum up heah the utha eenin afta quittin time an spent damn near two hours huntin fer last month's livestock report. Never did find the damn thang. I had to call his house. So learn that quick as you kin."

"Yessuh."

"Anutha thang, if I wuz you, I'd stay way frum 'at auditorium less you on office bizness. That way, you won' git in no more trouble."

"Yessuh."

He was gone when Boss Jack came and I was going through one of the four-tier file cabinets. "How'd you get in the file cabinet?"

"The warden gave me the keys."

"That's okay then, I just wanted to know how you got in

'em. Sit down and let me talk to you a minute. How far did you go in school?''

''I got a GED.''

''From what I gathered in the warden's office yesterday, you can type.''

''Yessuh. About forty words a minute.''

''Well, that's plenty fast enough. Do you know anything about debits and credits?''

''Not much, only whut I learned when I was takin a ICS course in accounting.''

He went to the closet and got a copy of every form used in the office. ''Here, take these and learn 'em by name and what each looks like. Afterwards, I'll show you how to fill 'em out. By the way, you better go put the flags up. You'll find them folded up in the back of the visiting room.'' As I was leaving, he added, ''I'll sure be glad when the warden decides to get another porter out here.''

I found Old Glory and Texas, ran them up the flagpole, and returned. ''I don't know if the warden told you anything or not,'' he continued, ''so I'll just start at the beginning. You work seven days a week. Until we get a porter, you have to keep the office clean, floors waxed and all. On Sundays, you work in the visiting room.'' He looked out the window, ''Say, did you know you got the flags upside down? The American flag should always be hung on the top. Do you know what it means when flags are flown upside down?''

''No sir.''

''It's a distress signal. If an airplane was to fly over and see those flags flying that way, the pilot would think we were in distress.''

''Well, Boss Jack, I don't know about you, but I'm sho in distress. I ain' never seen this many forms in my life.'' We had our first good laugh together.

''Well, don' worry, you'll get the hang of it.''

Boss Jack's persistence prevailed and the warden assigned Jewel to do the porter work, freeing me to concentrate on the bookkeeping. With his patience and instructions, in a couple of months I could handle all the paper work and knew the filing system.

He literally turned the work over to me, all the monthly reports, posting the inmate records, and even the employee payroll. This provided him with more coffee drinking time over in the guards' dining room. He wouldn't drink the coffee I made in the office for the others. "That belongs to them, and I don't want no part of it," he would say. After I got the procedures down pat, I had some free time too.

Big Devil liked to spend as much time driving in the fields as possible and was in and out of the office, mostly out. He didn't like the administrative "crap," and would much prefer seeing how things were running on the farm for himself. He'd walk through the building and kitchen or drive in the fields surveying the work needed to be done. Sometimes he came to the office on the weekends, but usually didn't stay long.

When working on the weekends, I had the office to myself. Jewel had no interest whatsoever in the office other than keeping it clean. He spent his leisure time sleeping in the visiting room. One Saturday after the warden had come and gone and Jewel was fast asleep in the visiting room, I decided to satisfy my curiosity and see what Big Devil had in his desk. While rummaging through it, I ran across the *Warden's Handbook* in his middle drawer.

Thumbing through it, I found a page marked with red pencil. At the top was written, "Handling Convicts." First paragraph, "Never give a white convict anything he doesn't ask for. Very proud, arrogant, and independent. Mexicans require close supervision, strict disciplinary procedures often necessary; cunning and rebellious. Negroes: treat like children."

Treat like children! I kept sneaking back until I read the whole book. The more I thought about it the more I realized that was exactly the way he treated us, "like children."

Rules regarding the employee payroll had been explained to me by Big Devil and Boss Jack. "Nobody" opened the big brown envelope containing the checks before the warden got it. The envelope was to be placed on his desk "intact." I had orders not to tell the bosses the checks were there until the warden left the office. He took his check, Cap'n Smooth's, Lieutenant Sundown's, Cap'n Foots', and Boss

Jack's. Because of their educational gap and varied social backgrounds, the warden made sure that he handed Boss Jack his check personally, just to keep it straight as to who was paying whom. Boss Jack didn't like being in the office with all the bosses either, so as soon as he got his check, he left too.

Buzzard stayed out of the way at the back of the crowd and waited for everyone to get their checks and leave. After the time in the warden's office when he had to "sign" some papers regarding his retirement, I knew the secret. When the warden handed him the pen, Sergeant Buzzard held it with a death grip and his hand convulsively trembled. It took him a good fifteen seconds to draw the two uncrossed streaks of lightning.

Boss Eatem Up couldn't read or write either, but could at least make an X. I signed his name on the payroll for him too. Cap'n Foots, with his seventh grade education, could only do a little better. The warden didn't have a single ranking officer on his immediate staff who had a high school education and none could put together a report on their operations without help from Boss Jack or me.

Boss Jack and I were caught up with our work in the office. As usual, to keep from being in the office while the warden was there, he was over in the officers' messhall drinking coffee. After Big Devil and I were left alone in the office, "Ol' Racehoss, cum in heah fer a minute."

"Yessuh."

"I wanna ask you sumthin. Who do you thank is th' ugliest, Ol' Cryin Shame or Ol' Pug?"

I didn't answer and just started laughing. Pug's face looked like a pekinese, especially around the nose and mouth, and Cryin Shame was just plain ugly.

"I'm serious nigguh, which one uv 'em do you thank is th' ugliest?"

"Warden, neither one wouldn' win no beauty contest."

Realizing I still hadn't caught his drift, he said jokingly, "Hell nigguh, I thought you wuz keepin up wit thangs heah in the office. I'm talkin bout that letter that cum in heah the utha week or so bout plastic surgery. Well, we got anutha one today."

As he talked on, I recalled the letter. It stated that one of the universities had gotten a grant to do research on the use of plastic surgery as a corrective measure for criminal behavior. According to the letter, the researchers deemed the way a person looks has a definite bearing on his/her personality and criminal behavior. They were asking for a volunteer to undergo the operation.

"I gotta pick sumbody to send up to them Walls. Hell, all the doctors in the world couldn' make Ol' Cryin Shame look no betta. Changin his face ain't about to stop 'at nigguh frum stealin. He needs a whole new head."

Pondering for a moment, "Ol' Pug's my choice cuz ain' nuthin gon' hep Ol' Cryin Shame. He's jes crazy is hell, the penitentiary's the best place fer 'em. So I tell you whut, go head an make out sum transfer papers on Ol' Pug an les git 'em on way frum heah on Black Betty."

15 ||||||||||||||||||||||| [   ]

From all indications, we were going to have a Big Juneteenth celebration. Being given a good meal and the day off was the warden's pre-cotton picking time "rally." This got our engines heated up. When the cotton blossomed, it wouldn't last long. That's when we repaid him.

Big Devil issued orders to Cap'n Foots to feed us fried chicken and watermelon, plus we had a big ballgame scheduled Saturday. Our team, the Yellow Jackets, was playing the Ramsey Hardhitters for the southern division championship.

Even though Mr. Meabs was the manager of the team, Big Devil did the managing. He made the final decision as to who played on the team using the Hog Law book to make most of his selections. "If a nigguh don' pick nuff cotton, he can' be on my ball team."

When the Yellow Jackets beat another team, it was ice cream and cake, but, when they lost, it was the soda water boxes for the rest of the night. He punished the whole team when they got beat and those who errored the game off were punished more severely. Being number one was an obsession of his, whether it was producing the first bale or winning a baseball game. Baseball was the only convict activity he showed an interest in.

A few intermittent showers started on the Thursday before the big game. Big Devil immediately called in the building for Mr. Meabs and told him to get some tarpaulins from the tractor shop and cover the diamond.

Friday afternoon the showers were gone. Big Devil began his usual roaming about the farm checking things out. He knew every inch of it, just like Road Runner and I did, only he drove it. While surveying his 16,000-plus acres he went down Hog Pen Alley and passed by the baseball field. He saw standing water on the diamond and no tarps.

When he returned to the office, he slammed the screen door behind him, went directly into his office, and called for Mr. Meabs. He crashed down the phone and sat at his desk cursing. "Gotdam diamond's jes full uv puddles. That sonuvabitch didn' do whut I tole him!"

Mr. Meabs stepped into the office with a big grin on his face. With both barrels, the warden let him have it. "You spose to be soooo Gotdam smart! Got a big ol' piece a' paper hangin on yore wall, but you ain' got sense nuff ta cover up a fuckin diamond!"

Mr. Meabs' small, pudgy frame shrunk six inches as he stood in the warden's doorway. "You know whut, Meabs? I don' know nuthin you KIN do cuz you ain' dun a damn thang since you been heah. Them nigguhs been arunnin 'at Gotdam school house. All you been doin is settin up there on the hard part uv yore rotten ass takin all the credit."

Mr. Meabs mumbled something, but was interrupted. "Shet yore mouth when I'm talkin to you!! Next time you disobey my orders, I'm gon' see that sumthin gits dun to yore ass!"

I stopped typing and looked into his office. I saw the back of Mr. Meabs' pants legs shaking from his trembling knees. During a pause in the blistering ass chewing, Mr. Meabs said in a soft whimper, "I'm sorry, Warden. I git busy an flat forgit."

"Busy my ass! You ain' never been busy a day in yore life." Sarcastically, "You spent alla yore time agoin to school gittin educated. Well, it sho as hell didn' hep you none. Meabs, I beena puttin up wit way mo uv yore shit than I oughta. Take yore Gotdam ass outta heah, an see if you got sense nuff to go roun to that messhall an git a mop an bucket, an git yore ass down to that ballfield an dry up 'at diamond. I bet not see a speck uv water on it when you git thru!''

Meabs left the office running. Soon after he left, I left. I made it my business to be standing by the backgate when he came out with his mop and pail hung over his shoulder. He was whistling like a jolly little elf on his way to cookieland with the mop balanced over his shoulder and the pail hanging from the mop head.

Being reduced to a molecule of shit just a few minutes ago didn't seem to have phased him one bit. Regardless, I hadn't felt this good about anybody getting eaten up and spit out since Big Emma sliced Arthur Johnson across the cheeks of his ass with that butcher knife. The score had been evened.

The Juneteenth celebration got underway as planned. A few trusties were still out working, but they would take off early for the ballgame. After the fried chicken lunch, we went out on the yard and ate our piss chunk. We were full as ticks after the watermelon and waiting for the main event.

EVERYBODY WAS THERE, the building was left empty. Whenever the Yellow Jackets played at home the warden demanded 100 percent attendance with the only exception being the picket bosses, and even they watched with binoculars. The whole ballfield was encircled by bosses on horseback.

Plenty of candy wrappers were rattling while our team was on the field warming up. Rat's on the mound for us today!

"RAT! RAT! RAT!" the chanting began.

He was the Satchel Paige of the prison system and could throw a ball hard as a mule can kick. When Rat was pitching, the warden wouldn't let anybody do the catching but Pee Wee, who stood about 4'1". The warden liked the way Pee Wee "talked it up" with Rat between pitches. Extra padding was sewn into Pee Wee's mitt, but with Rat on the hill, it would be all busted out by the end of the game.

The warden sat on the hood of his car going over the game plan with Mr. Meabs. "Heah dey cum," somebody in the bleachers shouted as the big caged truck bringing the Hardhitters turned onto Hog Pen Alley. The free world umpires arrived and held their conference with Big Devil,

Bear Tracks, Mr. Meabs, and the Ramsey team manager. After setting the ground rules, the game got underway.

The first three batters up for the Hardhitters, Rat mowed down. He threw nine pitches that sounded like nine cannon shots each time one hit the mitt. And he knocked Pee Wee back from home plate nine times. But Pee Wee jumped right up, dusted off the seat of his britches, and quickly resumed his catcher's stance, never missing a beat.

Pounding his mitt, "Thas th' way, baby kid! Turn over in yo hide! C'mon, baby kid! Turn me over—make me see upside down!" BOOM!! "Thas th' way!! Why don'tcha knock me down sumtime?!" BOOM!! "Thas th' one, baby kid! Put it rat heah! Lemme have that same one agin!" BOOM!! Down and back he'd go.

The bleachers bunch whooped and hollered, "Rodent's right today! Dey can't see it cuz dat nigguh's throwin dirt up dere!"

"Man, dat nigguh's kickin high!" referring to Rat's knuckles dragging the ground each time he cocked his leg and reared back.

The Hardhitters' best pitcher, Coach Whip, who was a sidearmer, was no less effective with our first three batters. The pitcher's duel went on inning after inning with only one scratch hit given up by Coach Whip. Through six innings, Rat struck out eighteen batters and was well on his way to breaking his own strike-out record.

Top of the seventh, their best hitter, Swahili, was up. Rat reared back and fired. The pitch was ripped into right center field. The outfielder bobbled the ball and it was a standup double. We let out an excited sigh in the grandstand.

The next hitter sacrifice bunted and the runner was safe at third. One out. Big Devil called "time out" and summoned Rat over to the car. "If you lose 'is game nigguh, I'm gon' do sumthin to yore Gotdam ass!" After the pep talk Rat bore down and the next batter went down swinging. Two away.

Rat went into his full windup. A bleacher fan yelled, "Look out!! Heah he cums!!" The third base runner was stealing home and Rat uncorked one to cut him down. The force knocked Pee Wee at least six feet back. The runner slid across home and was standing up dusting off his britches by the time Pee Wee got back to the plate. Rat struck out the next hitter for number twenty.

In our half of the inning, we got two hits but couldn't push anything across. On through the top of the ninth, Rat had a total of twenty-four strike outs, but we were still behind one to nothing. Rat was also the best hitter on the team and would be the second batter coming up in the last of the ninth.

Rock Island, our first baseman, was the first man up. He hit a long fly ball the center fielder ran down and caught. Rat was at the plate. First pitch, he smacked a double down the left field line. Big Devil jumped off the hood of his car shouting. Popeye, our next to the last hope, swung at and missed the first two pitches from Coach Whip. Then he hit a little blooper to the shortstop. Two down.

Big Devil headed for Mr. Meabs, who was standing next to our players' bench. If a rabbit was in the hat Big Devil was going to pull it out. Since the game had been so crucial throughout, both teams had exhausted their player rosters.

The Yellow Jackets had used every player, except West Texas. The warden held a strategy conference with Mr. Meabs. Pee Wee was scheduled to hit with the tying run still at second. West Texas couldn't help but overhear Mr. Meabs tell the warden that he had used all of his pinch hitters. West Texas butted in, "Warden, Suh, lemme take a bat."

"Git away frum me, nigguh!"

Mr. Meabs took his shot below the belt with a chance to voice his displeasure at having West Texas on the team, "Wes Texis, you can' hit no ball. You don' eben pra'tice when you out here."

Undaunted, West Texas pleaded, "Warden, Suh, I picks a lotsa cotton fer you. I ain' got to play in no game yet."

True, the warden knew he was no ball player to begin with, and let him sit on the bench and watch two practice days a week. At forty-five, West Texas was still one of the best cotton pickers on the farm. The warden kept him on the team because of that and to give him the two days to rest up. He had a way of looking out for the older convicts who were good cotton pickers.

Big Devil conceded, "I don' give a damn if he ain' been

practicin. Let 'em hit. Least he got sense nuff to do whut I tell him.'' *Touche!* ''He can' do no worse'n 'em utha rotten bastards who couldn't hit a Gotdam bull in the ass wit a base fiddle. Gitcha a bat an go on up air an lay into one!''

Since he'd never played a game, he'd never been issued spiked shoes. So he dug in at the plate with his heelless field brogans. He fouled off the first two pitches. Coach Whip got wild and threw three balls in a row. Things were so tense you could hear a boll-weevil piss on cotton.

The three-two pitch was on its way, and it was just what the warden ordered. SM . . . ACK!! He hit it deep. The outfielders watched as the ball flew over their heads. Because there was no fence, there were no automatic home runs. The center fielder was running full speed trying to catch up with the ball and the bosses were galloping their horses behind him.

It rolled damn near to the turkey pens, a good 600 feet from home plate. The center fielder finally caught up with it as West Texas was falling down rounding second. He'd already fallen going to first. The bleachers rocked with excitement as he stumbled to get up. Rat scored.

Three players lined up in the outfield for the relay back in. When West Texas rounded third, he was almost out of breath and looked like he was running in slow motion. The warden rushed out between third base and home urging him on, ''Cum on, nigguh! C'mon, git ready to slide!!'' The throw was finally coming in. West Texas fell again and started crawling. Big Devil ran up to him screaming, ''Git up! Git up! Git up, nigguh! Git uuuuup!!''

West Texas stumbled on toward home, collapsing head first at the plate and putting his hand on the bag. ''SAFE!'' by a hair.

We won two to one, ice cream for all. That is, except for the player who bobbled the ball and allowed their runner to reach second. He spent the rest of his Juneteenth standing on a soda water box.

16 ||||||||||||||||||||||||||||| [_____]

Big Devil was on the bright side of sixty. He enjoyed sitting around talking with his old law enforcement and hunting cronies who stopped by the unit on a regular basis for a free cup of coffee and meal. Reared back in his executive chair, he told them tale after tale about things that had happened during his illustrious career, which he had begun as a field boss on Ramsey. Then he was mess steward on Clemens, where he got promoted to warden. After the white cons were transferred away, he was sent to Retrieve to take over.

"They shipped off all 'em ol' white thangs befo I got heah, an when I took over 'is camp, they handpicked the worst nigguhs from the utha units an shipped 'em to me. So, I started out wit nuthin to begin wit," he told his full-bellied audience.

He pointed to the gruesome 11 × 25 framed photograph hanging on the wall behind his desk. It showed a headless convict sitting at the end of one of our messhall tables. In the photo Red Wine sat perfectly erect with his hands still resting on the messhall table, with a lighted Lucky Strike clamped tightly between his fingers. Except for his missing head, everything in the picture was normal.

Big Devil joked, "Sum flunky got tired uv bein Ol' Red Wine's gal-boy, an chopped his Gotdam head off!"

I had heard the story from the cons on their tank. Red

Wine, one of the building tenders on Number 1 tank, had been kicking the flunky's ass and raping him at will.

The decapitation took place at lunch after we'd passed through the chow line and were all seated and eating. As usual, the flunkies were bringing the steam pans up and down the aisles offering second helpings. When the victimized flunky walked down the row of tables where Red Wine was seated, he stopped behind him long enough to pull a meat cleaver from underneath his apron. He made one swooshing swing and BLOP! Red Wine's head hit the floor like a cabbage. Even though the blood was gushing out from where his head used to be, the photo showed Tarzan seated across from him still eating.

With a pompous air Big Devil chuckled and said, "It took awhile, but I dun tamed most uv these nigguhs." Then he hollered to me in the outer office, "Ain't that right, Ol' Racehoss?"

"Yessuh, Warden."

"Take Ol' Racehoss. When he first cum heah, useta git punished all the time. Turned out ta be my top hand. Would ya'll bleeve 'at nigguh won the cotton pickin championship 'ginst the top pickers frum Ramsey and Clemens? But he's dun got sum education now so I put him out heah to be my bookkeeper."

"Ol' Racehoss," he called out.

"Yessuh."

"Holler up air an tell 'at picket boss ta call in the buildin an have 'em send Ol' Steeple Head out heah."

"Yessuh."

After bragging about the gore and cotton picking, it was time to send for the unit jester to further prove how "tame" we all were.

Steeple Head was black as a crow, slightly built, and his records said he was forty-nine and a six-time loser. His most striking feature was the shape of his pyramidal head with little room at the top for any brains to be stashed away. He practically grew up in the Gatesville Reformatory for Boys. With six convictions for non-violent crimes, he'd spent most of his adult life in prison.

Regular as clock work every Saturday night, he dressed

up in his "hustlin rig" and took a seat on the bench at the front of Number 5 tank. With jockey drawers, a rolled-up T shirt around his chest, a pair of raggedy hose smuggled in by the trash wagon trusty, and some homemade garters, he was ready. Sometimes, his work brogans were still covered with dried mud and horse shit from his job at the horse lot. And to top it off, he tied a red bandanna around his bald, cone-shaped head.

Since he wasn't "classified" as one of Retrieve's star punks, he didn't rate room service in Doc Nolan's dentist office. So Steeple Head took care of business in the shower area obscured from the inside picket boss by a partial brick wall. He charged three packs of Bugler, two for him and one for the building tender, Ol' Bugs, for the use of the motel and posting a lookout.

When business was slow, the cons on the tank teased him just for the fun of it. "Say, pretty mama, you know my cred-it's good an I'll straighten you draw day" (pay day, the day cons receive their scrip books).

Jokingly he'd shoot back, "Naw baby," very submissively, "yo credit may be good, but I can' light it up an smoke it." Imitating a woman, "Sides, it's th' wrong time uv th' month."

As soon as I finished second handing Big Devil's command, the outer picket boss was third handing it to the inside picket boss. In no time at all, from the office window, I saw Steeple Head running at full speed down the sidewalk for the front gate. The lever was thrown; the gate flew open.

I heard the crashing noise of his fumbling and falling into the office screen door. It sounded like he was breaking in. He finally jerked the screen door open and entered. After slipping and sliding on the freshly waxed floor past my desk, he almost skidded right by the warden's door. He grabbed hold of the door frame; if not, he would have slid on by and hit the wall.

Panting, "Yassuh, heah I is Warden Suh."

"Whut took you so Gotdam long!? I sunt in there halfa hour ago fer yore rotten ass, an you jes now draggin in heah!"

"I cum fass as dey lemme out, Warden Suh."

"Jes shut yore Gotdam lyin mouth! You beena lyin ta me ever since I knowed you, nigguh. Whut makes you thank I bleeve ANY Gotdam thang you say?!"

Steeple Head started weeping. As Big Devil paced around him, his menacing 6'2" frame towered over Steeple Head, adding to his nervousness. "Ya'll know whut I dun fer this nigguh? I heped git 'em out uv th' penitentiary. Didn' I, nigguh?"

"Yassuh."

"I got a friend uv mine over in Brazoria to take him in an give 'em a job. The man paid 'em a salary an let 'em live rat there on the place. He even let this nigguh drive his ol' pick-up truck. An all the while he wuz bein good ta 'em, you know whut he wuz adoin? The rotten bastard wuz asneakin back out heah gittin in my hog barn. The sonuvabitch wuz brangin that ol' cheap wine out heah an him an the night hog nigguh would pile up in my barn, git drunk, and fuck all night. The lot boss wuz pullin down sum sacks uv feed an found this sorry nigguh alayin up there sleep, buck nekked. I had him 'rested; they 'voked his prole an sunt his rotten ass rat back heah to me," failing to mention Steeple Head's arrest cleared the livestock report of "unaccountables" from day one.

Steeple Head had been shamed to his knees and pleaded for forgiveness. Between sobs he begged some of the half dozen men in the office, "Ya'll pleeze hep me!"

One of them said, "You know, Zeb, I'm willin ta take a chance on this nigguh's word an say I beleeve he's atellin the truth when he says he wuz tryin' ta git heah fast as he could."

Big Devil joked, "Why Gotdam, Haley. You gittin weaker'n a bottle uv piss in yore old days."

They all laughed as Steeple Head sobbed on, puddling up the floor. Big Devil continued to conversationize with his buddies, ignoring him completely. "This nigguh's still crazy, but not as bad is he wuz. The rotten bastard never could keep up wit th' squads in the field, so even afta he fucked up 'n cum back, I give 'em an easy job in the lot squad. All he has to do is saddle 'em bosses' hosses ever mornin an have 'em ready by turnout time. Does the bastard

295

'preciate it? Why hell no! The sonuvabitch gits the bosses' saddles mixed up an puts 'em on the wrong hosses all the time.

"Ol' Steeple Head," Big Devil called to him in a milder tone.

"Yassuh?"

"That'll be enuff uv 'at now. You heah me talkin to you?"

Steeple Head sprang up, stood at rigid attention, the crying ceased.

In second gear, "Tell ease people jes how long I been aputtin up wit yore black ass."

"All my life, Warden Suh. You been had me all my life. You raised me to whut I is today," he said with pride.

"Nigguh, don' stand there an blame 'at shit on me!"

"Warden Suh, I do everthang you tell me to. You been my daddy."

Big Devil's buddies laughed and one of them joked, "Ah ha, so this is why you lookin out fer 'em." They laughed harder, all except Big Devil.

With no forewarning, 'Tell 'em how many times you been fucked. You bet not lie. You heah me, nigguh!?"

"Warden Suh, I ain' gon' lie ta you. Warden, is you talkin bout since I been heah altogetha, or since I been heah wit you?"

"See whut I been tellin ya'll. Did ya'll heah that? Naw, nigguh, I ain' talkin bout the number uv times you been fucked in yore whole damned prison career. Hell, this addin machine can't add up numbers 'at big. Jes stick wit who dun it since Sadday night."

Steeple Head began calling off the names one by one with Lassie-like obedience until Big Devil stopped him. "Ol' Racehoss, go over yonder ta them guards' quarters an tell the officer on duty ta git over heah!"

I returned quickly with the on-duty boss. He was in the warden's office getting instructions. "Git out yore pencil an pad an write these nigguhs' names down when Ol' Steeple Head tells 'em ta you. When you finish writin 'em, go in that buildin an put them nigguhs on sum soda water boxes. I'll let 'em down."

According to Steeple Head's tally, four cons had sex with him since Saturday night. After writing their names the duty officer wheeled around, headed to arrest the fingered ones.

Big Devil asked one of the law enforcement officers, "Didja brang that apparatus witcha this time?"

"Yeah, I did."

As pre-planned, an empty chair was left by the machine for Steeple Head.

"Got 'em all ready ta go!" one of them said.

"Okay, hook 'er up an plug 'er in. Les see how much she'll burn."

The polygraph machine buzzed and clicked with each adjustment. Steeple Head stood mesmerized, his watery eyes glued to the machine's dials flickering back and forth.

"Damn! She kicked all the way up ta fourteen-forty!" the officer adjusting the dials said dramatically.

"Thas enuff ta fry th' hairs off'n a gnat's ass three hunnerd feet away! He won't feel a thang."

Steeple Head's eyes got bigger and his ear-to-ear grin shrunk. Beads of sweat popped out on his forehead. Big Devil fixed an intent stare on him while waiting for the officers to finish their "adjustments." He got the "she's all ready to go" nod and lit into him again.

"Nigguh, how much mo uv yore shit do you thank I kin stand? How long do you thank I oughta wait 'fore I do sumthin bad to yore ol' rotten black ass?" Steeple Head tried to speak, "Jest shet yore lyin mouth up an set yore stankin ass down over there in that chair!"

This was the first time I ever saw Steeple Head balk at the warden's command. Big Devil spat out the order again, "Ol' Steeple Head, set yore ass down in 'at Gotdam chair lak I tole you! An cut out so Gotdam mucha that sweatin too, befo you trigger this damn thang off."

Scared and confused looking, Steeple Head backed slowly toward the chair and sank down in the seat. Pleading more desperately, "Pleeze, Suh, Warden! Don' let 'em do it! Pleeze Suh. Warden, I ain' lied to you bout nuthin. Pleeze Suh!" Tears streamed. His body shuddered and trembled uncontrollably.

With a deep sigh of faked remorse Big Devil ordered,

"Go head an hook 'em up. I've gone fer as I'm goin to wit this nigguh."

The officer began wrapping the long, black cords around Steeple Head's body. "Raise yore arms straight up, lak this," he said, showing Steeple Head what he meant. "Lak this, nigguh! Raise up yore Gotdam arms!" he said impatiently.

Steeple Head sat rigid as stone.

"This is the dumbest nigguh I ever seen in my whole life!" the officer said.

"Well, I dun already tole ya'll that. Tell you whut, if you can't git 'em wrapped roun his chest an under his arms, jes wrap 'em roun his fuckin legs. They'll git the job dun wherever ya put 'em."

The officer began again, but Steeple Head jumped straight out of the chair. "Warden! Oh Lawd! Have mercy Warden! Oh Lawd! Warden! Nawsuh, Warden! Pleeze don' let 'em wrap me up in dis stuff! Pleeze spare me, Warden! Don' turn yo back on me!"

"Set yore Gotdam ass back down in 'at chair! You bet not make me havta put you in it!"

Steeple Head sank back down into the chair. To intensify and prolong their game, the officer slowly wrapped the cords around him. First, his legs, then underneath the bottom of the chair, looping the cords around his lap and on up around his chest.

Finally, all systems were go. The warden issued the order, "Okay, go head an plug 'er up agin."

Just as the officer was about to plug the cord into the outlet, Steeple Head unzombiezized. In a terror-stricken voice, he screamed "OH NO!!" and bolted up with the chair still strapped to him. He fell down, kicked and hollered hysterically while rolling and twisting on the floor trying to free himself. He thought they were going to electrocute him.

He managed to get the chair off his back, but was still entangled in some of the cords. Struggling to his feet, he almost knocked me down as he broke for the door. Off the table crashed the polygraph machine, scaring him even more. Out the front door and down the sidewalk he ran, dragging the cords behind.

The game backfired. Big Devil's cronies were cracking up at the unexpected finale as the warden ran a short ways down the sidewalk chasing him and yelling, "Cum back heah, you crazy sonuvabitch! Cum back heah!"

Big Devil stopped after hollering out one more, "You betta cum back heah, you ignant bastard!" But it was useless. Steeple Head was long gone, heading down Hog Pen Alley. On his way back to the office, the warden told the outside picket boss, "Radio the lot boss and tell 'em I said go down to the lot an brang Steeple Head back."

When Big Devil got back to the office the officers assured him the equipment hadn't been damaged. A few minutes later, the lot boss escorted Steeple Head into the office, "I found 'em hidin in the loft in the hay barn."

"Whutta you thank I oughta do to yore crazy ass, nigguh?! You dun tore up a thousand dollars wurtha 'quipment."

Steeple Head trembled as he stood mutely.

"Tell you whut I'm gon' do fer you, nigguh. Hell, I ought not ta do nuthin fer yore rotten ass," he declared with a faked change of heart.

Steeple Head begged, "Pleeze, Warden Suh. I be merciful fer anythang you do fer me."

"Well," Big Devil continued, "I ain' gon' take it out on you fer ascarrin up my flo wit that chair while you wuz afloppin roun lak a damn chicken wit its head cut off. An I ain' gon' do nuthin ta you fer tearin up Guvment Property, but I am gon' havta do sumthin to yore rotten ass fer runnin outta heah 'thout permission."

"Yassuh, Warden. Thank you, Suh."

"See if you got sense nuff to go roun to that backgate an tell 'at boss I said put yore rotten ass in that pisser."

With a look of relief, Steeple Head left trotting off to the backgate. A small price to pay for proving we were all "tame."

Working so closely with Big Devil, I was afforded a bird's-eye view of his multi-chameleoned personality. His callous dealings with Steeple Head were just e pluribus unum in his repertoire of management styles. He was the best Dr. Jekyll I'd ever seen with Hip Cat.

After living on the tank with Hip Cat for a couple of years, I knew of his deep love for his mother. He was an only child. Unlike most of the cons on the tank, he never talked about old girlfriends and sex. Instead, he talked only about his mother and how close they were.

During one of our talks he told me, "I ain' seen her in twenty-fo years. I know how she feels Race; I know she wants to see me. I want to see her too, but not lak this. I tell her in ever letter I write to git that out uv her head, I don' want her comin way down heah. It's too far fo one thang an she's too old to make a trip lak that all the way frum Paris." (Paris, Texas, near the Oklahoma border.)

It was Wednesday. I was taking a break in the visiting room when I saw the taxicab pull up out front. An elderly black woman got out. Assisting herself with a cane as she walked toward me, I knew she was Hip Cat's mother because they sure did favor.

"Young man, can you tell me where the warden's office is?"

"Yes ma'am," holding the door open, "it's right here."

After we entered, "Wait here, ma'am."

"Thank you."

"Pardon me, Warden. There's a lady out here to see you."

"Tell her to cum on in. Whut kin I do fer you?"

"Are you the warden?"

"I'm th' warden."

"Well sir, I come down here to see my son, Alonzo Curlee."

Offering her a seat, "How long's it been since you seen him?"

"Twenty-four years," she said without a doubt.

Big Devil began telling her the visiting rules, "Sundays is visitin days an visitin hours is frum nine to 'leven in th' mornin, an frum one to three in th' eenin."

He hardly ever broke that rule unless prior written permission was granted through the Walls. I had seen him turn away lawyers who came down to the unit to see their clients.

"I didn' know ya'll had certain times," she said. Adding

sorrowfully, "an I came all the way from Paris. Warden, please sir, can't I see him even fo jus a minute?"

"Ol' Racehoss!"

"Yessir."

"Tell the picket boss to call inside and tell 'em to send Ol' Alonzo Curlee out heah."

While waiting, "I'm gon' let ya'll visit THIS time. Me an Ol' Hip Cat, thas whut we call him, go back a long ways," referring to being at Ramsey together.

The outside picket boss let him through the front gate. Hip Cat came in the office and stopped at the warden's doorway, "Yes sir, Warden."

"Cum on in. There's sumbody heah to see you."

When he stepped inside the door and saw her sitting to the side, he was totally speechless. She stood up. Then he cried out, "Lawddd!!" and wrapped his arms around her. They embraced. Weakened by the shock of seeing him, her legs gave way and they both almost fell when she went limp. Hip Cat gently helped her back into the chair.

He dropped to his knees weeping and she cradled his head against her bosom, rocking back and forth and stroking his head. Cooing, "Hush, hush. Les don' cry baby. The Lawd has brought us together agin. I been prayin so hard fo this day to come."

This was the only time I had ever seen a show of compassion in Big Devil. He was sniffling as he stepped out of his office. I was choked up too. "Don' let nobody in my office til I git back."

"Is it okay if I close your door, Warden?"

"Yeah, close it."

He got in his car and drove off. He'd broken another rule. A boss is supposed to be present during all visits with free world people. About thirty minutes later, he returned and took a seat in the outer office with me.

Hip Cat opened the door after awhile and Big Devil went back in and sat down behind his desk. I couldn't hear all of what they said, but I did overhear him telling her that the next time Hip Cat came up for parole, he had a good chance of making it.

Breaking another rule, offering hope.

While waiting for the taxi from town, she thanked him for his kindness. As Hip Cat assisted her out the front door, she looked over her shoulder and said, "I'm gon' pray fo you."

When she got to the sidewalk she stopped. "You keep on bein a good boy so you can hurry up an come home to Mama." Hip Cat did get out and we learned a short time after that he had died from natural causes.

And, the warden was the worst Mr. Hyde I'd ever seen two weeks later, on the Sabbath. The visiting room was packed. It was my responsibility to issue freshly starched and pressed whites to each con that the boss brought out for a visit. The cons had dressed out in the backroom, and were seated on one side of the long, glass-partitioned counter.

As a fringe benefit, Big Devil allowed me to be the runner to the coke machine for the cons and their visitors so they wouldn't lose any time visiting. Plus, it was a security measure since the visitors weren't permitted to hand anything to them. I was into my third or fourth trip, and busily passing out the drinks when unexpectedly, the warden stepped in.

He stood in the doorway for a minute or two, looking things over. A well-dressed, middle-aged, light-complexioned lady turned around in her seat and asked, "Pardon me, are you the warden?"

"Yeah."

With a friendly smile, "Do you mind me askin you how my son is doing down here? Has he been behavin himself?"

Still leaning against the doorway, Big Devil cast his eyes across the counter on her son, contemplated for a moment, then looked back at the mother. "How many chillun you got?"

"I have just the two. My daughter here," pointing to the teenaged girl sitting beside her, "and my son."

With the same empty face, he shook his head, "You ain' got no son. You got two gals . . .," turned and left. Exit Mr. Hyde, leaving the con's mother in a state of shock.

I had been working in the office almost four years now. For the past year it had been rumored that a warden rotation plan was in the making. The grapevine was right again. The administration assembly line rolled out the plan in a memo that sent Big Devil through the roof. It stated that he would be one of the first wardens rotated because he had been at one unit for so long, and henceforth, wardens would be rotated every five years.

Besides dismantling the long-time dynasties, Dr. Beto, the new administrator, would be assigning an assistant warden and farm manager to each unit to help free the wardens so they could focus more on their administrative duties.

Big Devil ranted and raved to Boss Jack and me, "I been runnin 'is farm over twenny years, an now they gon' ship me off summers else. Up til now I been goin 'long wit all their educated puke, but I'll be Gotdamned if they gon' start runnin me roun frum pillar to post!"

He fought the new policies tooth and nail, but he would be transferred to the multi-racial Eastham Unit, and the Eastham warden would be transferred here. The assistant warden and farm manager would be down within the month.

A mood of uncertainty swept through "hell." In addition to the warden rotation, the administration was raising the educational requirements of the prison employees and would be doing all future hiring rather than leaving it up to each individual warden. No more walk-ons like Boss Humpy. Current personnel would be frozen in their positions until they met certain educational standards and could pass written examinations for promotion. Long-time employees who were below the new educational requirements would have job performance evaluations done on their positions to verify their proficiency.

When the rest of Retrieve's personnel learned of the new orders, there was near pandemonium. Most of the officers and bosses were justifiably worried about their futures. Education was never one of Big Devil's main criteria for employee selection. He used to boast he had only completed the eighth grade himself. A large portion of his staff did not graduate from high school. Many didn't get out of grade school.

I knew Buzzard and Eatem Up were scared to death since they couldn't even write their own names.

With only a month left until the warden's transfer, things at Retrieve were sadder than the horses that pulled President

McKinley's casket down Pennsylvania Avenue . . . until Black Betty came. She left a lone passenger. On my way back to the office to deliver his record to the warden, I leafed through it and thought there must have been a mistake. After the warden looked at it, he phoned into the building, "Send Ol' Pug out heah."

I was looking through the file cabinet, and Pug walked by without my seeing him. He went directly into the warden's office. "Ol' Pug, is that you nigguh?"

"Yessuh, it's me, Warden!"

"Ol' Racehoss, cum in heah an look at this nigguh."

I definitely wanted to see him because I sure didn't recognize him at the backgate. I went in and after seeing Pug up close, it was still hard to believe it was him. Instead of looking like a pug-nosed pekinese, now he looked like Pinnochio with a long pointed nose, big ears, and thinned lips.

"Gotdam nigguh! If you wudn' black as th' ace uv spades, you'd look jes lak a white man."

Pug grinned.

"Do you lak 'is new face better'n you did that uth'rn?"

"Yessuh, Warden. I laks it jes fine."

"Lemme ask you sumthin. Where'd they git all 'at meat frum to make you that nose an them ears?"

"Mostly off my behind, Warden."

Seldom did the warden ever laugh out loud, but he laughed so hard he was in tears. "You mean to tell me, out uv all th' places on you, they had to take sum uv yore ass an put it on yore face an ears? You know whut that means, don'cha nigguh?"

"Nawsuh."

"Well, it means that you'll be walkin round asmellin yore ol' goatsmellin ass fer th' rest uv yore life!" Big Devil was still laughing when he said, "Go on roun to th' shop an tell 'at boss I said give you a tractor an send you on out to th' field. Be sho an tell 'em who you is an if he don' bleeve it, tell 'em I said call me."

That night on the tank, Pug stood before the mirror until count time, primping. Proud Walker and a few others went to the back purposely to tease him. Proud Walker asked,

304

"Pug, lemme axe you sump'n, man. Did you pick dis face or did dey do it? I lak'd you th' utha way when you look lak a bull dog. Now you look mo lak a ant eater wit dat long nose."

At last Proud Walker said something I agreed with. Pug was ugly as sin before his surgery, but now with his "new" Anglo features he looked like an uglier somebody else.

The same week Pug came back, Trigger Bill met his doom. He had finally convinced the warden to take him off as building tender and let him work in the shop squad. Big Devil still relied on Doc Cateye to run the hospital, so when he wanted to know, he called him. Cateye diagnosed Trigger Bill's death was due to poisoning. Explaining, "Sumhow he musta got into suma that cotton 'secticide cuz Warden, I smelt it on his breath. Smelt lak he'd been drinkin sump'n else too, lak that ol' chock."

The trial of the decade was underway. The warden interrogated the entire tractor and shop bunch. "Warden, dat nigguh had a bad habit uv slippin roun drankin utha folks' stuff. Das probably whut happen to him. Sumbody musta fixed up a special batch fer 'em," one explained.

Wash stated, "Warden, Suh, I ain' sayin I'm one uv 'em, but I know dat dem utha nigguhs chips in an buys sugar outta th' messhall an makes 'em up a batch uv chock. An dey say, Ol' Trigger Bill didn' never chip in. He snuk aroun watchin where dem utha nigguhs hid dey jugs at an he drunk it all up, and be blowin his breath in dem utha nigguhs' faces."

Trying to trip up the testifier, "How do you know he wuz sneakin round drankin up ya'll's homebrew?"

"Nawsuh, Warden, I wudn' watchin 'em. I wuz doin my wek lak I spose to, I jes heard dem utha nigguhs talkin dat wuz watchin 'em."

"An I don' spose you kin 'member none uv their names eitha?"

"Nawsuh, I sho don't, Warden. You knows me, I try to tend to my own bizness when I'm out dere."

Even though in a roundabout way every one of them confessed that Trigger Bill had been poisoned and gave their renditions of why, nobody knew who. So Big Devil ruled there was inconclusive evidence and the case was closed, "Death by suicide."

Security got its first slap in the face when Sergeant Buzzard and Rattler let one get away. This was the first successful escape from the burning hell in many years. Retrieve's once notorious reputation for not "lettin 'em git outta the bottoms" had been stained.

The warden's impending transfer caused an exodus of old-timer personnel, especially those he failed to get transferred to Eastham with him. The director stuck by his guns, that each warden would be allowed to take only their convict cook. Boss Jack was finally getting to have the last laugh.

Cap'n Smooth had in 37 years, and suddenly decided to hang up his spurs. Lieutenant Sundown, who had come to Retrieve with Big Devil over twenty years ago, resigned and went to work with the local sheriff's department. The laundry supervisor requested and was granted a transfer to another unit. The shop, lot, and garden supervisors all retired. Buzzard, after 30 years, was quitting the dog trail and put in for his retirement to begin the day that Big Devil departed.

Even the two old water wagon mules, Coal Oil and Fannie, got out a month before the warden was to leave. They rode off into the sunset for the soap factory and hopefully, were NOT pulling the water wagon in mule's heaven.

Big Devil stayed out of the office and kept mostly to himself. He went fishing a lot in "his" pond, the one I had helped dig. His move to Eastham was a bitter pill that he was forced to swallow. Starting over again at a multi-racial unit with over 2,000-plus untamed cons was going to be a real challenge to his wardening philosophy. *He sure better not leave his handbook behind!* I thought.

17 ||||||||||||||||||||||| ☐

1968

On the morn scheduled, the curtain fell on Big Devil's long reign over hell.

That evening the replacement warden from the "Ham" arrived. I recognized him from his photo in the prison administration's annual directory. But, I had no idea the face in the book would be attached to a giant's body, and I readily accepted the stories I'd heard about his prowess as a defensive lineman at A&M.

He walked into the Warden's Office and sat down behind the mahogany desk, "I am sitting in the right seat, ain't I?"

"Yes Sir," I answered, but he sure didn't look right sitting in it.

"How long have you been working in the office?"

"About four years, Warden."

"How much time you doin?"

"Thirty years. Warden, do you need me to get anything out of your car?"

"Naw, I got a lot of junk in there, but I'll take it on down to the house. The van will be here later tonight with the rest of my things; I'll git somebody to unload it tomorrow. That's a pretty long drive down here." Adding, "That'll be all."

Within a few months after the new one's arrival, he was baptized with a sit-down strike in the fields, an escape attempt, and a near riot in the messhall. Work slowed down in the fields for the first time in many moons. The squads no longer worked on Saturdays, and it didn't look like we would finish our harvest first. The unit fast lost its manicured appearance, as the weeds took over.

We were shown a *laissez-faire* style of "wardening." Each evening after he had supper, the warden routinely returned to the office to catch up with his paperwork. Afterwards, he headed for the building and went into one of the lower line tanks to play dominoes with the cons. With the door locked behind him, he stood at the domino table and waited his turn.

When he went in one of the eastside tanks, we could look down from the trusty tank and see him at the domino table. He seemed right at home, and made as much noise as they did slamming the dominoes and squabbling. At first, the cons were leary of him, but after he passed around his ready rolls freely, they were glad to have him in the game.

Boss Wise-em-up didn't dare holler, "Ya'll betta git down on it. Sum uv you ol' wild-ass'd nigguhs gonna havta talk to that warden in the mornin." We had gotten used to his evening tank visits and on Saturdays he spent practically the entire day inside the line tanks. Even though there was always a domino game going over at the guards' quarters, he preferred playing with the cons.

Sometimes, while waiting his turn at the table and rocking on his heels, he'd lose his balance and reel backwards. The cons standing around would catch him before he fell. He'd thank them and they laughed and kidded him about it, going so far as to say, "Warden, I sho wish I felt good as you feels."

In the office the assistant warden and Boss Jack were discussing him. Boss Jack commented, "His breath smells like a distillery."

"Yeah, I know. How in the hell can I maintain buildin security while he keeps volunteerin' himself as a potential hostage." A few days after their talk, the assistant warden made out a request for transfer, which was granted. He was sent to the Darrington Unit, and promoted to full warden.

The Walls administration got wind of the warden's tank

escapades. A few weeks after the assistant warden went to Darrington, a big sedan from the Walls kicked up gravel wheeling into the parking space. The three officials (one I recognized from the cane patch) walked briskly past the warden's office and on through the front gate.

Once inside, they struck up a trot hurrying down the sidewalk and on into the building. It was Saturday. About ten minutes later, four were coming back. They had busted the warden red-handed in Number 3 tank playing dominoes. He led the way into his office; they closed the door. After the officials sped away, he walked down the sidewalk headed to his house, with his shoulders sagging. The outside picket boss got a radio message about four hours later and hollered it down to me. "The movin van'll be here Wednesday."

Monday in the truck mail a letter came from the Walls' Education Department. I had been selected to attend heavy equipment school at A&M, and was to be transferred to the Walls on Thursday. I had no idea how they came up with my name; I hadn't applied for anything.

Later that day it came in on the teletype that the warden from Central would be the next replacement and was scheduled to arrive on Thursday. We'd probably pass one another along the highway, I figured.

Wednesday afternoon I helped the warden put his trophies and other personals from the office into his car. That night I packed my little shit and was ready to vacate hell too.

After the heavy equipment school ended, I was assigned to a bulldozer sitting idle at the Darrington Unit. When the work was completed at Darrington, I was sent to work at Pre-Release, Ramsey, Ellis, Ferguson and then on to Eastham.

Whatever cost factors were involved for the training I received, they were certainly getting their money's worth out of me. When my mail finally caught up with me, I wasn't surprised that I had gotten another year's parole set off. The Board read their Hog Law book on me and determined that being back five more years wasn't "near bouts enuff," as Cap'n Smooth would say.

The truck-driver guard slowed the diesel transport to a stop in front of the Eastham Unit tractor shed. I unchained and quickly unloaded the machine. Finished, he took me to the backgate and had me put on the count, then checked me into the building.

The building officer told me to sit down in the hall against the wall and walked away down the long hall. About half an hour later, another officer walked over and ordered, "Come with me."

I walked slightly behind him for at least two city blocks down the main artery before we made a sharp left into a smaller hallway. When we reached the closed door with "Warden" written above it, he knocked lightly.

"Yeah, cum on in." I recognized his voice immediately.

When we entered, the officer quickly removed his cap, placing it under his arm, "Is this him, Warden?" he asked.

"Yeah, thas him. That'll be all."

The officer politely closed the door on his way out.

"Ol' Racehoss, Gotdam nigguh, been a long time since I seen you," in a tone that sounded like he was glad to see me.

"Yessuh, sure has Warden. How you doin, Suh?"

The spark in his once fiery eyes had dwindled to a flickering ember. The lines of time threaded his face and his hair was white as snow. He looked tired and old.

"Aw, I'm doin pretty good, I guess. Lotta diffrunce in this farm an that utha one tho," he added.

"Yessuh, I imagine it would be."

"Almost fo times as many heah an most uv 'em young ones that ain' learnt how to do time yet," he commented. Taking a look at my record there on his desk, "Looks lak you been movin roun quite a bit."

"Yessuh, I sure have."

"You had a chance to go back down there yet?"

Jokingly, "Warden, I doubt if I'll be sent back to Retrieve. We did all the heavy equipment work with our hoes and shovels befo you left."

He smiled, "Set down," motioning toward one of the office chairs. "Ya'll run that utha warden way frum there in a hurry. Didn' ya? Got 'em busted to 'sistant warden. Whut wuz th' matta? Wuz he to hard on ya'll?" he asked sarcastically.

"No suh, I don' think that was it."

"How cum they sunt you over heah?"

I already knew I wouldn't be here if he hadn't requested me from the master list of heavy equipment operators. "They said you needed some work dun with the dozer."

"Yeah, well, I got a little drainage work an sum clearin I wontcha ta do."

He leaned back and began naming off the Retrieveites who had gotten out, come back in, and were here with him. "Ol' Proud Walker, Ol' Bay City, Ol' Steeple Head, and Ol' Cryin Shame." Then, bragging, "Them ol' bastards got word to me soon as they asses landed in them Walls, wantin to cum where I wuz. So I tole 'em to send 'em on. Ol' Forty's over heah too. Have you heard whut happen to Ol' Pug?"

"No, suh."

"Well, that new face didn' hep him much. That ignant bastard didn' last a hot minute after he got out. He went to Houston an got to big-assin wit sum ol' woman an she stabbed him in the heart wit a ice pick an kilt him. An you'll never guess whut Ol' Bay City dun. He's gotta be one uv th' craziest nigguhs I ever seed. As good a damn mechanic as he is, he got busted in a cafe. The owner caught him drunk, settin down in front uv th' juke box takin the screws out uv it to steal the nickels an dimes. The owner held a gun on him til the police got there. I can unnerstand it when suma these nigguhs that ain' got no talents cum back, but there ain' no excuse fer a nigguh lak Ol' Bay City to keep runnin in an out uv heah.

"An Ol' Steeple Head shouldn'a been sunt back at all fer whut he dun. That crazy sonuvabitch wuz runnin frum a nigguh who'd whupped his ass. 'Thout even lookin back, Ol' Steeple Head shot over his shoulder and hit that nigguh rat betwix the eyes, kilt 'em dead as a hammer." Laughing,

311

"That nigguh cried an begged th' judge out uv a measly three years.

"Ol' Cryin Shame robbed a man's place, then set down on the steps an waited fur th' police to cum take 'em to jail. I always knowed that nigguh couldn' make in in the free-world." Adding, "He don' hafta worry bout it no mo. They filed the bitch [habitual criminal] on 'em an give 'em life 'is time."

After bringing me up to date on the old stomping ground cons, he put on his hat. "Cum on, I'll show you roun the farm."

He drove up and down turnrow after turnrow, pointing out all the agricultural improvements he'd made. "When I furst cum heah, trees an underbrush wuz growin all up to there," pointing over to some freshly plowed land. "I dun added more'n two thousand new acres uv farm land to this place. Tell you sump'n else, I put these sonsabitches to wek too. It wuz sum bastards up heah who'd been layin up on they asses in that buildin so long, they'd dun flat furgot how to wek!"

Boasting, "I put a stop to 'at shit in a hurry. Ol' Race-hoss, when I cum up heah, they had bout 300 nigguhs and meskins wekin in the fields. None uv them ol' white thangs wuz wekin atall. Now, I got over forty squads."

"Warden, do they work together in the same squads?"

"Well, not zackly. They wek in the same cut sumtimes, but I ain' got roun to mixin 'em up yet. Course when one uv them ol' white thangs fucks up in his squad, I take him out an put his ass in a squad wit them nigguhs for a couple uv weeks. Weks ever time. Don' take much uv that to git his heart right and make him put his ass in high gear."

When he reached the place where he wanted me to start working the dozer, he stopped the car and told me what he wanted done to prevent water from standing in the area after it rained. He said I'd be working under the farm manager, and would be coming out in the mornings with the tractor squad.

As we were driving away, he continued, "Tell you sump'n else too, most uv these bosses wuz doin jes lak they damn well pleased, which wuz nuthin. It took sum

312

doin, but we got it straight that I wuzn' gon' put up wit they trifflin shit. They got the message afta I run off a batch uv 'em.''

When he ended the tour, I was let out at the backgate, "Boss, put this nigguh on yore trusty count an let 'em go on in the buildin.''

The trusty tank was empty except for the building tender, Ol' Forty. The warden had given him the same job he'd had in the hell. As soon as I put my belongings away, we sat down and had a long chat. He told me he had filed a writ because he had observed his forty-year sentence, explaining, "Hell, Racehoss, it don' take but twenny-fo calendars to do forty. I dun nine years fo I made prole an I been back over seventeen. Sumbody fucked up, man. I been heah two years too damn long! Dumb as I is, I kin figure dat out.''

Forty reaffirmed what the warden told me earlier. "Big Devil put dese muthafuckas to wek, an I mean everbody. Ain' no mo uv dat layin-roun shit.''

The next morning when the call came for the tractor squad, I caught out with them and headed for the tractor/shop area. I was checking the fuel and oil in the dozer when an officer dressed in snappy western wear, who looked to be in his mid-forties, walked up, "I'm the farm manager. You gon' be runnin 'is thang?''

"Yessuh. The warden told me what ya'll want done.''

His expression flashed anger, "Ain't you th' nigguh I seen ridin round wit th' warden yestiddy?''

"Yessuh, he had me in the car with him.''

"Whut's yore name?''

"They call me Racehoss.''

"Well, Mister Racehoss, when you git thru dilly-dallyin round wit 'at machine, do you thank the warden would mind if I told you to go on an git started?''

I got on the machine, fired it up, and walked it down the turnrow. After twenty days, I had the big drainage ditch cut and was ready to start clearing stumps.

Then, when the equipment service truck from the Walls arrived on its regular run, they brought along my trainee-helper, a young white con. In the training program I had been instructed how to train new operators. While two of my former A&M classmates who were assigned to the service truck were checking the machine, the service truck boss went over the trainee details with me.

"They want you to let him ride on the machine with you while you're operatin so you kin tell an show 'em what you're doin. Then let 'em run it with you ridin. When he gits to where he can handle it pretty good, let 'em do it by himself much as possible so he can git the feel uv it. With you watchin, uv course.

"I think he knows the front end frum the back. He told me when we wuz comin out here that he had run a front-end loader once. You don' need filters or nuthin, do you?"

"No sir," I said.

He and his two helpers left.

My new helper told me he was twenty-four, that this was his first time in the pen, and that he was from some little town in northeast Texas, serving three years for burglary.

The on-the-job-training was paying off. Gene was getting better and better as the days went by and could run the machine alone, but wasn't quite good enough yet to work it in close quarters. I was leaning against a tree no more than fifteen feet away watching him spread some backfill when the farm manager drove up.

He stopped and shouted to me, "Ol' Racehoss, git over heah! Gitcha Gotdam ass on the back uv this pickup! I'm takin you to that buildin."

Climbing onto the back, I asked, "What for?"

"Jes shut yo damn mouth an git on!"

He drove off, spinning the wheels. On the way in he radioed ahead that he was bringing in one of the heavy equipment operators. When he stopped at the backgate, Big Devil drove up at the same time. He must have intercepted the message. The farm manager got out of his truck and walked the few feet around to the driver's side and leaned on the door.

"Whut's th' matta?"

"Warden, I wuz brangin this nigguh in to have 'em put in the pisser."

314

"Fer whut?"

"Fer one thang, when I drove up out there in th' field awhile ago, Ol' Racehoss wuz standin off up under a shade tree makin 'at white boy do all the work."

The warden beckoned for me. I jumped off the truck bed and walked over to his window, "You heah whut th' farm manager said?"

"Yessuh."

"Is he tellin th' truth?"

"Yessuh," I answered, totally surprised that he'd ask. Never had I heard Big Devil question an officer's word. "Warden, my helper had only been on the machine bout five minutes when the farm manager showed up. I was doin what I was told to do by the service truck boss who brought 'em. He told me to let 'em run the machine much as possible. I'd dug the stumps up and he was spreadin some backfill when he drove up."

Leaning on the steering wheel and never looking up, "You kin go on back to doin whutever you wuz adoin, cuz I know you musta been mighty busy." The farm manager's face reddened more when Big Devil said, "Git in th' car, Ol' Racehoss," and took me back to the machine.

The warden kept finding little projects, keeping the machine busy, overextending his allotted time limit. The farm manager started driving out almost daily, taking Gene off in the front seat of his pickup. Sometimes they'd be gone for over an hour. When he'd get back, he said the farm manager had him doing "somethin." And I left it at that.

At the hearing, my two former A&M officer classmates testified that they did indeed find a new oil and air filter buried. The farm manager and my helper took them to the "exact spot." My reason for burying the filters, Gene said, was, "I didn' feel like messin wit 'em."

The warden questioned me. "Didja do that, Ol' Racehoss?"

I looked him straight in the eyes, "No sir." I turned and looked across the office into the face of my helper. "Warden, why don'cha ask him how they got there. He's the one that's been ridin aroun in the pickup with the farm manager, an they the ones who found 'em."

Big Devil smelled a rat. He mulled over the testimony a few seconds then said, "Since ya'll's the ones," pointing to the two service truck bosses, "that brung this ol' thang over heah, ya'll take 'em back witcha when you leave." He yelled out of his office to his clerk to start processing transfer papers.

One of the bosses ventured to ask, "What do you want us to do with him when we get him back to the Walls? Warden, sir, we need to have some reason for brangin 'em back."

"Do th' same thang wit him ya did fo you brung him over heah."

The boss went a step further, "But Warden, no disrespect sir, what's th' reason?"

"Oh, I see. You hafta have a reason to give 'em? Well, tell 'em th' reason is I don' wont the rotten-assed bastard on my farm, an if they have any problem wit that, tell 'em to call me."

After being caught in the middle of a power struggle, the day to leave Eastham couldn't come quick enough. Orders finally came from the Walls to transfer me and the dozer to Coffield, the new unit under construction. As we turned onto the iron-ore covered road, the compound of galvanized buildings loomed ahead. The truck driver followed the road around the buildings and stopped at the shop. At the loading dock, a truck from Wisconsin that had brought down a monstrous Number 9 Caterpillar was waiting to exchange it for my smaller one.

The normal check-in procedure at all the other units I'd been on began at the backgate. Instead, the driver now drove to the office. No one was in the outer office when we entered. He called out, "Is anybody in here?"

From inside the warden's office, "Whutcha got?"

The driver handed him my records, then left. It was Silly Willy, the former Clemens warden. He was rotated in the first round too. He glanced through my papers briefly, then looked over his horn-rimmed glasses, "Ol' Racehoss, kin ya still pick 'at cotton?"

"No sir, not like I useta. That was a long time ago, Warden."

"They tell me you're a pretty good 'quipment operator. Well, you sho cum to th' right place. Plenny uv work heah to keep ya busy; you kin plan on stayin heah a while.''

He asked me what I thought of my new dozer. He said there was enough work here for a regular heavy equipment squad and assigned me to it. After our chat, he phoned inside and had an officer sent to his office.

I followed him through the long, barn-like galvanized building with chicken-wire-covered windows, surmising security wasn't the long suit for this unit. With so much construction work, most of the 500 cons were of trusty caliber, if not already trusties.

Each hanger-type building was divided into two tanks. A tin wall with an open doorway separated the tanks. Only a barber was in the tank when I arrived. This was my first unit without building tenders. He walked with me down the rows, pointing out the vacant bunks. There looked to be about 100 bunks in all.

I read the tank's bulletin board and saw that college classes would begin soon. I had been traveling around so much I was never at one unit long enough to take some courses. Silly Willy seemed certain I would be here awhile, so I decided to enroll.

He was right. There was plenty of work to do on the 23,000-acre unit clearing timber, plowing root stumps, building roads and bridges, getting the land ready for farming. I was putting in a lot of hours and worked seven days a week. But the warden worked out a schedule allowing me to come in at four o'clock on the afternoons I had classes. I continued the writings I started a few years earlier and had filled up ten composition tablets.

The much-traveled letter caught up with me, and was lying on my bunk when I came in from work. I opened it cautiously, the way they did those eyes and teeth boxes. ''Dear Bubba, I hope you doin fine. It took a long time for me to find where you was. It's Mama. She just hanging on. She got gangrene in one of her legs from the phlebitis and she got kidney failure to. They got her hooked to a machine. I talked to a lawyer about gettin you out to come see her. The doctor say he would *personally* call the Board to request that you

317

come. I hope and pray they let you. I want to see you so bad. Been a long time, hasn't it. I love you, Bubba. Your sis, Pat.''

I was called out that evening. Letters containing news of illness, death, or other urgencies are viewed as motivations for escape attempts. The warden told me to lay-in the building tomorrow, and phoned inside to inform the building major.

Back on the tank, I got it from under my pillow and reread it. It had been so long since I'd seen Emma, I was unable to picture her clearly. My mind slowly drifted back over the years.

The next morning I was called out to the laundry and issued some free-world khakis, shirt, and shoes. I'd been granted a five-day emergency reprieve. The deputy sheriff from Gregg County was waiting for me in the warden's office. After being shackled for transport, he led me to his car. The trip from the Coffield Unit near Palestine to Longview took about an hour and a half.

In the Good Shepherd Hospital parking lot, he removed the leg and waist chains, but left the wrist cuffs. I got slightly nauseated by the strong hospital odors when we walked through the sliding glass doors. A brief stop at the admissions desk; the deputy got directions to her room. We were on the right floor, and walked briskly down the wheel chair and gurney-lined hallway.

Pat looked up the hall, saw us, and came running. After the kisses and hugs, she asked the deputy, ''Do you have to keep the handcuffs on 'em?''

''Mam, these are my orders. If you want to talk to the sheriff bout it, that's alright with me.''

Pat told me that Emma had been in a coma for three days. Walking toward the room Pat said, ''Befo we go in, I'm goin over here an phone th' sheriff.''

While she was phoning, I waited in the hall exchanging greetings with her boyfriend T.J., and Emma's three sisters Pat had summoned from Dallas. I hadn't seen any of them since I was a kid.

Pat's conversation with the sheriff's department necessitated the deputy going to the phone. Before I entered

Emma's room, he removed the cuffs and left the hospital.

I was startled by how old and frail she looked, more like ninety than sixty-six. I reached over the railing and touched her. Her eyes opened slowly. Barely able to move her fingers, she motioned for me to come closer. I held her hand and leaned my face close to hers.

Struggling to speak, her lips trembled. In low, short whispers, "Mama knowed you wuz comin, I wuzn' bout to go nowhere til you got here. Move back a little so Mama kin look atcha."

Still holding her hand, I straightened my body. Opening her eyes wider, she looked me over through the flowing tears, "Is me an you still buddies?"

The life-light in her eyes waned. Fighting back my own tears, "The best kind, Mama."

A faint smile crossed her lips. With her gaze fixed on me, she drifted off into death. Thank God! we got the chance to make our peace. My turning point had been five years ago in solitary. If I hadn't changed, there's no way I could have responded quickly enough. The feelings were there; I loved her. I only regretted she beat me asking.

Pat bought me a navy blue suit and the accessories, and put some money in my pocket. It surprised me that the funeral was held in a church and not at the funeral home.

The pastor began the service by saying, "A member she may not have been, but I can say one thang for Emma Sample, she give mo to this church in dollars an cents over the last few years than fifty percent of the membership. So do she have a right to be in this church fo her funeral? I just wanted to clear th' air on that point."

He said he had visited with her twice a week over a long period of time and had gotten to know her. "I can tell the bereaved I know in my heart Emma Sample is in Heaven. If there was ever anybody I been close to as they neared death that I felt been saved, it was her. In the last few months befo her death, she got close to her God and was prepared to die. She was not afraid. As she put it, 'I'm a big girl.' "

The small church was filled. I had no idea this many cared enough to attend. Even Mr. Milton, the liquor store man, closed up and came. The faces of the congregation were somber. Emma had told Pat she didn't want "no whoopin an hollerin," just organ playing. She even picked the music the organist played throughout the service. I could almost hear her singing along.

As I stood at the casket for the last viewing, I pulled out TWO one dollar bills, folded them neatly, and slid them underneath her hand. I knew she wouldn't want to run into Blue and not have any money to bet she "bar it."

Pat offered to be my parole plan, but because she had been busted a couple of times for gaming operations at her house, I felt living with her would be unacceptable to the Board. Besides, I didn't want to put any heat on her by having a parole officer coming in and out. Instead, I submitted a plan to go to a halfway house in Houston.

It was December and the snowflakes were soft-peddling their way to the ground. The heavy equipment boss came to the tank and called for me. Since it was Sunday I was on towing stand-by. When we got in the pickup, the boss took me to where I had parked the machine the evening before. Once I got to the bogged-down truck, it only took a few minutes to hook on the cable and pull it out. I towed it far enough up the road so the driver could make it the rest of the way to the sawmill on his own.

The equipment boss said he had to drive to the other side of the unit and close some cattle gates, reminding me, "We're tryin to git everthang closed up. Ain' gon' be many uv ya'll wekin next week cuz most uv th' bosses'll be off fer Christmas. Why don'cha go over in the woods an make yoresef a far. I'll be back adder while an gitcha."

It didn't matter; I was in no hurry to get back. The tank was heavy laden with holiday melancholy and I felt better being outside. The woods had become a refuge. I pulled Big Bertha off the road and walked her through the sparse timberline of spruce and speckled ash. Deeper into the woods, I came upon a little stream and stopped.

I saw movement in front of the small brush pile on the other side, a brown cottontail. I shut the engine down to low idle and quickly got my three-foot rabbit stick from behind the seat. I eased out of the cab onto the dozer track. Just as it jumped, I threw my stick and turned it a flip. I was on it like a duck on a june bug.

From the cache of tools in my toolbox, I quickly had it skinned, gutted, and washed in the stream. Seasoned with the salt and pepper I stockpiled from my sack lunches, it was roasting on a tree-branch rotisserie in no time.

Leaving my fire, I crossed the stream and got on the dozer to walk it over. Pausing for a moment, I looked at the pictur-esque winter wonderland and felt like I was in the middle of a Christmas card. The crystallized flakes splashed off the naked branches and sparkled like Roman candles before joining their snowflake pals blanketing the forest floor. I didn't want to disrupt the little stream's serenity and decided to leave Big Bertha where she was and walked back.

Occasionally, one of the icy pellets found its way down my shirt collar, but for the most part, the yellow slicker suit kept me dry. I squatted, turning my rabbit slowly over the flames. A break in the silence. Squinting, I saw a man ap-proaching on horseback.

He stopped his horse eight or ten feet from the fire. He said amicably, "Hello there, how you doin? I could smell it cookin all over the woods." Smiling, "All I had to do was follow my nose. Got enough to share?"

"Sure, come on. It's almost ready," I answered, sur-prised that anyone was nearby but glad to have his company, even though I'd never seen him before.

Finished with tying the reins, he came over and squatted beside me, ungloved his hands, and warmed them over the fire. "Merry Christmas to you, pardner," he said.

"Same to ya."

"Is that yore dozer parked over yonder?"

"Yep. That's Big Bertha."

We gazed into the flames and took turns picking off bits of the rabbit. "What're you doin out here in th' snow? I thought everybody was in watchin th' football game," I said.

"Roundin up some strays."

"If you hadn' smelled this rabbit, you might've missed one," I joked.

I got around to telling him about being out nine months

321

earlier for my mother's funeral, and "I talked to the parole man back in September, but ain't heard nothin yet."

He stopped chewing and said with an air of certainty, "Don' worry bout a thang. You'll make it." We finished our rabbit feast. "I thank you fer sharin with me. I guess I betta be movin on."

"Yeah," I said, "good luck with yo roundup."

He mounted and headed back through the thicket. Stomping out the fire, I remembered and hollered out, "What's yo name! What buildin you on?"

I guess he didn't hear me, I thought, and resumed my fire stomping. It started snowing much harder so I climbed on Big Bertha and waited until the boss came and took me in.

Monday evening when I got to the building, an inner unit truck mail envelope was on my bunk. When I opened it and saw the parole release slip inside, I got weak in the knees. I'd be out in less than a month.

Every morning when the trusties went out, I watched for my rabbit eating "pardner" to tell him the good news, but never did see him again.

I finally gave up trying to find the ghost rider in the snow.

The day before my release I arrived at the Walls, and was ready for shake down. The bunch of us who came in on Black Betty were quickly herded into the security station for the strip-search. Looking down the line while waiting my turn, I noticed those ahead inspected by the older guards moved through the line much faster. The younger bosses were more thorough.

My turn came, I put my clothes, shoes, and other personals on the counter. I completed the "open your mouth, spread your cheeks" part as the young guard watched. He raked my shoes and clothes to one side, indicating it was okay to start putting them back on. I was almost finished buttoning my shirt and cramming my cigarettes and Zippo back in my pockets when he began to leaf through my composition tablets stacked on the counter.

"What're these?" he asked.

"Jus some books I've been keepin notes in."

"How long you been here?"

"A long time, Boss, seventeen years altogether."

He pitched them into the barrel with the rest of the things they'd confiscated. Five years of writing tossed into the trash.

"You ought not have no trouble rememberin."

18 ||||||||||||||||||||||| [   ]

January 12, 1972, 9:45 A.M.

Twenty-six days prior to my forty-second birthday, with the
ten bucks mustering-out money in my pocket, I was paroled
to New Directions ex-offender halfway house in Houston.
The second day, I enrolled in night classes at the University
of Houston, financed by the Department of Vocational Rehabilitation. The fifth day, I got a job working for a black
newspaper, a hundred bucks a week. Two of my parole
criteria had been satisfied: I had a place to stay and a
job.

The dice "started hittin." I moved out of the halfway
house after a month into my own apartment. I had never
been in a newspaper plant before, let alone worked in one.
But, in about a year and a half, I was promoted to general
manager. In the meanwhile, I'd put together a very decent
wardrobe and bought a new car.

I could hardly wait for the weekends. Soon as five o'clock
Friday came, I headed for Longview to be with Pat. We had
been apart for too many years. With each visit we grew
closer and closer. We were the only family left, and really
enjoyed one another.

She had managed to go to cosmetology school and ran a
beauty shop in her house. But like Emma, she also ran dice
games on the weekends. I usually managed to arrive right in
the middle of the crap game, but she'd leave the table and

we'd sit in the living room talking and laughing until we both got in the game.

During one of my weekend visits, it was nearing dawn and the crap game had finally ended. All the players were gone, except the few who couldn't make it. Three of them were piled up on the daybed in the back room. After losing all their money, they filled their bellies with Pat's collard greens and hamhocks, fried fish and hot water cornbread. They were drunk and sleeping peacefully.

Pat and I talked and she explained the relationship she had with Roy Lee, her ex-husband, as well as the one she had with T.J. She interrupted herself, "Boy, am I glad I got a big Bubba I can tell all my secrets to, th' way they do in them love story books I read all th' time."

She started crying; I went to her and put my arms around her. With her head buried against me, she whimpered like a little child, "Bubba, I want you to always know one thing, I love you with all my heart." Crying more profusely, "We're all we got." After blowing her nose and wiping away some of the tears with the hankie I'd handed her, "God, I miss Mama. Sometimes I feel so all alone, Bubba."

Holding my sister close and crying too, "You're not alone, Pat. I'm right here with you. C'mon, cheer up. We're gon' make it jus fine. Watch an see. C'mon now," I urged, "les stop cryin an have a drank together."

After sharing a small shot of vodka, "I'm okay now," she said. "I guess we been needin to cry together for a long, long time."

Sunday morning when I was ready to head back to Houston, she walked out to the car with me. "Bubba, don' stay away long."

I stuck my head out the window, "Don' worry, I'll be back soon. You got me hooked on them collard greens."

I worked hard during the days and was tired at the end of them. One night the phone woke me. Half-asleep, I picked up the receiver, "Hello."

"Bubba, is that you?"

I glanced at the radio clock, 2:15. "Hello," I repeated, "Pat? Speak up, I can hardly hear you, say that again."

"This is Clara, Pat's friend across the street."

"Okay, I'm with you, what's up?"

"I'm callin bout Pat. She been shot."

"Is she dead?"

"I don' know, but you betta cum quick. The police and ammalance is over there now. They brangin her out on th' stretcher."

"Where will they take her?"

"Good Shepherd."

"Who shot her? Do you know?"

"Naw. Wait a minute! I see 'em; the police is puttin Roy Lee in the car."

"Thanks for callin, Clara. I'm on my way!"

I threw a few things in my bag, and hit the road. It had just been a week since I was up there. About four hours later, I was exiting onto Highway 80 on the outskirts of Longview heading for the hospital. Once through the familiar electronic doors, I walked up to the admissions desk. The corridors were empty, and the big clock on the wall showed 6:23.

"Pardon me, ma'am. Do you have Patsy Hicks here?"

"Just a moment," and she fingered through the cards. "Yes, she was brought in a few hours ago. Are you a member of the family?"

"Yes, I'm her brother. Can you tell me anything about her condition?"

Reading from the record, "Multiple gunshot wounds. She's in ICU. Her doctor will be in around nine."

"Can I see her?"

"No sir, the doctor left strict orders not to allow any visitors until he sees her again this mornin."

She directed me to an area where I could get some coffee and wait, assuring me that when the doctor came in, she'd let me know. Waiting for nine o'clock, I drank a gallon of coffee and went to the john a half dozen times.

"Doctor," the nurse said, "this is Miss Hicks's brother."

"Hello, come this way." He placed the folders he was carrying on the desk, "I'm gonna level with you. Pat's been very seriously injured, so seriously, I dare not tell her just yet. She's got fifteen gunshot wounds from a small caliber weapon scattered over her body. Fortunately, all the bullets went through and didn't hit any vital organs. But she lost a lot of blood. If we can make it through the next week or so without complications, she's got a fair chance. But in situations like this where the patient is totally immobile, there's always a possibility of blood clotting. Her being a diabetic could also cause problems with the clot-preventive medication."

"Is she conscious?"

"Yes, she's conscious. She's sedated, but I talked with her just a little while ago. She's fairly coherent."

"Can I see her? Just to let her know I'm here. I won't disturb her."

"All right, but only for a few minutes."

The admissions nurse directed me to the Intensive Care Unit. When I entered, the green-clad nurse met me at the door, "I'm here to see my sister, Patsy Hicks."

"Okay, she's in that room," pointing through the glass window.

"Is it alright if I go inside?"

"Yes, but don't touch anything," she warned and returned to her station.

Stepping inside, a cold chill ran over me. There were tubes in her nose, both arms, and lower body. I quietly approached the big-wheeled gurney, "Pat, Pat," I said softly, "can you hear me? It's Bubba, I'm here."

She turned her head ever so slightly in my direction and whispered out, "Oh Bubba, I'm so sorry I had to worry you."

"Hey buddy, you can't worry me. I love you."

"Bubba, that sonuvabitch went crazy," she said weakly. "Mama warned me," and a tear trickled down her cheek.

"Was it Roy Lee?"

"Yeah, I want you to promise me you won' git in no trou-

327

ble.'' She was fading out, ''It ain' worth it . . . don' go back down . . .'' The drugs took over.

After leaving ICU, I saw T.J. ''Hi man. I got here soon as I heard bout it. Is she gon' be awright?!'' he asked.

We stepped to one side of the hall. I told him what the doctor told me.

Over the next few days either T.J. or I remained at the hospital. On the fifth day, she was moved from the ICU to a room that I realized was right next to the one Emma had died in. I saw her doctor and expressed how good I felt about how she was doing.

''Don't get too optimistic just yet,'' he cautioned. ''The next few days will be the most crucial. It's a miracle she's made it this far.''

Regardless of what he said, I was optimistic. She looked so much better as the days wore on, and had even sipped a little soup. She seemed to be gaining strength.

The next three days she was in very good spirits. We talked and she told me the whole story. ''I was in a financial bind Bubba, and needed six hundred dollars right away to take care uv some bills. Roy Lee came by the house and we got to talkin an I mentioned I needed to borrow six hundred dollars frum somewhere—and quick. He offered to lend me the money and said to pay 'em back whenever I could. He'd been after me to take him back, but we been divorced for nearly six years, and I don' love him. He knew that, but he couldn' stand that I was in love with T.J.

''We had a good game goin and T.J. was at the house when Roy Lee came over. He got in the game, and befo long him and T.J. were arguin. And there I sat in the middle. It was gettin mo serious and I knew T.J. was gettin ready to jump on 'em. I felt like he would really hurt Roy Lee so I asked him to leave. He thought I was takin sides with T.J., which I wasn't. But he couldn' see it that way and stormed outta the house.

''It was past midnight Sunday when I got home. I got a funny feelin, specially when Buster didn' bark. I figured he must be sleepin an didn' hear me, he's gettin old too. I unlocked the door, stepped inside, and locked it behind me befo I turned on the lights.

"There sat Roy Lee on the couch with a rifle layin cross his lap. It scared me so bad, all I could think to say was, 'Whatcha doin sittin up here in the dark? How'd you git in?' Bubba, he never said a word. I started fo my bedroom, but befo I could reach it, he got up and started shootin. I tried to grab him. I managed to git my hands on the rifle barrel, but he kept on shootin. I remember him knockin me back away frum him. I don' know how many times I was shot, but I could feel the burnin inside me. I fell to the flo'. He reloaded, stood over me, and shot sum mo times. I played dead. I believe if I hadn', he would've reloaded agin. Then I passed out. How many times did he shoot me?"

"The doctor said it was more than a dozen."

"Damn, I sure was lucky."

"Yep, you sure are."

She was more cheerful on the sixth day than she'd been since it happened. But she did mention that if she didn't make it, she wanted me to give her rings to Mae Rose, T.J.'s sister. "She's been a real good friend to me." Joking, "You git everything else, the house with the mortgage and all the unpaid bills. But at least that o' car's paid fo.'"

I emphasized, "But you gon' make it, Sis. You're comin 'long fine."

"Yeah, but just in case."

She took a turn for the worse on the ninth day and grew much weaker. The blood clotting was out of control. The next day she lapsed into a coma. Standing at her bedside, I watched her chest rise and fall for the last time.

Never before had I felt so helpless. We'd had so little time together since I'd been out of prison. My heart ached and I felt near collapse as I helped lift her body into the ambulance and rode along to the funeral home to make arrangements.

The chapel overflowed. There wasn't enough seating room. People lined the walls. I fulfilled my promise to her and gave the eulogy. She was buried next to Emma. I settled her financial matters and left. Pat's death was a shattering, unexpected blow that left a hollow hole in my chest. I could hardly get my breath as I looked down the highway before me.

I had to somehow put the painful loss in a safe place in my mind. I threw myself into my work. I didn't go back to Longview for Roy Lee's trial, but after it was over T.J. called me at work one day and told me Roy Lee had been sentenced to thirty years. How ironic: the same sentence I got for robbery.

In 1974, three months after Pat died, the director of the halfway house program, Sonny Wells, came to my office at the newspaper and offered me a job. I accepted and became the business manager for the Criminal Justice Division–funded ex-offender program. In December of the same year, the miracle of miracles happened. A statewide search had been launched by a very popular "maverick" state representative, Ronnie Earle, to find an ex-convict to direct a program out of the Governor's office. After a lengthy interview he passed the dice to me; I was appointed project director of Project STAR (Social Transition And Readjustment).

Governor Dolph Briscoe had signed the Controlled Substance Act (possession of four ounces or less of marijuana is a misdemeanor) retroactive and effective immediately. Even court cases where small quantities were used as enhancement to get stiffer sentences were affected. This meant that a lot of cons would be released as a result of the new law.

"Effective immediately" meant that those affected would bypass the six-week pre-release program designed to plug them back into society. This was my job, to provide counseling and job placement assistance. It also meant that since I was the program I had to hurry!

By the first of the year when it kicked off, I had contacted literally hundreds of potential employers across the state by phone and in person regarding hiring ex-offenders. Much to my amazement, after some straight talk about the matter and

330

answering questions about the "risks," the majority were willing to "take a chance."

By the time the first prisoners were released under the new program, I had job possibilities and somebody for them to contact already lined up. Of course the individuals still had the responsibility of nailing it down; that's where the "how to" and "sharing personal experiences" counseling came in. Armed with "big papers" bearing the governor's signature, I was authorized to enter the prisons and counsel my clients prior to their release.

At the guard level I was "that nigguh frum th' Guvner's Office," but in the wardens' offices I was "Mr. Sample." The convicts viewed me with pride, "a stone-down gorilla," and called me "Mister Racehoss." As for me, it was an emotional high every time I entered the gates simply because I knew I could leave when I was ready.

Three hundred and five of the 476 prisoners affected under the new ruling needed assistance. At the end of 1975, follow-up data on those who had been assisted by Project STAR showed it was a success. Of the 305 I assisted, only three had been rearrested.

On my final trip to the Walls to visit my last client, I recognized somebody I hadn't seen in years, Big Devil's son. I remembered when he was just a kid and used to come up to the office and hang around hoping I could come out and toss the football with him.

I walked over to the security desk where he sat and spoke. He recognized me, "Hi, Racehoss," reaching out his hand to shake.

"Hi, Zeb Jr. How long you been workin for the prison system?"

"Aw, bout two years. Ever since I got outta the Navy."

"How's your dad?"

"Aw, jus fine. He retired, you know."

"Naw, I didn' know. When?"

"Been bout two years now. Him and Mama got 'em a little place in Lovelady an settled down."

The doors were unlocking, "Say Zeb Jr., I gotta run.

331

Here comes my client. When you see the warden, tell 'em hello for me.''

"Okay, sure will.''

After seeing that the new releasee was safely on the bus at the station, I got in my car and drove away from Huntsville. Driving along the highway listening to the music on the radio, mind wandering, I realized I had made a wrong turn somewhere when I saw the sign, "Lovelady 24 miles.'' That sure wasn't the way to Austin. I started looking up ahead for a place to turn around. Then decided "what the hell.''

Five hundred yards after I entered Lovelady, I pulled in an Atlantic-Richfield service station. The attendant came out, "Yessir.''

"Hi, I just need some information. Can you tell me where the Chambers live?''

"Sure kin,'' pointing, "see 'at little road,'' no more than twenty feet away, "jes turn rat there an follow it on roun til you cum ta a big oak tree. Thas where it makes a Y, stay ta th' right an you'll dead end in they front yard.''

It was no road, it was a path. I followed it as directed and ended up in the front yard of a white frame house with a big porch with a swing. I parked in the driveway and walked up to the front door.

KNOCK! KNOCK!

His wife came to the door, "Yes?'' She didn't recognize me, but I remembered her.

"Is Warden Chambers in?''

"Yes.''

"Would you tell him somebody's here to see him?''

"Jesta minute. Zeb, Zeb.''

"Yeah?''

"There's somebody heah to see you.''

"Okay, be there in a minute.''

After stepping onto the porch, "Ol' Racehoss!''

"That's right, Warden.''

"Damn! When did you git out?'' Motioning toward the porch swing, "Have a seat.''

"In '72.''

332

"Well," he said smiling, "you beat me out by little better'n a year."

"I didn' know you retired til I saw Zeb Jr. over at the Walls."

"Yeah, I heped git him on over there," he boasted jokingly. "Whut wuz you doin over at th' Walls?"

"Meetin a convict."

"I see. Whut kind uv work you doin?"

"I work out of the Governor's Office, the Criminal Justice Division."

"Is that so? Whut all do you do?"

"Well, have you heard about the marijuana release program?"

"Yeah."

"I'm the project director."

"Well, I'll be. I didn' know you wuz headin up 'at program."

"Yessir, I left the Walls after my client got out, made a wrong turn, an ended up on the road to Lovelady."

"Well, Racehoss, I'm glad you did. Where you livin now?"

"I moved from Houston to Austin about a year ago."

"Frum whut I heah, Houston ain' nuthin but a trusty shack. Half the people who git out wind up in Houston. I betcha a third uv Houston's population is ex-convicts. When you wuz livin in Houston, didja ever run 'cross any uv th' ol' timers?"

"I sure did," adding, "I went to a halfway house for ex-cons when I got out. Know who was runnin it?"

"Who?"

"Ol' Sonny Wells."

"You don' say? I heard Ol' Cateye went to Houston too. You ever see him?"

"Yessir, I saw him. Last I heard he was working for Dr. Gates. Ol' Ottie Dottie works for Sonny at the halfway house, and I saw Flea Brain standin on a street corner in Galveston. He's still just as funny as ever. An Ol' Forty's workin at the halfway house too, got him a buildin tender job. Ol' Thirty Five's preaching in Fort Worth. An let me see, who else? Oh, you'll never guess who else I saw."

"Who?"

"Pork Chops. I went to a movie one night and after takin my seat, I heard somebody sayin, 'Racehoss, Racehoss!' I looked around and it was Pork Chops. He said he had a job workin at a cafe an doin just fine."

"I'm glad to heah that. I hope they all kin stay out."

We sat in the swing chatting just like two old cons. "Last time we wuz together, Ol' Racehoss, that damn farm manager wuz afta yore ass."

"Yessir, that's right." His memory was uncanny as we talked and talked about yesteryears.

"Warden, how come you hung 'em up? I thought you would probably stay around til they tore all the buildins down."

"Yeah, well, I planned to, but then I thought about it an talked it over wit Ol' Miss. I decided it wuz time fer me to git out. I spent the betta part uv my life in prisons. I don' wanna have nuthin else to do wit 'em. I'm thru. I dun my time." Adding humorously, "Hell Racehoss, I did mo time then you did. But I got my belly full in a hurry afta they let th' convicts take over. Fo I lef the Eastham farm I had a dozen lawsuits filed 'ginst me."

"For what?"

"Violatin sumbody's civil rights, brutality, all kinds uv stuff.—Say!" he said smiling devilishly, "since you wek fer th' Guvner an everthang, I might need you to testify fer me."

"Aw, you don' need my testimony. You'll make it alright," I kidded. "Warden, do you remember that time you put me in solitary when Mr. Meabs ran me in?"

"Yeah. Why?"

"God came to me while I was in there that time, and my life hasn't been the same. I just wanted to tell you that."

He sat silently for a moment, "Ol' Miss," he hollered into the house, "brang us two glasses uv 'at lemonade," rocking the swing gently.

After Ol' Miss handed us the frosty glasses, "Ol' Racehoss, I bleeve you gonna make it this time. And I'm glad I had sump'n to do wit hepin git yore heart right."

"That's where you're wrong Warden, you didn't have shit to do with it," and sipped my lemonade.

Bama, Sally and Elzado (in that order) died within a ten-year period after Emma's death in 1971. God bless their souls.

The
Retrieveites

Ol' Cadlack, Florine, High Pocket, Pile Driver, Dog, Mae Perl, Cuero, Bull, Sally, Big Six, Chicken, Judy, Mellaman, Fort Worth, Fistfucker, Marble Eye, Piss Ant, B. C., Jelly, Round Head, Navasota, Misusin Slim, Annie, Look Em Down Red, Lil Chicken, Big Low, Skinny, Maude, Tangle Eye, Road Runner, Bernice, Gilflirt, Texicana, Cattle Gap, Fish Head, Brass Mouf, Flea Brain, Calf Eye, Choppin Charlie, Garden Slim, Middlebuster, Crip, Baldy, Lil Alfonso, Flyin Home, Pickhandle, Big Mama James, Track, Beaumont, Mushavit, Rags, Mufflejaw, Sarge, Cuz, Filet Mignon, Spider, Slopediddy, West Texas, Kotch Tom, Moon, Bighand, Doc Cateye, Lunchmeat, Hound, Motomouf, Skeet, Pork Chops, Chubby, Doc Nolan, Trigger Bill, Snake, Cowboy, Runnintime, Forty, Lil Hand, Rabbi, Hawk, Ape, Pig Eye, Unca Moze, Dumplin, Round Rock, Good Eye, Rooster, Iron Head, Mattie, Stump, Walkie-Talkie, Cornflakes, Bugs, Toesucker, Shadow, Dead Man, Skindown, 84, Polly, Buster, Hook Em Bill, Swapout, Big Louzanna, Wetback, Beer Belly, Mae West, Buckjump, Wild Man, Lay Em Down Shorty, Rev, Duck Eye, Bird Eye, Yaller Gal, Fishgil, Water Boy Brown, Ax Man, Cross Cut, Soda Cracker, Dishpan, Turkey Slim, Rock, Whickabill, Kilgo, Rastus, Two Moufs, Cap Rock, Chinaman, Scrapiron, Mule, Tin Horn, Coon, Rock Island, Moose, Sleepy, Corsicana, Bones, Tree, Buttermilk, Ox, Dragline, Sardine, Gatermouf, Polecat, High John, Gypsy, Bad Eye, Mama Good Drawers, Ollie, Crazyfolks, Owl Head, Cutbelly, Naomi, Tarzan, Guvner, Black Pete, Firebug, No Ass, Crosshauler, Korea, Speedy, Halfahead, Rat, Mama Better Drawers, Lookinback, Cowfucker, Jaybird, Candy, Babysetter, Airhammer, Onegone, Calico, Gotcheye, Mammy, Gravedigger, Sue, Goat, Railhead Shorty, Cablecar, Spriggs, Polkadot, Chili, Dakota, Gilamonster, Pauline, Cresote, Dangalang, Squatlow, Glodine, Pulldo, Lil Hal, Big Time, Short Shorty, Witherspoon, Fartnot, Eel, Talco, Shadrack, Bloodeye, Black Rider, Tennessee, Birdseed, Whitefolks, Elifin, Sicamo, Jackhammer, Booty Green, Snot Man, Maewidder, Scarecrow, Koolade, Tiny, Fo Eyes, Slocum, Radio, Feets, Peebaby, Rapehead, Peewee, Slats, Lillian, Fishhook, Cryin Shame, Gallopin, Three-eighty, 44, 35, Hut, Hole in the head, Ostrich, Pank Eye, Dreamer, Elefinhead, Happy, Sopeter, Carnival, Water Well, Crybaby, Braggs, Nose, Sheep Shit, Brady, Collard Greens, Hammerlock, Pick a head, Racehoss, Space Man, Baby Raper, Killa, Snout, Mable, Pug, Hollywood, Backsticker, Peckahead, VD, School Teacher, Sof Head, Midnite, Way Lay, Skintight, Proud Walker, Rearback, Rockinchair, Box, Midget, Soapsuds, Earthworm, Amarilla, Big Ear, Bow Wow, Frenchy, Police, Eaglepaw, Fenderbender, 7 fangers, Knees, Neck, Nellynuthin, Old Folks, Backtrouble, Dizzy, Lil Ear, Claw, Kangaroo, Hip Cat, Watermelonman, Tumbleweed, Pitchfork, Alabama, Popeye, Squarehead,

Eightball, Duckbutter, Arcola, Snakedoctor, Jewel, Greyhound, Rabbit, Big Ada, Stripes, Possum, Jesse James, Ticktock, Hiwatha, Choker, Waco, Gasoline, Bat Man, Hercules, Bay City, Wolf, Pincushion, Top N' Bottom, Red Wine, Sparkplug, Appleass, Spooky, Waterbaby, Ragmouf, Ottie Dottie, Corinne, Halliburton, Steeple Head, Blacknite, Waxahachie, Goldfront, Shine, Picklehead, Molehands, Underground, Meat Cutter, Ace, Big Cross, Bubble Eye, Wash, Kong, Waskom, Jabbo, Sonny Wells, Razorback, Goosey, Monkey Man, Bulldog, Tomball, Preacher, Rosebud, Twin Chin, Black Scotty, Penny, Smallchange, Liverlips, Grunt, Big Mex- ico, Dolly, Butterbean, Tarbaby, Peanut, Goree, Doubledeuce, New York, Earlytime, Bugeye, Grasshoppa, Bicycle, Minnie, Patch over the eye, Arkadelpha, Packrat, Mank, Picturedrawer, Logcabin, Unca Frown, Smiley, Crazy Mo, Nicklehead, Sack Man, Tadpole, Jap, Bummabee, Flagpole, Gladiola, Willie B, Saddlehead, Teacake, Buttcut, Blackgal, Deepwalkin Dad, Copout, Monkeywrench, Dallis, Shot Man, Hambone, Willie Mae, Cornbread, Ragmop, Squirrelhead, Gertrude, Cave Man, Suzy Q, Prizefighter, Storyteller, Angola, Broth N' Law, Fly, Flea, Montana, Speck, Hop, Deathrow, Frostbite, Blaine, Minnow, Dummy, Yo-Yo, Lurline, Puppy, Pillowcase.

About the Author

After seventeen years in prison, Albert Race Sample was the first ex-convict in Texas to work out of the Governor's office and serve as a probation officer for Travis County. He has also served on the staff of the State Bar of Texas and appeared as the keynote speaker at the Texas Corrections Association convention.

He has also received the prestigious Liberty Bell award, two Services to Mankind awards, and a Speaker of the Year award in recognition for his work in the field of corrections and rehabilitation of ex-offenders. In 1981, Mr. Sample was recognized as the Outstanding Crime Prevention Citizen of Texas.

Albert Race Sample received a full pardon and restoration of all civil rights in 1976. He resides in Austin, Texas, with his wife and daughter.